FAITH AND HUMAN TRANSFORMATION

A Dialogue Between Psychology and Theology

James Forsyth

University Press of America, Inc.
Lanham • New York • Oxford

Copyright © 1997 by
University Press of America,® Inc.
4720 Boston Way
Lanham, Maryland 20706

12 Hid's Copse Rd.
Cummor Hill, Oxford OX2 9JJ

ISBN 0-7618-0739-X (cloth: alk. ppr.)
ISBN 0-7618-0740-3 (pbk: alk. ppr.)

∞™ The paper used in this publication meets the minimum
requirements of American National Standard for information
Sciences—Permanence of Paper for Printed Library Materials,
ANSI Z39.48—1984

To Stephen and Sarah

Contents

List of Tables

Preface

The context of this work is the rift, conflict or dichotomy experienced by many including many of the conventionally religious, between religion and life, between human and religious values, between the goals of human and religious development. In this latter form, the conflict is of particular interest to the psychology of religion and in particular to what we might call the developmental psychology of religion which is concerned with relating the stages of religious development to those of human development. Using the developmental models of Jean Piaget and Erik Erikson as a starting point, a number of scholars have proposed corresponding models of moral, religious and faith development. The present work originated in the author's view that these works are elaborations of the basic principle: healthy human development is the natural foundation for authentic religious development; that mature faith takes root in the mature human personality. In the thirteenth century St. Thomas Aquinas made the same point in broader terms, that is, in terms of the relationship between nature and grace, when he enunciated the principle *gratia praesupponit naturam* (grace presupposes or builds on nature).

But for Aquinas that was not the end of it, for he saw the relationship of nature and grace as reciprocal. Therefore he added a second principle: *gratia perficit naturam* (grace perfects nature). Translated into developmental terms this would mean that grace, and therefore faith (the human response to grace) orients the believer towards the goals of authentic human growth and therefore makes one more fully human. In this work I would like to elaborate on the developmental implications of this second principle, since it is for the most part underdeveloped in the literature on religious and faith development. Our focal point will be Christian faith experience and our question will be: Does faith, understood as a human experience and as the human response to grace, involve the same kind of transformation and self - transcendence as the experience of authentic human growth? Where it does, one may argue that grace perfects nature.

Acknowledgments

The author is grateful for permission to quote from the following source: *Life and Faith: Psychological Perspectives on Religious Experience,* (Georgetown University Press) by William W. Meissner, S.J.   Copyright 1987 by William W. Meissner.   Reprinted by permission of the author.

Introduction

Of all the temptations besetting organized religion one of the most insidious is the recurring need felt by church leaders to make religion "relevant." Insidious because it so often appears on the scene as a devil in the guise of an angel. What, after all, could be more desirable than to make religion more relevant to the lives of its adherents? The problem is that our good intentions are so often betrayed. The attempt to make religion more relevant to life often seems to result in making it more irrelevant. Indeed, in the contemporary religious scene, the sometimes insidious attempts by the church to make religion and worship more "user friendly" seems to have only added to the number of those who seek spiritual goals apart from the structure of organized religion. Paradoxically, this disaffected group includes a large number of young people and of self - styled religious "liberals" - the very groups to whom innovations in religious life and worship were meant to appeal. Among the more prominent of such innovations, for instance, are the revisions of Catholic liturgy initiated by the Second Vatican Council. These revisions were clearly intended to bring the mass closer to the people, but in fact, seemed to have produced a liturgy of such sheer banality as to constitute as much of a "turn off" as the alleged incomprehensibility of the old Latin mass.

Why does it happen so often that our attempts to make religion relevant leave us with a feeling that we have, in the process, robbed religion of something essential - denied something of its essential character? I would suggest that the answer lies in the fact that while religion must of itself be relevant to conditions of human existence if it is to command our total response, nevertheless, so many of our attempts to make religion relevant attempt to legitimate religion with reference to something beyond religion, to a set of human or social needs. This is precisely the view of religion which Freud[1] proposed - religion as an agent of civilization in curbing instinctual appetites - and concluded that religion was infantile and illusory. It is now fifty years since Dietrich Bonhoeffer reflected on the paradox of making God less relevant by trying to make him more relevant.

We have come to think of God and religion, he proposed, as the *deus et machina*,[2] as that which we turn to as the answer to our human and metaphysical concerns only when our human resources prove inadequate.

Such a faith, however, removes the "problem - solving" God and religion from the centre of life to the borders or extremities of our lives as we more and more learn to solve our own human problems and rely on our own human resources. Bonhoeffer's solution to this dilemma was to propose a "religionless" form of Christianity, i.e., a Christianity not based upon the "religious" premise that humanity "needs" God.

But surely this solution strips religion of one of its essential features; for our experience of religion tells us that it is indeed relevant to our human existence and answers to a variety of human needs.

Or is there a middle ground between divorcing religion and human need, on the one hand, and authenticating it on the grounds of human need, on the other?

Admittedly, the demand that religion be relevant to human life often reduces it to the level of a problem - solving agent in one's life. This we recognize as being in conflict with another aspect of our religious experience. Authentic religion, we know, is not a means to an end; it is not an agent offering us its services in the pursuit of purely human values. Religion may indeed give us peace of mind, comfort, security, human fellowship, etc., but we are not religious because of these benefits. If this were the case, religion would be analogous to an addiction; one would be religious because of religion's side - effects just as an alcoholic or dug addict is addicted to the substance he is abusing because of its side - effects. Authentic religion, however, is not essentially a problem - solver or a need - fulfiller. It is self - authenticating; it confronts us in such a way as to challenge us to make a decision about our existence and a genuine commitment of our lives to the transcendent ground of that existence. One does not achieve psychological maturity by consciously pursuing it but by transcending oneself through self - commitment. Likewise one does not achieve religious maturity by seeking the various forms of human fulfilment which might be the side - effect of religious commitment. Indeed, the act of faith may be made contrary to all considerations of human wisdom; but, paradoxically, it is through such a self - transcending commitment that the believer achieves authentic human existence. This paradox is expressed in the New Testament in such images as losing one's life in order to find it, the seed which dies in order to bear fruit, forsaking human goals for the sake of the kingdom and thereby receiving the very things one has forsaken.

I have suggested the possibility of a middle ground between on the one hand, divorcing God and religion from human need, and on the other, legitimating God and religion because of their relevance to human needs. Is there a way of speaking of the relevance of religion for human existence which does not reduce religion to a function within human existence? In this work, I want to reflect on the relevance of the Christian faith experience for human existence from the perspective of the psychology of religion, i.e., by bringing together in dialogue theological descriptions of the dynamics of the faith experience and psychological descriptions of the dynamics of human growth. The attempt to demonstrate such relevance, to demonstrate that the faith experience is relevant to the process by which one achieves human maturity and fulfilment, does not necessarily reduce faith to something having merely a humanistic value. It merely attempts to restate, in a contemporary, existential way the traditional theological theme of the relationship of nature and grace. In this work we shall attempt to come to an understanding of the human experience conveyed by the word faith by examining the dynamics of that experience as described by four Christian thinkers: Sören Kierkegaard, Karl Barth, Rudolf Bultmann and Paul Tillich. We shall then examine the dynamics of human growth towards psychological maturity as described by four leading theories of personality: those of Alfred Adler, Erich Fromm, Gordon Allport and Viktor Frankl. Our question then becomes: are these two experiences - the psychological and the religious - fundamentally the same kind of human experience involving the same type of human transformation? This question of the possible relationship between human growth and Christian faith is, as I have already suggested, a restatement of the age - old question of the relationship between nature and grace, religion and life, and there are at least two possible ways of describing this relationship.

At the very beginning of his *Summa Theologiae* Thomas Aquinas describes the relationship between nature and grace as reciprocal. On the one hand he states that:

> ...faith presupposes natural knowledge even as grace presupposes nature (*gratia praesupponit naturam*) and perfection presupposes something that can be perfected.[3]

presupposes some kind of natural human capacity for such a commitment. Aquinas maintained that there is not a complete discontinuity between nature and grace; that there is a natural predisposition for grace and, therefore, the gift of grace can be greater in one than in another.[4] More contemporary authors have elaborated on this Thomistic principle by demonstrating the importance of maturity, freedom and responsibility as the natural foundation for the life of faith. Conversely, they have shown the detrimental effect of human maladjustment, of immaturity, narcissism and over - dependence on the possibility of a genuine commitment of faith. As St. Paul remarked (Hebrews V:12 - 14), one must be a mature adult to receive the solid food of the Christian message.

It is the premise of the present study that most of the work that has been done in the area of the developmental psychology of religion has been of this nature, i.e., an elaboration in human developmental terms of the Thomistic axiom - *Gratia praesupponit naturam*. Using Erik Erikson's stages of psychosocial development,[5] Jean Piaget's stages of cognitive development[6] and Lawrence Kohlberg's stages in the development of moral reasoning,[7] various authors have attempted to demonstrate that healthy human development provides a natural foundation for healthy religious development and the achieving of religious maturity. Erikson. for example, identifies the challenges of each stage of psychosocial development as the acquisition of a particular human virtue, quality or "ego - strength" appropriate to that stage. Each ego strength is the result of the successful resolution of a psychosocial conflict. Thus, in the first year of life, the quality to be built into personality is hope which is the result of a predominance of "basic trust" over mistrust - the psychosocial conflict of infancy. Donald Evans sees in each of these psychosocial conflicts the psychological or experiential foundation for a religious/moral conflict between what he terms an "attitude - virtue" and "attitude - vice." The attitude - virtues are described as "ways of being in the world which have both a religious and a moral dimension,"[8] i.e., basic human stances toward reality which translate into religious attitudes and moral virtues. Thus, the psychosocial ego - strengths become the natural foundation and experiential root of religion and morality. In a similar vein, Heije Faber[9] seeks in each of the psychosocial stages a pattern of relationship with one's social environment which becomes the prototype or model for a particular way of relating to reality as such and to ultimate reality. In this vein the psychosocial stages are the psychological foundation for religious development understood as one's developing relationship with God. Walter Conn offers "a distinctive interpretation of conscience in terms of self - transcending similar vein, Heije Faber[9] seeks in each of the psychosocial stages a pattern of relationship with one's social environment which becomes the prototype or model for a particular way of relating to reality as such and to ultimate reality. In this vein the psychosocial stages are the psychological foundation for religious development understood as one's developing relationship with God. Walter Conn offers "a distinctive interpretation of conscience in terms of self - transcending subjectivity"[10] and finds evidence of a drive toward such self - transcendence in the developmental theories of Erikson and Piaget as well as in Bernard Lonergan's philosophical analysis of conversion. In this case moral maturity is seen as having its roots in authentic human development understood as the drive toward self - transcendence.

James Fowler[11] has outlined the stages of faith development. Faith is here understood as "human faith" - trust in and loyalty to "a transcendent centre of value and power"[12] which gives meaning and coherence to life and the development of which Fowler sees as an accompaniment of a person's cognitive, moral and psychosocial development. For Fowler, then, the various levels of faith ("Intuitive - Projective, mythic - literal" etc.) reflect the levels of a person's development in these other areas and this "human faith" is in turn the natural foundation of religion which Fowler, borrowing the language of Wilfred Cantwell Smith, describes as a "cumulative tradition" which through doctrine, ritual etc. gives expression to what is a "quality of human living."

From a theological perspective - or more accurately, from the perspective of the dialogue between psychology and theology - all the above mentioned theorists seem to share a common methodological stance. Their approach to the question of the relationship between human and religious growth translates the Thomistic principle *gratia praesupponit naturam* (grace presupposes or builds on nature) into the principle that authentic religious growth and maturity presupposes the natural foundation of authentic psychological growth and maturity. The theologian, however, might object that to limit our understanding of the relationship between human and religious growth to this one principle is to put limitations on the grace of God (by reason of the limitations of the natural foundation which it presupposes) and to ignore the reciprocal relationship between nature and grace. For in addition to the above - mentioned principle, Aquinas also said "...grace does not destroy nature but perfects it" (*Gratia perficit naturam*).[13] When this axiom is translated into developmental language it implies that grace not only presupposes a certain degree of human freedom, responsibility and maturity, but also has the effect of orienting the believer towards the goal of authentic human becoming. To ignore the principle that grace presupposes nature turns the grace of God into something magical whose effects have no basis in nature. But to ignore the principle that grace perfects nature is to ignore the dichotomy experienced by many people today between religion and life, between faith and human values.

It is true that the commitment of faith demands a degree of personal maturity but this leaves open the further question as to the direction and orientation which this commitment gives to further personality growth. In other words, grace presupposes a certain natural foundation or predisposition, but in what sense does it perfect it in some human sense? In this work, I would like to reflect on this further question of whether the life of faith is, in itself, experienced as human growth and authentic human existence. Does the believer experience his faith as the overcoming of threats to, and the achieving of authentic existence and personal growth? In other words, does grace perfect nature? If this question may be answered in the affirmative, it is thereby implied that the believer does not achieve human maturity and then make the commitment of faith; nor does he pursue faith - existence and human maturity as separate though compatible goals. It implies, rather, that he achieves authentic human existence precisely through his act and commitment of faith. If then we accept both principles - that grace both presupposes nature and perfects nature - there is implied a reciprocal relationship between human and religious growth or as William Meissner[14] (14) phrases it between psychosocial and psycho - spiritual development. This means, for Meissner, that for each psychosocial "ego strength" there is a psycho - spiritual analogue. Thus, for example, there is a reciprocal relationship between what Erikson calls "basic trust" and religious faith. This means on the one hand that religious faith is psychologically more possible for a person who possesses the natural human capacity for basic trust than for someone who is unable to trust and, conversely, that faith development is impeded by the inability to entrust oneself to anything outside of oneself. (Grace presupposes nature). On the other hand it means also that grace does not depend entirely on the development of basic trust; that where faith develops through grace it can create or expand one's capacity for basic trust (grace perfects nature).

In this work I want to reflect on this reciprocal relationship between human and religious growth. Part A will review those aforementioned authors whose work reflects the first principle of this reciprocal relationship between human and religious growth, i.e., that authentic human development is the natural foundation for authentic religious growth and the life of faith. (*Gratia praesupponit naturam*). Part B will attempt to test the validity of the second principle of this reciprocal relationship (at least in reference to the Christian understanding of faith) i.e. that authentic religious growth and maturity is productive of authentic human growth and maturity (*gratia perficit naturam*). I would maintain that this side of the reciprocal relationship between human and religious growth has remained underdeveloped in the literature on this question in part, perhaps, because it involves a serious dialogue with theology.

In testing the validity of this principle as it applies to the Christian experience and life of faith, our question becomes: Does faith existence, by its very nature, involve growth towards human maturity and fulfilment? Is the call to faith also a call to the realization of one's full humanity? Most believers, of course, would maintain, on the basis of a conviction of faith verified by personal experience, that through their faith they have become more fully human. Our discussion will be an attempt to test the objective validity of this subjective conviction of faith just as other psychologists of religion have tested the validity of the conviction that authentic humanity is the natural foundation for authentic religion, and just as philosophers of religion have tested the rational validity of the metaphysical truth claims of religion.

Does faith - existence, by its very nature, involve growth towards human maturity and fulfilment? In trying to answer this question we shall, as mentioned above, bring together in dialogue, theological descriptions of the Christian faith experience and psychological descriptions of the dynamics of human growth. In doing so, we shall be concerned with two specific questions: First, do these psychological and theological interpretations of human existence describe the same kind of human growth experience? Do the two forms of discourse refer to the same experiential substratum? Secondly, if we answer our first question in the affirmative, may we then proceed to describe faith - existence in the context of and using the terminology of the personality theories we have examined? For example, is the life of faith, rightly understood, characterized by what Adler called "social interest" the hallmark of the mature adult? What I want to suggest in this work is that the human dynamics underlying the experience of faith are the same as those underlying authentic human growth. I am not suggesting that faith and human growth are the same reality but that each involves the same experience of transformation. That transformation, as we shall see, is a self - transcending transformation of motives. From this point of view, what distinguishes the adult from the child is the quality of self - transcendence and the type of motivation which inspires his action, not chronological age. Similarly what distinguishes the believer from the non - believer is, again, a type of self - transcending motivation, not formal adherence to religion.

ENDNOTES

1. Sigmund Freud, *The Future of an Illusion.* (New York: W.W. Norton & Co., 1961).
2. Dietrich Bonhoeffer, *Letters and Papers from Prison.* (London: S.C.M. Press, 1953) pp.90 - 93.
3. *S.T.,* I, q.2, art 2.
4. *S.T.,* I a - II ae, q.112, art 2 and art 4.
5. Erik Erikson, *Identity and the Life Cycle.* (New York: W.W. Norton & Co., 1980).
6. Jean Piaget, *Six Psychological Studies.* (New York: Random House, 1967).
7. Lawrence Kohlberg, *The Psychology of Moral Development: The nature and Validity of Moral Stages.* (San Francisco: Harper & Row, 1984).
8. Donald Evans, *Struggle and Fulfilment: The Inner Dynamics of Religion and Morality.* (New York: Collins, 1979). p.16.
9. Heije Faber, *Psychology of Religion.* (Philadelphia: Westminster Press, 1975).
10. Walter Conn, *Conscience: Development and Self - Transcendence.* (Birmingham, Alabama: Religious Education Press, 1981), p.1.
11. James Fowler, *Stages of Faith: The Psychology of Human Development and the Quest for Meaning.* (San Francisco: Harper & Row, 1981).
12. *Ibid.,* p.14.
13. *S.T.,* I, q.1, art 8.
14. William W. Meissner, *Life and Faith: Psychological Perspectives on Religious Experience.* (Georgetown University Press, 1987).

PART A

HUMAN TRANSFORMATION AS FOUNDATION OF FAITH

(GRATIA PRAESUPPONIT NATURAM)

CHAPTER 1

Human Development and Religion.

A work which proposes to reflect on the dynamics of change and transformation in human development and on the relationship of that development to religious growth and maturity, must begin by differentiating the various aspects of human development and their relationship to one another. Our inquiry then has to do with the relationship between cognitive, moral and psychosocial development and religious development. In the Introduction I have suggested that this relationship is reciprocal, i.e., religious growth and maturity presupposes and builds on the natural foundation of authentic human growth, freedom and maturity, while at the same time orienting the religious believer toward the goal of authentic human growth and maturity. This statement of reciprocal relationship is based on the twofold theological assumption, as enunciated by Thomas Aquinas, that grace both presupposes and builds on nature (*Gratia praesupponit naturam*) and perfects nature (*Gratia perficit naturam*).

William Meissner, after relating Erik Erikson's stages of psychosocial development to aspects of "psychospiritual" identity, translates the theological axiom concerning nature and grace into developmental terms:

> It should be evident from this partial analysis, that there is a reciprocal relationship between personal identity on the natural level and spiritual identity on the supernatural. In psychological terms, then, spiritual identity builds on personal identity. There are two consequences of this relationship. First, the degree of spiritual identity which one can achieve may be limited by, or related to, the degree of prior personal identity achieved. Second, spiritual identity is in some sense perfective of personal identity.[1]

This first part of our discussion will seek to illustrate the first principle of this reciprocal relationship - that authentic human development is the natural foundation for authentic religious growth and the life of faith - by focusing on the work of certain authors (notably, Heije Faber, William Meissner and Donald Evans) who interpret the stages of human psychological development as establishing a foundation for religious growth. Specifically, these authors discuss the relationship of religious growth and the life of faith to Jean Piaget's theory of the stages of cognitive development (see Table 1), Lawrence Kohlberg's theory of the stages of moral development (see Table 2) and especially Erik Erikson's theory of the stages of psychosocial development (see Table 3).

TABLE 1. STAGES OF COGNITIVE DEVELOPMENT

	STAGE	APPR. .AGE	CHARACTERISTICS
I	SENSORI - MOTOR	0 - 2	- Egocentrism - child is center of objects which make up his up his/her world. - Learning about physical objects in environment by acting on them. - Gradual differentiation of self from objects in environment
II	PREOPE - RATIONAL THOUGHT	2 - 7	- Development of language means 1. Naming objects and talking about them 2. Learning not restricted to physical activity - Thought is egocentric and therefore 1. Prelogical - absence of logical operations (E.g. seriation, conservation, classification, reversibility). 2. Intuitive - Perceptions of world not governed by logical laws and relationships, age of wonder, fantasy, imagination.
III	CONCRETE OPERA - TIONAL THOUGHT	7 - 12	- Ability to think logically about concrete things. - Ability to see logical relationships among objects which at first were merely acted upon. - Ability to organize and classify in the mind rather than experience things in concrete ways. - Concrete understanding of causality, conservation, time space etc. - Intuitions become logical operations.
IV	FORMAL OPERA - TIONAL THOUGHT	12 - ADULT	- Ability to apply logical operations in absence of concrete objects, i.e., to think abstractly. - Thinking about logical possibilities rather than concrete objects. - Equilibrium achieved when adolescent belief in "omnipotence of reflection" is balanced by reflection more grounded in reality and experience.

See: Piaget (1967) and Wilcox (1979).

TABLE 2. STAGES OF MORAL DEVELOPMENT

LEVEL	STAGE	APPR. AGE	CHARACTERISTICS
PRE - CONVEN - TIONAL		10 - 13	- Moral reasoning based on consequences and physical powers of those in authority. - Society seen as alien authority
	1) PUNISHMENT AND OBEDIENCE		- Morality of obedience to rules because of superior power of authorities and to avoid punishment. - Actions judged according to physical consequences.
	2) INDIVIDUAL, INSTRU - MENTAL PURPOSE AND EXCHANGE		- Morality based on desire to satisfy one's own needs and occasionally the needs of others. - Right is what is fair - an equal exchange. - Being good to others so that they will be good to you.
CONVEN - TIONAL		ADOLE - SCENCE	- Desire to fulfil expectations of others or of groups regardless of consequences for oneself. - Based on need to belong which is becoming more important than concrete rewards. - Society seen as that entity of which I am a part and which must be maintained.
	3) MUTUAL INTERPERSO - NAL EXPEC - TATIONS, RELATION - SHIPS AND CONFOR - MITY		- Morality based on desire to please and help others and receive esteem and approval. - Maintaining relationships of trust and affection. - Behaviour judged by intention as well as consequences.
	4) MAINTE - NANCE OF SOCIAL SYSTEM AND CONSCIENCE		- "Law and order" orientation. - Doing one's duty for maintenance of social order. - Loyalty to society as a whole, not just interpersonal relationships.
POST - CONVEN - TIONAL		ADULT - HOOD	- Autonomous moral reasoning based on principles that are valid and applicable beyond the authority of groups. - Social perspective which is "prior to society."

5) SOCIAL CONTRACT	- Moral reasoning based on standards agreed upon by the whole society. - Possibility of changing law on basis of common good.
6) UNIVERSAL ETHICAL PRINCIPLES	- Moral reasoning based on universal ethical principles which apply to all of humanity and every society. - Abstract principles rather than concrete rules. - Right behaviour is adherence to self - chosen principles i.e., integrity.

See Kohlberg (1981) and Duska and Whelan (1975).

TABLE 3. STAGES OF PSYCHOSOCIAL DEVELOPMENT

STAGE	APPR. AGE	PSYCHOSOCIAL CONFLICT	EGO - STRENGTH
ORAL	0 - 1	BASIC TRUST vs MISTRUST	HOPE
ANAL	1 - 4	AUTONOMY vs SHAME AND DOUBT	WILL POWER
OEDIPAL	4 - 5	INITIATIVE vs GUILT	PURPOSE
LATEN - CY	5 - 12	INDUSTRY vs INFERIORITY	COMPE - TENCE
ADOLES - CENCE		IDENTITY vs ROLE CONFUSION	FIDELITY
YOUNG ADULT - HOOD		INTIMACY vs ISOLATION	LOVE
MIDDLE AGE		GENERATIVITY vs STAGNATION	CARE
OLD AGE		EGO - INTEGRITY vs DESPAIR	WISDOM

(See: Erikson, 1980)

In relating his stages of moral development to cognitive, religious and psychosocial development, Kohlberg suggests the following relationship among these various aspects of human development:
1. Moral development presupposes cognitive development. Since stages of moral development are, for Kohlberg, stages of moral reasoning and reflect varying degrees of maturity in one's moral judgements, then the level of moral development will reflect one's level of cognitive development. Thus, one who cognitively is at the stage of "concrete operations" lacks the capacity for abstract thought required for stage 6 moral reasoning based on universal principles of justice. As Kohlberg states:

> Since moral reasoning clearly is reasoning, advanced moral reasoning depends upon advanced logical reasoning. There is a parallelism between an individual's logical stage and his or her moral stage.[2]

2. Religious development presupposes moral development. Kohlberg proposes that moral development is necessary but not sufficient for religious development. He bases this principle on two philosophical assumptions. The first has to do with the autonomy of morality vis - à - vis religion. In discussing the relationship of morality to religion he rejects both the "divine command" theory (all morality is based on divine command) and "emotivistic" theories as in the Freudian notion that moral judgements are expressions of a "constellation of emotional structures termed the superego."[3] In this latter view, morality would be the result of socialization, i.e., of internalizing through emotional identifications, the moral rules of a given society, which rules are then reinforced by religion. Kohlberg favours a "natural law" theory which sees the development of moral reasoning as a structural development which is independent of particular religious and societal codes. The goal of this development is a set of self - chosen universal principles of justice. These moral principles, he argues, are the "outcomes of universal human nature" and are found to be "in harmony with our consciousness of the ultimate power or laws governing the larger extrahuman or cosmic order."[4]

The proposition that religious development presupposes moral development is based also on a second philosophical assumption, namely, that metaphysical or religious reasoning presupposes the development of moral reasoning. Kohlberg reminds us that even after one has attained the stage 6 level of universal moral principles, there still remains the further question: Why be moral at all? This, he argues, is not a moral question but an ontological or religious question.

> Thus, ultimate moral maturity requires a mature solution to the question of the meaning of life. This, in turn, we argue, is hardly a moral question per se; it is an ontological or a religious one.[5]

In other words, the religious question, "Why be moral?" presupposes a normative structure of morality, i.e. a criterion for making moral judgements, which is being called into question. Kohlberg's empirical investigations have led him to conclude that one's stage of religious development is never higher than his or her stage of moral development. Thus, there is a correlation between one's stage of moral reasoning and one's understanding of God. For example, the stage four concern for law and order as necessary for maintaining the social system is reflected in an understanding of God as lawgiver for the social and natural order.

In coming to grips with the question "Why be moral?" and, therefore, with the question of the meaning of life, "religious thinking involves a reflection on moral reasoning such that one's moral understanding is given a religious significance." In so doing, religion provides "a transcendent or infinite ground for rational human activity."[6] Morality, then, is related to religion as a necessary preamble, i.e., as that "rational human activity" which seeks its own transcendent ground or meaning by asking the question "why be moral?"[7] This suggests to Kohlberg the possibility of a further stage of development - "stage 7" - which however is "a religious or ontological stage, not a purely moral one."[8] This stage begins, in Kohlberg's view, with the despair we feel "when we begin to see our lives as finite from some more infinite perspective" and when we "identify ourselves with the cosmic or infinite perspective" and "value life from its standpoint."[9] We might add that this despair is an accompaniment of what Paul Tillich has called "ultimate concern" and what we shall refer to later in this study as the inadequacy of the ethical life. This religious orientation which lies beyond even the highest level of moral development (universal principles of justice) may involve a type of moral action motivated by self - transcending and self - sacrificing love. The term for this kind of love is *agape* which Kohlberg describes as "responsible love." This type of moral motivation, he maintains, is not an alternative to stage 6 since it presupposes universal principles of justice as love presupposes duty, but a higher stage of morality involving "acts of supererogation," i.e., "acts of sacrificial love and human brotherhood" which cannot be demanded of people in justice. *Agape* goes beyond duty and justice and, therefore, beyond the limits of natural moral development. It is the result of a new cosmic or infinite perspective which transcends the ethical.

> The center of the highest stage is experiences that are most distinctively religious experiences of union with deity, whether pantheistic or theistic....We term this new perspective `cosmic' and `infinite'...The attainment of this perspective results from a new insight. Using Gestalt psychology language for describing insight, we term it a shift from figure to ground, from centering on the self's activity and that of others to a centering on the wholeness or unity of nature or the cosmos.[10]

Later in our discussion I shall attempt to describe the experience of grace and faith as precisely this type of religious experience which results in a new perspective which takes the believer beyond the ethical.

3.   Both moral and religious development presuppose psychosocial development, i.e., the development of social perspective. Kohlberg's term for social perspective is "role - taking." A role - taking stage is "the level at which the person sees other people, interprets their thoughts and feelings, and sees their role or place in society."[11] Role - taking or social perspective is the result of environmental stimulation and as such acts as the link between cognitive and moral development.

> Role - taking level, then, is a wedge between logical or cognitive level and moral level; it is one's level of social cognition.[12]

In other words, it is precisely the environmental stimulation provided by social interaction and the development of social perspective which accounts for the individual's ability to apply his or her developing cognitive capacities to the solution of moral problems. Kohlberg cautions however, that cognitive and moral development are not thereby to be considered simply as aspects of the socialization process.

> Basic moral norms and principles are structures arising through experiences of social interaction rather than through internalization

of rules that exist as external structures; moral stages are not defined by internalized rules but by structures of interaction between the self and others.[13]

What then is the role in moral development of those emotional identifications and internalizations which are part of the socialization process? They are not the cause of morality as Freud had maintained. Morality is not simply the result of internalizing parental and societal commands and prohibitions; it is the result of the whole process of social interaction and the development of social perspective and "role - taking" stages. What identification does supply - in addition to giving morality some specific content - is to "deepen its affective significance."[14] This means that when moral obedience is, in part, obedience to a loving parent or a loving God, whose representation is a projection of the parental figure, then there is added to moral motivation the added affective dimension that "someone else cares" whether one is good. Thus Kohlberg points out that when young people leave home and experience independence there is frequently either regression to a preconventional hedonism because "no one cares" or progression to principled morality which is not dependent on external approval.

We might describe, then, the relationship between the various aspects of human becoming as follows: religious development presupposes moral development which in turn presupposes psychosocial development or the development of social perspective. Kohlberg, for instance, describes each level of moral development as characterized by a particular social perspective.[15] The preconventional level is informed by a concrete, egocentric, individualistic perspective in which society is perceived as an objective force, even to the individual, and imposing rules from without. At the conventional level law and order become the norm for morality because it is good for the maintenance of society, perceived now as that entity of which I am a part. Thus my own welfare and the good of society coalesce. In postconventional morality, however, there is a return to an individual perspective, not in the child's sense of being alien to society but a perspective which is, to use Kohlberg's phrase "prior to society." This means that the individual has made a commitment to self - chosen universal moral principles on which, it is believed, any good society must be based. The laws of any particular society are thereby relativized; they must reflect and be judged in the light of such universal principles.

The development of social perspective, then, would seem to be the most basic requisite of moral and religious development. In saying this we are stating a variation of the theological axiom *gratia praesupponit naturam.* And if we further apply this to the psychosocial theory of Erik Erikson it would mean the resolution of each psychosocial conflict and the acquisition of each psychosocial ego - strength or virtue becomes the natural foundation for some aspects of religious development, or as the theologian might say, for the "action of grace." In the remainder of this first section of our discussion I would like to review the eight stages of Erikson's psychosocial model of human development and, in so doing, to summarize the way in which this theological axiom is illustrated in the work of some of those who have commented on the religious significance of Erikson's stages. Most notably we shall examine the manner in which the stages of psychosocial development are interpreted by Heije Faber as a growing pattern of relationships which are the natural foundation for one's growing relationship with God; by William Meissner as bearing a reciprocal relationship with "psychospiritual" development; and by Donald Evans as the psychological foundation for the development of the "attitude - virtues" which are the foundation of religion and morality.

1. *ORAL STAGE - BASIC TRUST VS. MISTRUST* (HOPE)

In Erikson's stages of psychosocial development, the focus is clearly on human relatedness, on the conflicts that result from the interaction between the individual self and others (both significant others and the society as a whole) and therefore on the "virtues" or ego - strengths which develop as a result of the successful resolution of such conflicts. In this respect it represents a twofold extension or elaboration of Freud's psychosexual schema of human becoming. First, human development is seen not merely as the maturing of the sexual instinct but as the development of a personal identity in relation to one's social environment. Accordingly, adult characteristics are the result of such social interaction and not simply refined and sublimated ways of gratifying primary instincts. Secondly, it means that human development does not reach its goal in the attainment of sexual maturity but continues through old age and includes all stages of the life cycle.

Thus, for Erikson, the first year of life can be described not only as the "oral incorporative" stage with all the modes of adaptation which that term implies (taking in, holding on, biting etc.) but also as the stage of total dependency which requires "basic trust" in the mother or mothering person on the part of the neonate. The human infant remains dependent for a longer period of time than other animals, perhaps in order to learn to trust his or her human environment, for trust is basic to that human experience of belonging which Erich Fromm calls "rootedness" or "brotherliness" as opposed to the instinctual rootedness of the animal. In the infant's growth toward an attitude of basic trust Erikson sees the role of mother or the mothering person as crucial. The quality of the mother's response to the infants's needs will to a large extent determine whether the child will feel secure or threatened - secure in the impression that the world (for mother *is* the infant's world) is a benign place and that he is important, or threatened by the impression (through neglect, harshness, etc.) that the world is a hostile place and that he is not important. The infant will accordingly respond with either a trusting attitude towards the world and towards himself (self - confidence) or a mistrusting attitude towards the world and himself. Herein lies the psychological root of the inability to entrust oneself to anything or anyone beyond the self - the characteristic of what Fromm calls the "hoarding" character who clings to what he has (ideas, beliefs, tastes) and perceives the world beyond the self, especially those aspects of it that are new and novel, as a threat.

The conflict between this general mistrust of one's environment by which one perceives everything as threat and cannot accept change and the attitude of basic trust by which one accepts life as it is and is open to life, change and process is one that we begin to experience in infancy but which continues through all stages of the life cycle. An attitude of basic trust towards one's world is rooted, says Erikson, in the conviction

> That you can trust the world in the form of your mother, that she will come back and feed you, that she will feed you the right thing in the right quantity at the right time and that when you're uncomfortable she will come and make you comfortable, as so on. That there is some correspondence between your needs and your world, this is what I mean by basic trust.[16]

But Erikson warns that all of this does not mean that one must develop a completely trusting attitude towards life to the complete exclusion of mistrust. For complete trust can result in an uncritical acceptance of fashionable ideas, dependence on popular opinion and gullibility while the absence of mistrust can mean the elimination of that wariness that is necessary in the face of the real dangers that threaten us. The developmental goal is rather a favourable balance between trust and mistrust.

> Actually a certain ratio of trust and mistrust in our basic social attitude is the critical factor. When we enter a situation we must be able to differentiate how much we can trust and how much we must mistrust, and I use mistrust in the sense of a readiness for danger and an anticipation of discomfort.[17]

Or as Jesus cautioned his disciples, they must not only be "simple as doves" but also "wise as serpents" (Matthew 10:16).

The developmental goal, then, of this first stage of development is not the complete elimination of mistrust but the predominance of trust over mistrust. This balance in favour of basic trust makes possible an attitude of hope which is the virtue or ego - strength which the infant begins to develop at this stage. We might say that hope is a trusting attitude toward the future; without it there is no moving forward for which reason Erikson refers to it as "the basic ingredient of all strength" and "a very basic human strength without which we couldn't stay alive."[18] It is, then, as if the child in whom trust predominates over mistrust "decides" to live. This basic human capacity for hope must be reaffirmed by the human subject throughout life, Erikson notes, "because of his lifelong struggles between trust and mistrust."[19] He stresses that hope is a basic human strength "and not something invented by theologians or philosophers." Thus when religions speak of the virtue of hope they "only sanctify what they recognize as given."[20] Hope as an ego strength is the natural foundation of the theological virtue of hope (*gratia praesupponit naturam*). This principle is recognized by proponents of the theology of hope whose theological reflection begins with an analysis of hope as a basic structure of human existence. The God who is the object of hope - who is described in terms of humanity's hope for the future - then becomes humanly as well as theologically meaningful.

As a way of elaborating on the religious significance of this and each succeeding psychosocial stage, I suggest that we reflect on a series of statements from Erikson and his commentators.

(1) *Religion is the institutional safeguard of the child's growing sense of trust* (Erikson).

When Erikson says that religion is "deeply related to the matter of trust" it is important to note that he is not speaking of religion in some private and personalized sense but of religion as a "cultural and traditional institution."[21]   There is a twofold significance in this. First it reminds us that for Erikson psychosocial development stresses not only the social interactions with an individual's intimate circle of significant others but with the larger society and its institutions. Secondly, it assigns a role in human development to the currently much maligned "institutional" religion.   While it is true that institutional religion has been psychologically damaging to some of its adherents and it is also true, in Erikson's view, that "there are millions who profess faith, yet in practice mistrust both life and man,"[22] nevertheless religion at its best serves "to restore a sense of trust at regular intervals in the form of faith."[23]   It must be remembered that trust is the formal element of faith, that faith is essentially an act of trust in another and of entrusting oneself to another.   Thus the basic trust learned by the infant is the psychological foundation - the "raw material" as it were - of religious faith.   Just as hope as a basic human strength has to be reaffirmed throughout life, so the basic trust which is the source of that hope has to be similarly reaffirmed.

In the process of the reaffirmation of trust the basic trust which the infant experiences toward mother on the psychological plane eventually becomes in time a sort of "ontological" trust towards one's world, towards reality as such - what Erikson describes as a conviction "that there is some correspondence between your needs and your world." When this trust is expressed religiously, it becomes faith in an ultimate trustworthy object and source of security. In inculcating such faith, institutional religion reaffirms and reinforces that attitude of basic trust which is basic to life.   Erikson identifies some ritual expressions of trust characteristic of religion: childlike surrender to the divine, a humble attitude in prayer, the confession of sins and appeal for divine forgiveness.[24] It is important to notice that these elements of religion do not create basic trust but reinforce an already existing attitude of trust.   It is not difficult to see that for one dominated by an attitude of mistrust the effect of these elements of religion might be just the opposite. For Erikson what is important for an adult is a kind of faith which reaffirms and maintains that basic trust which can be transmitted to infants, whether that faith be derived from religion or some other form of human fellowship or endeavour.

> Whosoever says he has religion must derive a faith from it which is transmitted to infants in the form of basic trust; whosoever claims that he does not need religion must derive such basic faith from elsewhere.[25]

(2) *Religion is the result of a positive experience in relation to the mother which conquers the negative one* (Faber).

This statement implies that the infant's experience of mother is ambivalent. Erikson explains the ambivalence of the infant's feelings by pointing to those experiences which are the inevitable sources of mistrust. These are the experience of being deprived resulting from the temporary frustration of the infant's hunger drive; the experience of being divided resulting from the infant's increasing self - awareness (and therefore separation from "maternal matrix"); the experience of being abandoned resulting from the mother's preoccupation with other duties and interests. Basic trust must be maintained in spite of these physiological, psychological and environmental sources of mistrust.

> It is against the combination of these impressions of having been deprived, of having been divided, and of having been abandoned, all of which leave a residue of basic mistrust, that basic trust must be established and maintained.[26]

This "residue of basic mistrust" leaves the child with a sense of "paradise lost." Basic trust must maintain itself in spite of this sense of loss which is reinforced by all of life's negative experiences. Basic trust enables the child to move forward into life with hope in spite of the regressive desire to recapture the lost paradise. Religious faith also has this "in spite of" quality for religion turns the nostalgia for a paradise lost into hope for the future, a hope expressed in symbols such as the "Kingdom of God."

Heije Faber suggests that in this ambivalent experience of the child the mother can be seen as a prototype of reality. In this experience of the mother as both the nourishing mother (object of trust) and the threatening devouring mother (object of mistrust) "the child," he maintains, "learns to experience its most fundamental relationship to reality."[27] Throughout life, one's experience of life and reality will have this same ambivalent and "in spite" of quality. The experience of trust vs. mistrust becomes the "ontological" anxiety of being vs. non - being; and the affirmation of basic trust in spite of mistrust becomes what Paul Tillich calls the "courage to be," i.e., the affirmation of being in spite of the "threat of non - being." In the same way, one might say that religious faith involves a sense of oneness with the deity that conquers the sense of separation. As Tillich maintains, faith involves the courage to be on the basis that one's being has been affirmed and accepted by the ground of all being. This experience of being "grasped by the power of being" overcomes the threat of non - being.[28]

(3) *The religious pattern of obedience and achievement is based on the foundation of basic trust* (Faber)

According to Erikson, psychosocial development takes place according to an "epigenetic" principle, which means that it follows a ground plan according to which, of all the ego strengths which make up the healthy personality as a whole, each has its own "time of special ascendancy" - a point in the developmental schema which is critical for its development.[29] This further implies that development of ego strengths is cumulative in the sense that the achieving of the developmental goal of each stage depends on the successful resolution of the previous stages as on a foundation. Thus the development of a healthy sense of autonomy in stage 2 presupposes and is dependent on the foundation of that basic trust which is developed in stage 1. Since the toddler is obviously not completely independent, her efforts to be autonomous and do things on her own must be sustained by a sense of basic trust in the support and help of the adult which enables her to control failures rather than be controlled by them. Paradoxically, the child needs the sense of oneness with mother - even in her absence - to sustain her in her attempts to be independent of mother. Otherwise autonomy becomes an isolated attempt to do things on one's own which cannot sustain itself.

The toddler is saved from the fate of facing reality alone, depending only on her own inner resources, by an attitude of basic trust which is rooted in a sense of oneness with mother, of participating in the "being" of mother. The ontological analogue to this infantile experience might be found in Tillich's analysis of the "courage to be" in which he reminds us that the "courage to be as oneself" (autonomy) is essentially inseparable from and must be complemented by courage to be as part," i.e., the courage that derives from the experience of being part of a reality greater than the self.[30] This, in turn, is an essentially ontological or religious kind of experience best exemplified in the mystical or unitive kind of experience of union with God, nature or the cosmos. It is from this sense of oneness or participation in a reality greater than the isolated self that one derives a sense of ultimate security and the ability to face reality alone and assimilate the negative experiences which inevitably result from that venture. Faber employs W.D. Winnicott's concept of the "transitional object" to interpret the child's attachment to such things as teddy bears and "security blankets" as an attempt to make mother present. In the same way, he suggests, the use of images in religion makes God present for the believer.

> In religion the image is also an 'intermediate or transitional object.' Rationally speaking, the image can be seen as a representation. But even superficial observation shows that the emotional side is much more important. The image makes the deity present.[31]

He further points out that where the religious desire is identified with "nostalgia for the experience of oneness" (whose psychological root is the experience of oneness with mother of the first phase), then the process of secularization, with its stress on the autonomy of the secular realm, amounts to a loss of "transitional objects," i.e. the religious forms, images, symbols and rituals "in which we preserved the basic trust of the first phase.[32] Those theologians who offer a positive evaluation of this process explain it as a development towards a more authentically "biblical" type of religion which is based on the self - revelation of the God who alone is holy and which therefore desacralizes our relationship to all other reality. In the context of his discussion of the relationship between basic trust and autonomy, Faber sees it as a shift from a maternal to a paternal structure or from "naturalistic" religion to a "religion of the word." Naturalistic religion represents God as an original all embracing unity, the totality of being, of which the mother - figure is the experiential prototype and who reveals himself in images. In religions of the word, God is the supreme being rather than the totality of being in which we participate, a creator and lawgiver who communicates (through the revealed word) over the distance that separates the infinite from the finite and of whom the father - figure is the experiential prototype. This is the God who commands and calls his people to an historical task and destiny. This makes for the religious pattern of obedience and achievement to which Faber alludes. His point, then, would seem to be that this type of "religion of the word" with its emphasis on obedience and achievement requires as a necessary foundation a sense of oneness with God perceived as the totality of being, just as the exercise of autonomy requires an attitude of basic trust rooted in a sense of oneness with mother. In this way the anxiety of separation from God is overcome by a sense of oneness with the ground of one's being. Again, the philosophical analogue to this might be found in Tillich's insistence that the understanding of God as supreme being (the cosmological method) must be complemented by the understanding of God as the "ground" or totality of being (the ontological method).[33]

(4) *There is a reciprocal relationship between basic trust and religious faith* (Meissner)

For William Meissner there is a reciprocal relationship, as previously noted, between the ego - strengths acquired in the process of developing a psychosocial identity and the virtues which make for the development of a "psychospiritual" identity. Thus when the principle "grace presupposes nature" is applied to this first stage of growth his conclusion is twofold: (i) Religious faith which, as we have seen, is essentially an act of trust in and of entrusting oneself to another, is psychologically more possible for a person with the natural human capacity for basic trust. (ii) Faith development is impeded by basic mistrust, i.e. "the inability to confide oneself in a trusting relation to anything outside of oneself.[34] On the other hand, the principle that "grace perfects nature" in this context means that the grace of God does not *depend* on the development of basic trust. Where faith develops through the action of grace it can create or expand the capacity for basic trust. It is grace, in the theological view, which makes the response of trusting faith possible, for by grace one is "drawn to, loved and accepted by the most trustworthy of objects."[35]

This reciprocal relationship also obtains between the ego - strength of hope and the theological virtue of hope for both are rooted in trust or faith. Meissner describes hope as "a basic quality of experience which is made firm by the satisfaction of desires, from the infant's primitive desire for nourishment and affection to the adult's deepest, most soulful cry for strength and spiritual consolation."[36] As the infant's developing attitude of hope is rooted in basic trust towards a trustworthy mothering person, so the hope of the adult believer is "rooted in our trust and in the trustworthiness of God and His fidelity to His promises."[37] Meissner concludes:

> It seems then that both faith and hope build upon the capacity of the personality for trust and confidence. If the person has developed this capacity, his spiritual disposition through faith and hope is more secure, and the extension of basic trust to an infinitely loving Father and God is thus made easy. Where the initial crisis has been resolved in favor of basic mistrust, however, the capacity for entrusting oneself to God through faith and hope is impeded. Conversely, by reason of the principle of reciprocal influence, the implied disposition of trust and confidence in God through faith and/or hope will exercise a reciprocal influence on the orientation to basic trust in the personality.[38]

From a theological perspective this reciprocal influence of grace on one's psychological well - being points to the healing or "sanating" (to use Meissner's term) influence of grace by which it is believed to reintegrate the personality which suffers the disintegrating effects of sin.

(5) *The constituent elements of trust and mistrust are a set of attitude - virtues and attitude - vices which are the experiential foundation of religion and morality* (Evans).

For Donald Evans religion comprises a set of attitudes which are expressed in beliefs and worship.   By "attitude" he means a fundamental way in which the self relates to its environment, i.e., a mode or pattern of adaptation.   Such a fundamental attitude is "pervasive" both internally and externally: it is the response of one's total personality to all life situations. Morality, on the other hand, is made up of a set of virtues which are expressed in moral beliefs and conduct. Virtue here is understood not just as a disposition to follow certain rules of conduct but a way of *being* in the world, a pervasive stance toward the world which results in certain kinds of behaviour. "Attitude - virtues," then, are defined as "ways of being in the world which have both a religious and a moral dimension."[39] These attitude - virtues, therefore, constitute the human and experiential basis or foundation of religion and morality. Human existence is seen by Evans as a struggle between the attitude - virtues and the opposing attitude - vices (e.g. trust vs. mistrust), and human fulfilment is the result of the "predominance of attitude virtues over attitude - vices."[40]

It would appear that this interpretation of psychosocial development is less nuanced than that of Erikson himself because of its apparently simplistic identification of the poles of each psychosocial conflict as "virtue" and "vice." Erikson, as we have seen, does not see the apparently "negative" attitudes such as mistrust, shame, doubt, etc., merely as "vices" but as necessary components of psychosocial identity. The "virtue" proper to each stage is, for Erikson, that attitude which results from a proper balance between the poles of the conflict. Thus "hope" is the result of the predominance of trust over mistrust. In the main, however, Evans is faithful to Erikson's insight when he speaks of human fulfilment as the predominance of attitude - virtues over attitude - vices. Thus in reference to our first stage, the developmental goal is the predominance of trust over mistrust. In this regard, Evans' contribution to our discussion consists in his identification of those attitude - virtues and attitude - vices which make up the constituent elements of trust and mistrust. In other words trust and mistrust translate into a variety of conflicting attitudes - conflicts which we experience throughout life. Evans lists the constituent elements of trust vs. mistrust as follows:

(i) *Assurance vs. Anxiety.* Rooted in the experience of basic trust is "the assurance that life is worth living because it has already received the meaning and reality which are necessary for human fulfilment."[41] The assurance of one's identity, genuineness and worth ("reality assurance") and of an overall ultimate meaning to reality as such ("meaning assurance") is received as something already given, not something for which I anxiously strive. In this sense, it has a religious quality since it is perceived as a gift from an ultimate meaningful reality, an ultimate ground of being. This carries with it the assurance of being confirmed, accepted and valued which is analogous to the experience of grace and whose moral consequence consists in that degree of self - transcendence - freedom from self - preoccupation and concern about one's self - worth - which it makes possible. This means, as Sam Keen states, (in a passage quoted by Evans), that "my action may spring out of what I am rather than arising out of a desperate need to establish myself."[42] The opposing attitude - vice is anxiety in the sense of "ontological anxiety," i.e., the fear of non - being, nothingness, meaninglessness and worthlessness - constituent elements of basic mistrust and part and parcel of human existence.

(ii) *Receptivity vs. wariness.* Wariness is an expression of basic mistrust and is described by Evans as an attitude of defensiveness against one's world which is seen as threatening and intruding. It includes *resentment* (reaction against the threat of being deprived), *hostility* (reaction against the threat of being destroyed) and *miserliness* (protecting what one has).[43] These qualities link the meaning of wariness to what Erich Fromm calls the "hoarding" character type with its orientation toward destructiveness.[44] The self - defeating quality of this attempt to hoard and preserve and protect rather than to reach out, assimilate and grow (Fromm calls it "non - productive") is reflected in the enigmatic words of Christ: "for the man who has will be given more; from the man who has not, even what he has will be taken away" (Mark, 4:25). Receptivity, on the other hand, refers to an attitude of openness to the world as a gift. One who receives the world not as a threat or even as deserved but as the gift of something good is thereby enabled to respond with *gratitude* (by giving freely in return), and with *confirmation* (of the worth of other people who are received as gifts).[45]

(iii) *Fidelity vs. idolatry.* Fidelity here refers to a faithful commitment to that which is seen as the source of the assurance of both reality (personal self - worth) and ultimate meaning. It is a kind of faithful persistence in that assurance which is maintained in spite of the anxiety of meaninglessness and nothingness and which, therefore, allows for the experience and expression of that anxiety. It is only when such ontological anxiety is repressed that one falls into idolatry which is the attempt to eliminate anxiety not through the assurance of worth and ultimate meaning but by seeking total satisfaction in some substitute good or, as Evans puts it, by the "focusing of limitless needs on a limited object."[46] In the absence of an absolute and unlimited source of meaning and worth one feels total fulfilment and security in some substitute object such as work, pleasure or possessions which then becomes the object of an addiction. When such idolatry is focused on a single substitute good it corresponds to what James Fowler calls "henotheistic faith" i.e., "a pattern of faith and identity in which one invests deeply in a transcending center of value and power, finding in it a focal unity of personality and outlook, but this center is inappropriate, false, not something of ultimate concern. The henotheistic god is finally an idol...It means the attribution of ultimate concern to that which is of less than ultimate worth."[47] For Evans, the psychological function of such idolatry has to do with the repression of anxiety. If the idolatry is not focused on a single object, it may take the form of what Fowler calls "polytheistic faith" which he characterizes as "a pattern of faith and identity that lacks any one center of value and power of sufficient transcendence to focus and order one's life."[48] This provides, to use Evans' term, only a pseudo - assurance" since a less than ultimate object of commitment cannot provide ultimate and unlimited security and fulfilment.

(iv) *Hope vs. despair.* Hope, which Erikson sees as the ego - strength resulting from the favourable balance of trust and mistrust is described by Evans as the forward looking dimension of assurance, the hope that the assurance of meaning and worth which exists in the present will continue into the future.[49] This kind of hope, he maintains, is maintained through involvement with others (with one's world) and hence takes two forms: a passive "openness to liberation" which involves a willingness to receive "the essentials of life" (assurance) from others as well as a more active "initiative towards encounter" by which one reaches out to others to create personal encounter through which "meaning and reality and life energies can be experienced."[50] Despair, therefore, is equated with a kind of self - imposed isolation based on the absence of any hope for human relations in which the essentials for life (a sense of worth and ultimate meaning) can be received. To someone in the grip of such despair, depression and self - isolation, the "summoning of the self to move outwards into encounter" - even in the simple form of picking up the phone to call a friend - "may seem like climbing Everest."[51]

(v) *Passion vs. apathy.* The apathetic absence of feeling results, in Evans' view, from the fact that one's feelings are perceived as threatening. The response to such a threat is a lack of openness towards one's feelings or detachment from them. Sometimes one's most intense feelings such as loneliness, helplessness, grief or rage threaten to overwhelm us. Even feelings of tenderness and love can be threatening because of the interpersonal commitment and responsibility they imply. Apathy is the bulwark we erect against such a threat and Evans suggests that there is a kind of religious apathy which constructs for itself an image of God as neutral (unconcerned with and unresponsive to his creation) or impersonal ("energy" or "life force"). Such a god is a projection of the detached apathetic person and is described by Evans as an "Ideal World Observer," and, since apathy is born of distrust, such a god is a "Deity of Distrust alongside resentful mans's Grand Depriver, idolatrous man's omnipotent Fairy Godmother and despairing man's Wheel of Fate."[52] In addition to its religious implications, apathy has the quality of a moral vice by reason of its attitude of cold detachment toward others, by reason of its "law and order" style suppression of the feelings of others, and finally, by reason of the destructive forces that erupt when the repression of feelings breaks down.

The opposite of apathy is passion a constituent element of trust which is an openness to one's feelings (including feelings of mistrust). It is "the aspect of trust which allows mistrust to come out into the open."[53] Evans finds a pre - eminent example of passion in Jesus' words of seeming despair from the cross: "My God, my God, why hast thou forsaken me?" (Mark 15:34) Evans comments:

> In a little while Jesus feels serenely confident and says, "Father, into they hands I commend my spirit" (Luke 23:46). But at the moment he is overwhelmed by almost intolerable feelings: a terrible agony as he experiences abandonment, a heavy helpless despair, a bewildered resentment at being deprived of all consolation. Jesus is able to feel and express his distrust, because at a deeper level he can still trust. He is not afraid that he will drive God still further away by blurting out what he feels. He appeals to a God who is still there though not near. He is assured that his whole self has been affirmed and accepted by God, so he need hide nothing from himself and God. The most trusting of men can acknowledge the depths of his own distrust.[54]

The same may be said of all human relationships. Much is heard today about the necessity of trust and communication especially between spouses. What makes possible the honest communication of the sometimes negative feelings of anger, resentment, etc., is the presence of still deeper feelings of love, trust and loyalty.

2. ANAL STAGE - AUTONOMY VS. SHAME AND DOUBT (WILL POWER)

In the Freudian, psychosexual view of human development, the anal modes of adaptation - elimination and retention - become respectively the psychosexual prototypes for, on the one hand the adult character traits of freedom of emotional expression, disorderliness, emotional outbursts etc., and, on the other hand, the traits of thrift, frugality, neatness, orderliness, cleanliness etc. Erikson's psychosocial interpretation of the anal modes of adaptation is apparent in the following passage:

> This stage, therefore, can be decisive for the ratio between love and hate, for that between cooperation and wilfulness, and for that

between the freedom of self - expression and its suppression. From a sense of self - control without loss of self - esteem comes a lasting sense of autonomy and pride; from a sense of muscular and anal impotence, of loss of self - control, and of parental overcontrol comes a lasting sense of doubt and shame.[55]

The anal stage, then, is not just the striving for pleasure through the experiences of elimination and retention, which in time becomes sublimated into adult character traits; it is the conflict between the child's striving for autonomy which derives from "a sense of self - control without loss of self - esteem" and the feelings of doubt and shame that might result from the failure of his attempts at autonomy.

The child of approximately age one to four wants to move out of the complete dependency of the oral stage. He wants to be on his own and do things on his own; he wants a degree of autonomy of which he is not yet completely capable. Therefore, as we have already seen, he needs basic trust in the willingness of others to help in order to control his failures. This striving to be on one's own, when it is carried on against the background of basic trust, leads to the development of normal autonomy and will power. If basic trust is lacking, the child will be inhibited in his striving for autonomy by feelings of shame, fear and timidity. Instead of controlling his failures he will be controlled by them. This leads him to overmanipulate and overcontrol himself through a precocious conscience and an obsession with compulsive rituals which becomes "the infantile model for a compulsion neurosis." The result, in time, is an adult whose "precocious conscience does not really let him get away with anything, and he goes through life habitually ashamed, apologetic, and afraid to be seen." The failure to achieve a healthy autonomy might also be expressed by developing a defiant kind of autonomy by way of overcompensation. "Real inner autonomy, however," says Erikson, "is not carried on the sleeve."[56] Let us turn now to our commentators for insight into the religious significance of this stage.

(1) *If autonomy develops without a foundation of basic trust, the ego feels isolated and is exposed to the fear of having to assert itself alone. This pattern is the psychological root of a perversion of religion or a breach with religion* (Faber).

In the previous section we discussed the predicament of the person whose striving for autonomy and achievement is not rooted in the experience of basic trust and who must therefore experience the anxiety of facing reality on his own, relying solely on his own inner resources and deprived of that experience of basic trust which inspires the confidence necessary to do and achieve and be independent. Faber sees such a person as experiencing a threefold conflict.[57] First, there is the conflict of activity vs. passivity which results in a person whose compulsive activity masks a secret longing for passivity, or who is unable to be passive or dependent. Secondly, the conflict between dependence and independence resulting in repression of one's dependency striving. Thirdly, the conflict of defiance vs. shame and doubt in which apparent pride in one's achievements masks a certain doubt about their worth and therefore shame. The shame experienced by the toddler at this stage is not to be confused with guilt which for the child is the fear of punishment. It is rather "the fear of standing alone and feeling defenceless," with the accompanying "fear of the loss of security and love."[58] As with the child, so also with the "self - made" adult whose striving for autonomy and achievement have an over - driven quality.

It must be reiterated, however, that the developmental goal of this stage is the proper *balance* between autonomy and shame and doubt. As Erikson points out, while shame "can be a terrible form of self - estrangement for the human," a certain capacity for shame is a necessary ingredient for a healthy personality, for "one cannot imagine a human who is not afraid of being embarrassed - afraid of being in a situation in which other people will find him shameful."[59] The same is true of doubt, as is well know by anyone who has had to deal with someone who never has a moment of self - doubt. The problem lies not in experiencing shame and doubt but in being *controlled* by such feelings which happens when one's sense of shame and doubt is not outweighed by a sense of basic trust. For the religious person this means, as we have seen, that the sense of separation from God is not outweighed by the sense of oneness with and participation in the being of God. Such a person lacks the sense of what Donald Evans calls the "assurance" of one's genuineness and worth as a "given" that does not have to be earned, and therefore must constantly strive to establish her own worth and acceptability through autonomous achievement. For Faber, this represents a "perversion of religion" which is exemplified by the Pharisee and the Puritan.

Whatever the merits of those who made up the historical Jewish sect known as the Pharisees, Jesus' criticism of their religious mentality has led Christians to apply the term "Pharisaism" to any type of religion which is extremely legalistic and which is motivated by the desire to justify oneself, i.e., to earn God's love and acceptance through moral and religious achievement.   The Christian sees this as the antithesis of the religious relationship of grace in which God's acceptance is seen as freely given; it need not and, indeed, cannot be earned.   From this perspective, Pharisaism reverses the true order of things by believing that moral and religious observance will lead to God's acceptance, whereas in faith (the response to grace) one believes that God's prior and freely given acceptance inspires moral and religious observance.   For this reason, Faber calls it a "perversion" of religion and interprets it psychologically as a case of autonomy and achievement not developed on the foundation of basic trust (faith).   If I do not have the assurance of worth and acceptance that is the result of basic trust, then I must work to earn and establish that acceptance.   In the religious sphere this translates into a religion based on excessive self - justification, because, as Faber points out, in the absence of basic trust, "fear and doubt of the self will turn autonomy into a perverted self - justification."[60] In the anal stage, self - confidence grows on the foundation of the confidence in another experienced in the oral stage. Without this foundation of confidence, self - confidence becomes "desperate self - assertion in the face of fear and self - doubt."[61]

Faber also sees Puritanism as psychologically rooted in the pattern of the anal phase. He points to the following "anal" characteristics of the Puritan mentality: the emphasis on doing, producing and achieving through a sober industrious lifestyle; the desire for purity and getting rid of the impure and the dirty; holding fast to money; the desire to confirm one's status with God (as one of the elect); and all of the above as masking feelings of self - doubt.[62] The theological root of such a mentality is to be found in the Calvinist doctrine of predestination according to which the eternal and unchangeable will of God predestines each human soul to either eternal salvation or eternal damnation.   One therefore cannot earn salvation but only examine one's own life for the evidence of salvation or "election," namely, a clean, sober, industrious lifestyle. It is not difficult to understand how for some this would become an anxious attempt to create such signs of election in their lives by pursuing such "worldly asceticism" (to use Max Weber's term). It is also not difficult to understand how for some the material prosperity which followed from such a lifestyle would also come to be regarded as a sign of election. Hence for many a life of ceaseless effort, achievement and success become the foundation for a religious sense of security. Since, moreover, the wealth accumulated through such effort was not to be squandered on enjoyment and self - indulgence (which implies idleness), it was reinvested. In this way, according to Max Weber,[63] the so called Protestant work ethic became the moral and spiritual infrastructure of the capitalist economic system. Perhaps it is an illustration of our principle that grace presupposes a natural foundation that Calvin's doctrine, the intent of which was to place salvation beyond the realm of the humanly achievable, was received in many cases by minds with a craving for certainty and, therefore, transformed into the basis of a lifestyle the purpose of which was to assert and affirm, through autonomous human achievement, one's spiritual election. In this respect, it is not unlike the Pharisees' desperate attempt at self - justification and fits the pattern of autonomy and achievement without a foundation of basic trust.

This same pattern may result not in a perversion of religion but in a "breach" with religion. In normal development, autonomy develops on the foundation of basic trust and one develops a healthy balance between trust and autonomy, dependence and independence, confidence and self - confidence. In abnormal development one does not achieve this balance because autonomy loses its connection with basic trust and develops on its own. Hence the "desperate self - assertion" of which Faber speaks. The excessive emphasis on autonomy may coincide with a loss of the religious attitude which is based on basic trust toward an ultimate trustworthy reality and participation in the being of that reality. When there is a too one - sided emphasis on autonomy, Faber remarks, the religious pattern of trust and participation "recedes into the background."[64] When this happens on the social level, the result is the process of secularization in which secular society regards itself as autonomous or independent of religion, living according to allegedly self - discovered human values and no longer looking to God and religion for moral and spiritual guidance. This declaration of the autonomy of the secular order, the liberation of society from the tutelage of God and the sacred and the Church amounts to a loss - at least in the sphere of public and social life - of the religious dimension. This spirit of autonomy is what Tillich calls "the spirit of the finiteness which rests within itself" (i.e. the finite, temporal and secular is sufficient unto itself) or "the courage to be as oneself." Some theologians such as Bonhoeffer see in this spirit of autonomy a welcome rejection of the "religious premise" that humanity "needs" God. Others, such as Faber, point to its roots in an anal pattern of autonomy deprived of basic trust and see, therefore, the possibility insecurity and the sense of "being condemned to freedom."[65]

In all of this, Faber has pointed to a pattern of human development which constitutes an impediment to authentic religious development, thus illustrating in a negative way our principle that grace presupposes nature.

(2) *The psychospiritual complement of basic autonomy is contrition* (Meissner).

For William Meissner sin is "capitulation and self - debasement before inferior forces."[66] This amounts to a lack of integrity, a failure to be true to who I am and to my own deepest convictions; in other words, a surrender of my autonomy. It follows, therefore, that contrition or sorrow for sin is a reclaiming of one's integrity and, therefore, one's autonomy. It involves a return to a true sense of self esteem and a realization of the true dignity of the self. It further implies a recognition of the self as the ultimate source of personal and moral responsibility. In contrition the ego assumes responsibility for its moral failures and does not blame external forces. An illustration of Meissner's point might be found in the text of the Catholic mass. Since the mass is an act of public worship the prayers are in the first person plural. In the penitential rite with which the mass begins, however, the congregation recites the *confiteor* - the confession of sins - in the first person singular, thus signifying that each one takes personal responsibility for his own sins. In this context, Meissner also points to the Catholic emphasis on the "purpose of amendment" as an integral part of contrition and by which one assumes personal responsibility for the damage one has caused and for one's own future development.

Contrition, therefore, is seen as "an extension in the spiritual order of the fundamental dispositions of basic autonomy" or "an expression of spiritual autonomy."[67] In keeping, then, with his notion of the reciprocal relationship between psychosocial and psychospiritual growth, Meissner's conclusion is twofold: First the development of autonomy on the psychosocial level facilitates the expression of true contrition. Secondly, when one fails to develop true autonomy, the resulting sense of shame and doubt makes the expression of true contrition more difficult. Shame makes it difficult to face one's failures. It is "the reaction of the guilty soul trying to hide its face from God."[68] Similarly, self - doubt implies insecurity and lack of resolve. Doubt about the moral quality of one's action makes clear self - appraisal, and therefore true contrition, difficult.

(3) Autonomy vs. Shame and doubt is the experiential foundation of the religious/moral conflict of humility vs. pride and self - humiliation (Evans).

In Evans' view, humility is an "attitude - virtue" because it represents a positive way of responding to the problem first experienced in the anal stage, namely, the tendency to feel ashamed because one's attempts at autonomy (power, achievement, status) are limited and meet with limited success. In the end, it is the problem of how to deal with one's finitude. Humility is therefore defined as a "realistic unashamed acceptance of my finitude."[69] This includes not only the acceptance of what I cannot do but also of what I can do and, therefore, a spur to effort. Humility, therefore, "includes an active exercise of the limited power which I actually have, changing the world and myself as I am able."[70] Adrian Van Kaam, speaking of the realistic kind of self - acceptance which is at the heart of humility, describes it as an acceptance of my "unique but limited task" in life.[71]

The opposite "attitude - vice" to humility - the negative response to the problem of shame over one's limitations - takes either of two forms. On the one hand, pride involves a denial of the reality of one's limitations to the point of indulging in delusions of grandeur. The proud person cannot bear to confront his limitations and the accompanying shame because they are too threatening to his self - esteem. He therefore represses awareness of them by means of a "self - deceptive attempt to act out one's fantasies of infinitude, of divinity, of unlimited power and status."[72] Self - humiliation, on the other hand, is the opposite but equally negative reaction to shame. It is complete surrender to feelings of shame, a reverting to a state of infantile helplessness in the face of the problem of one's limitations. While pride is a refusal to recognize limitations, self - humiliation is a refusal to recognize strengths, and both therefore, represent a failure to realize true humility, which is both a religious attitude and a moral virtue. It is a religious attitude in that it involves an at least implicit recognition of a power or unifying reality which is the source of both one's limitation ("the Limiter") and of one's strengths ("the Enabler").[73] It is also a moral virtue because the self - acceptance which is the essence of humility produces a realistic acceptance of others as what they are and not merely as a function in one's own life, to serve one's own sadistic (pride) or masochistic (self - humiliation) fantasies.

3. THE OEDIPAL STAGE - INITIATIVE VS.GUILT (PURPOSE)

Both Freud and Erikson see the oedipal stage as significant for moral development. Freud sees conscience or the superego as an outcome of the Oedipus complex and the processes of identification and internalization which are a necessary part of the resolution of the conflict. Conscience, resulting as it does from the internalizing of parental and societal commands and prohibitions, is a by - product of the socialization process. For Erikson, the significance of this stage for moral development is to be found in the psychosocial conflict between the initiative of the child of approximately 4 to 6 years of age and the restraints imposed by parents. The child's initiative is expressed through imaginative play and intrusiveness. Imaginative play is termed "symbolic" by Piaget who reminds us that it is an expression of the child's egocentric cognitive activity and a "deforming assimilation of reality to the self," by "transforming what is real into what is desired."[74] Eventually the child will have to find an equilibrium between this desire to assimilate reality to herself and the need to adapt oneself to reality. We might say that parental restrictions confront the child with that reality to which she must adapt. The child's intrusiveness is described by Meissner as "intrusion into other bodies by physical attack, into other people's attention by activity and aggressive talking, into space by rigorous locomotion, and into the unknown by lively curiosity" which includes a growing sexual curiosity.[75]

The conflict between the child's initiative and the parental restraints has at least two consequences. First, it channels the child's energies, partially at least, away from fantasy and towards reality by encouraging the completion of realistic projects. This is at the same time a turning away from mere pleasure which results from the gratification of instincts towards some genuine experience of happiness which results from making progress toward a goal. In other words, some sense of purpose and direction begins to develop. Secondly, the child begins to internalize the parental restrictions which marks the beginning of moral development and the formation of conscience which, Erikson notes becomes "the great governor of initiative." If initiative is too severely restricted either by the parental restrictions or by an uncompromising infantile conscience the result may be "a self - restriction which keeps an individual from living up to his inner capacities or to the powers of his imagination and feeling."[76] Again, the developmental goal is the proper balance between initiative and guilt.

Freud believed that the psychological roots of religion lay in the dynamics of the Oedipus complex, i.e., in the male child's sexual rivalry with his father and the projection of the resulting ambivalent feelings onto God as a surrogate father.   Since this projection perpetuates the ambivalent feelings of love and hostility as well as the resulting guilt feelings, religion is seen as rooted in and an expression of the guilt which is experienced in the oedipal phase. The following propositions interpret the oedipal stage as the natural foundation for religious development in more broadly psychosocial terms.

(1) *The oedipal phase emphasizes the relationship with the father which becomes the pattern for a new kind of relationship with God* (Faber).

The focal point of Faber's discussion of each stage of development is the pattern of relatedness which becomes the prototype for a way of relating to others, to one's world to reality and to ultimate reality or God. Thus in the oedipal stage it is the new developing relationship with the father which is of particular interest "because it is the medium through which it becomes possible to enter into a new relationship to the divine reality."[77] The relationship with mother in the oral phase was characterized by basic trust and a sense of oneness and participation.   Even after mother is recognized as a separate and distinct person the sense of participation remains because "the basic feeling in contact with the mother is safety, security, and the knowledge that we belong to her."[78] This is followed by the stage of autonomy, a distancing of oneself from mother in order to achieve a degree of autonomy, though, as we have seen, an autonomy always rooted in and determined by basic trust.

Just as autonomy develops on the foundation of basic trust, so the developing relationship with the father in the third stage presupposes a certain degree of autonomy. This is so because this new relationship is characterized by distance rather than participation in the sense that the other is not someone with whom I was originally one but rather, in some sense, a "stranger" whom I encounter. To use Faber's term, the other is discovered as a "counterpart." To be sure, there is a sense of participation in the relationship to the father but, as Faber points out, it is a sense of participation or oneness which must be established "over a distance." Thus it is a relationship that combines in some way the features of the first two stages: participation and distance, trust and autonomy, dependence and independence. The child at the oedipal stage has experienced two different types of relationship: a relationship with mother rooted in a sense of oneness and participation and a relationship with father based on distance, separation or what Faber calls a "cleft." Borrowing from Emmanuel Levinas, he suggests that these relationships are the experiential prototypes for two kinds of "metaphysical thinking." The first "proceeds from totality" and stresses the fact that I and that to which I am related (others, reality, the cosmos, God) make up one reality or totality. The second, stresses the distinct otherness of that to which I am related. In this latter kind of relationship the other is not that together with whom I make up a totality but a "counterpart" whom I encounter face to face, with whom I must communicate through language over the distance that separates us and whose reality, by reason of either its power, authority, dignity or need, makes an ethical demand upon me.[79]

Accordingly, these two types of relationship become experiential prototypes for ways of thinking about God and one's relationship to the divine reality. The relationship to mother is the prototype for an understanding of God as the "ground of being" (Tillich), the totality of being as such in which every particular being participates. Awareness of God as this all - embracing totality, Tillich argues, comes not by way of rational argument, but by an immediate awareness and experience of the self as participating in a reality greater than itself. He compares it to the experience of overcoming estrangement, i.e., of becoming aware of that of which I was always essentially a part but from which I had become existentially separated or estranged.[80] Gordon Kaufman sees in this way of thinking about God a "teleological" model of transcendence which is based on the notion of the self as incomplete in its individuality and as striving toward God as that totality in which it essentially participates as the goal or *telos* of its becoming.[81] It is finally, the experiential prototype for what Faber calls naturalistic religions which are based on the experience of oneness and participation in the all - embracing totality of God or nature, i.e., on a timeless and universal human experience which transcends history.

The relationship with the father, on the other hand, is the prototype for an understanding of God not as the ground of being but as the Supreme Being who is know not through immediate awareness but by inferring, through observation of creation or the cosmos (Tillich calls this the "cosmological" method) the existence of a creator. This God is not a totality in whose being I participate, but a separate and distinct entity from whose being I am excluded. As with the child's encounter with the father, one's encounter with this God is like "meeting a stranger," and participation in the being of this God is always through communication (revelation) which bridges the infinite distance which separates humanity and divinity. Such an encounter represents what Kaufman calls the "interpersonal" model of transcendence. As in interpersonal life our knowledge of other persons depends more on what they do than what we do, i.e., on their honesty in revealing themselves through communication, in the same way the inaccessibility of God is overcome only by his self - revelation. If the relationship with the father with its emphasis on overcoming distance or separation is the prototype for this way of thinking about God, it is therefore the prototype for what Faber calls revealed or "prophetic - historical" religions in which God is seen as bridging the distance between himself and his creatures by communicating his revealing word through a prophet or historical founder and calling his creatures to some historical task and destiny [82]

(2) *The psychospiritual analogue of initiative is penance.* (Meissner).

The developmental goal of the oedipal stage is a balance in which initiative predominates over guilt. A realistic sense of guilt which results from a recognized violation of the moral order is not incompatible with initiative. A harsh or punitive superego, however, which afflicts the ego with guilt feelings which derive from oedipal conflicts and are not reasonable or realistic has an inhibiting effect which blocks the exercise of initiative. Meissner believes that this predominance of initiative over realistic guilt "seems to extend itself to the spiritual level through the fundamental orientation of penance."[83] In other words, initiative, as a fundamental ego - strength, is the natural foundation for the psychospiritual virtue of penance which, in turn, is an exercise in initiative, just as contrition is an exercise in autonomy. Contrition, as we have seen, is the recognition and assuming personal responsibility for one's moral failures. Penance, Meissner notes, is a "prolongation and consequence" of contrition since it represents a "permanent disposition" to do what is necessary to correct the disorder recognized in contrition. In contrition the ego exercises its autonomy by assuming responsibility for moral failures; in penance the ego "assumes responsibility for its own regulation and discipline," i.e., for maintaining ego control over libidinal drives.[84]

Meissner distinguishes between true and false penance by pointing out that true penance is an ego function and, therefore, is guided by a sense of balance and realistic proportion. True penance, therefore, is in the service of the ego and aims at authentic self - discipline through ego control. The aim of false penance is not self - discipline but self - punishment based not on realistic guilt but on guilt feelings originating in the superego. Ultimately, true and false penance are differentiated on the basis of the source of the initiative for self - discipline: the controlling and regulating ego or the severe and punishing superego.[85] In keeping with his principle of "reciprocal influence," Meissner concludes that where the natural capacity for initiative predominates over guilt a natural foundation exists which facilitates the exercise of true penance. Where this capacity for initiative is blocked by the domination of the superego "one cannot expect a facile response to the more demanding initiative inherent in true penance."[86] On the other hand, where true penance is achieved through grace "the implicit exercise of spiritual initiative in the ego can produce an effect on the basic disposition to initiative itself."[87]

(3) *Initiative vs. guilt is the experiential foundation for the religious/moral conflict of self - acceptance vs. self - rejection* (Evans)

We have seen that the encounter between the child's initiative and parental restrictions is productive of guilt. We have also seen that such guilt may be neurotic guilt experienced as pervasive feelings of guilt resulting from an overdeveloped superego and issuing in "over - controlled" behaviour which inhibits the development of initiative. On the other hand this psychosocial conflict can and should result in a realistic sense of guilt which represents a balanced sense of right and wrong derived from a healthy internalizing of reasonable parental restrictions.   In recent years we seem to have been culturally conditioned to think negatively about such things as shame and guilt. Some would almost have us believe that we would never experience these darker moods were it not for authoritarian structures which make us feel "ashamed of our bodies" or impose "guilt trips" on us. Erikson, however, maintains that the capacity for shame and guilt are essential to a healthy personality when they exist in proper balance with their psychosocial opposites - autonomy and initiative. A person who cannot experience shame and guilt is not a complete person.

For Donald Evans, what is crucial in our experience of both shame and guilt is the nature of our response to it. As the positive response to shame is humility so the positive response to guilt is "self - acceptance in spite of feeling guilty." As the negative response to shame is pride or self - humiliation, so the negative response to guilt is "self - rejection because of feeling guilty." The self - acceptance here described is both a religious attitude and a moral virtue. It is a religious attitude to the extent that one's self - acceptance is seen as being dependent on "being accepted" by another. Self - acceptance derives from the fact that "I accept the acceptance of another."[88] This requires an attitude of faith or trust toward the other which calls to mind Tillich's definition of faith as "the courage to accept oneself as accepted in spite of being unacceptable."[89] Self - acceptance, then, is made possible by the "grace" of anther's acceptance. Evans argues that there is implicit in self - acceptance a recognition of an ultimate source of grace or acceptance. This ultimate source of acceptance is "whatever reality unifies the whole environment" and he refers to this reality as the "cosmic Acceptor."[90]

Seen in this light, there is an implicit religious attitude in self acceptance which may become an explicit religious faith in an accepting and forgiving God. But self - rejection because of guilt may also translate into explicit religious convictions.

> Self - acceptance is a religious attitude, though it is not necessarily accompanied by conscious religious convictions. For some people, however, the whole struggle between self - rejection and self - acceptance is understood in explicitly religious terms. The issue is whether an accusing, condemning voice of an alleged God pervades my life, crushing me or compelling me to futile and destructive attempts at atonement, or whether I hear and identify with the accepting voice of God so that I am continuously liberated and converted and renewed.[91]

The moral significance of both self - acceptance and self - rejection has to do with their positive and negative impact respectively on human fulfilment. They are also morally significant in terms of human relationships. Feelings of self - acceptance and self - rejection are projected onto others producing attitudes towards others which are, respectively, open and accepting or "accusatory and punitive."[92]

4. *THE LATENCY STAGE - INDUSTRY VS. INFERIORITY* (COMPETENCE).

This stage which covers the elementary school years (approximately 6 to 12) was not developmentally significant in Freud's psychosexual schema since it is a period of sexual latency. From Erikson's psychosocial perspective, however, the early school years are exceedingly important for the process of socialization and the development of social perspective. The child's transition from home to school is in some respects a transition from play to work. It is a task oriented stage in which the child is exposed to supervised training in the mastering of right techniques for carrying out real tasks. Erikson sees this as a kind of basic training in the skills (e.g., literacy) necessary to function in society. It is also a psychologically significant time in that the child's need for esteem and approval is now satisfied, at least partially, by producing good work rather than through play or simply by being someone's child. In this period of sexual latency, pleasure comes in the form of joy in work completed and well done. Hence the importance of learning good work habits so as to acquire a degree of competence and efficiency. The developmental goal of this stage is competence and it is a psychosocial strength since it amounts to a desire to be socially useful. This drive toward competence is what Erikson calls industry which he describes as "a sense of being useful ... a sense of being able to make things and make them well and even perfectly."[93] Industry can be described as an extension of autonomy and initiative; it is autonomy and initiative expressed in a disciplined way.

The hazard of this developmental stage is the failure to produce which inspires feelings of inadequacy and inferiority. We might say that inferiority is the result of personal failure within the competitive atmosphere of the school. Erikson points out that the sense of inferiority - "the feeling that one will never be any good" - emphasises the value of a teacher who focuses on what the child can do and who can discover the child's hidden talent. A further hazard is experienced by the child whose "sense of identity can remain prematurely fixed on being nothing but a good little worker or a good little helper, which may not be all he *could* be."[94] This child links his sense of identity and self - worth to what he can do or produce. Such a child may become the adult workaholic still trying to manufacture self - esteem and the approval of others through work or the practitioner of a very moralistic and legalistic type of religion whose aim is to earn the approval and acceptance of his God through religious and moral observance. In all such cases what seems to be lacking is what Evans calls "assurance," the sense of acceptance as a given and which is therefore not threatened by the experience of failure. It includes the conviction that what I am is more important than what I do or accomplish; that what I do or accomplish does not earn acceptance and approval but is motivated by a sense of acceptance and approval which is already given.   This prior, unmerited acceptance is what Christianity calls grace and it is the reason why Jesus could tell his followers not to be "anxious" about providing for their material needs such as food and clothing (Matthew 6:24 - 34). It is significant that he warns against anxiety rather than worry. Worry would seem to be a natural reaction to unpaid rent or mounting bills. Anxiety, however, is another matter since it implies not just worry about objective circumstances but about oneself and one's self - worth. Our lack of material success, he seems to say, may cause us to worry but it does not affect our worth in God's eyes.[95] One might say that the parents and teachers of the child at this stage must in some sense be "god - like" in that they must demand that the child measure up and produce satisfactory work while at the same time communicating to him that their love and acceptance does not depend on what he achieves. In this task they are trying to be like the God who is both the God of law and the God of grace. Meissner and Evans offer some further insight into the religious significance of this stage in the following propositions.

(1) *The spiritual analogue of industry is fortitude* (Meissner).

For Meissner, industry involves "a certain capacity within the ego not only to direct its energies to a goal, but also to maintain that mobilisation of resources until the goal is achieved or the task is completed."[96] This implies an ongoing effort in spite of difficulties, opposition and resistance and in this regard it is analogous to the moral virtue of fortitude. In the ego which has developed a sense of industry there is a natural foundation for the development of fortitude which represents, for Meissner, an advance over previous phases of psychospiritual development in that "the capacity for prolonged effort implies a deepening and closer organisation of the entire psychic structure."[97] Where, on the other hand, there is a defect of industry because of the predominance of a sense of inferiority, the development of fortitude will be correspondingly more difficult. According to the principle of reciprocal influence the converse is also true. Through the development of fortitude on the psychospiritual level through grace the resources of the ego can be mobilised in such a way as to "mitigate the results of the initial developmental failure to resolve the industry crisis successfully."[98]

(2) *Industry vs. inferiority is the experiential foundation for the religious/moral conflict or responsibility vs. pseudo responsibility and irresponsibility* (Evans).

The sense of industry implies the assuming of responsibility for completing a task or achieving a goal. Evans therefore describes the responsible person as "someone who can be counted on to do a good job when tasks are assigned to her or undertaken by her."[99] It is psychosocial strength because it involves learning "how to be competent in performing tasks within and for the community."[100] For Evans, responsibility amounts to a religious attitude when it becomes not just a sense of responsibility for this or that task but a "pervasive life - stance" in which life as such is seen as a task or calling and one assumes responsibility for becoming what one is called to become and completing the life task one has been assigned. When responsibility reaches this point of development it implies, as Viktor Frankl has pointed out, that one interprets his existence "not only in terms of being responsible *for* fulfilling his life tasks, but also as being responsible *to* the taskmaster."[101] The point made by both Frankl and Evans is that while the religious person explicitly acknowledges the divine Taskmaster, the "non - religious" person who nevertheless sees life as a task for which he is responsible is demonstrating an attitude which is essentially religious.

The development of such an attitude of responsibility presupposes the prior development of trust, humility and self - acceptance. If trust is lacking, one works only to become as autonomous as possible. If humility is lacking, one is either too proud or too self - humiliating to work under the authority of others. If self - acceptance is lacking one's work is a way of atoning for guilt "by scrupulous rule observance and self - punishing service."[102] In all these cases the apparent attitude - virtue of responsibility is in fact the attitude - vice of pseudo - responsibility. Work for such a person is not the responsible exercise of freedom but an expression of bondage to his inner insecurity.

Work for him is not a blessing but a curse. It is not a joyful expansion and expression of his capacities, but a bondage and a burden. He does not work as one who is at home in Eden, but as one who has been forced into exile.[103]

The above describes a person whose attempts at assuming responsibility for his life tasks is flawed by the lack of those ego - strengths which are the necessary precondition for a true sense of responsibility. In the absence of trust and humility and self - acceptance, self - rejection may be so dominant that one becomes irresponsible, i.e., incapable of assuming responsibility, so that life becomes "an undisciplined meandering, an unboundaried drifting."[104]

5. *ADOLESCENCE - IDENTITY VS. ROLE - CONFUSION* (FIDELITY)

The adolescent's well know self - consciousness - concern with how one appears to others - manifests a deeper, inner search for one's identity, a looking for the real essence of oneself which lies behind the various roles one has played and a desire to be known by others as that essence. All the preceding psychosocial stages, each of which confirms one's sense of self - esteem in some way, contribute to and culminate in the adolescent sense of identity which Erikson describes as "the accrued confidence that one's ability to maintain inner sameness and continuity (one's ego in the psychological sense) is matched by the sameness and continuity of one's meaning for others."[105] These words suggest that the need for a sense of personal identity is twofold; it includes not only the need to discover my identity - to discover who I am - but also the need to have that identity confirmed by others. It is not enough to know who I am; society must confirm that it is O.K. for me to be who I am, that the person I am has meaning for others. Hence, the adolescent sense of identity is related to discovering one's role in society and the hazard of this stage lies in failing to discover that role or "role confusion". Erikson explains the well known adolescent tendencies to overidentify with heroes or with an "in group" of peers with the accompanying tendency to be "clannish, intolerant, and cruel" towards outsiders as a "defense against a sense of identity confusion."[106] The significance of this stage for religious development was a preoccupation of some early psychologist of religion who were interested in the phenomenon of religious conversion. The following propositions focus on the religious significance of the adolescent search for identity as expressed in fidelity.

(1) *Religion is a source of ideologies for those who seek identities* (Erikson)

We might say that in the search for a sense of identity the adolescent needs three things:

(i) Acceptance.   Adolescence is characterized by a kind of idealism on both the cognitive and the moral level. Piaget has pointed out that the adolescent's new - found capacity for abstract thought may lead to a "belief in the omnipotence of reflection" by which the adolescent subjects reality to his own thought processes, "as though the world should submit itself to idealistic schemes rather than to systems of reality."   In time the adolescent must achieve an equilibrium between this egocentric desire to assimilate reality to his own thought and the necessity to adapt to reality as it is.   This equilibrium is attained "when the adolescent understands that the proper function of reflection is not to contradict but to predict and interpret experience."[107] A similar confrontation with reality occurs in the realm of the adolescent's moral idealism by which he seeks to actualize the ideal image of himself, and which will render him acceptable to himself and to others.   Like the adolescent's thought patterns this desire to live up to one's ideals through one's own human resources is egocentric and it fails in face of the realistic awareness of his own limitations.   It is at this point that the adolescent needs the experience of being accepted for what he is   -   including limitations and shortcomings - and not for what he can become.   The significance of religion for this stage consists in the fact that, in the face of the failure of idealism, it offers the adolescent an ultimate source of acceptance or grace.   Erikson's focus however, is on the following two adolescent needs.

(ii) Values.   One's identity is reflected in one's deepest convictions, those assumptions about what is and what ought to be which form the basis of one's life and which Erikson refers to as "ideology."   Therefore, with the emerging sense of identity there develops a capacity for fidelity to a set of beliefs and values. This capacity for fidelity is an ego - strength we need in order to adapt to the human world of ideas and values just an animal's instincts are necessary for adaptation to the natural environment.   Erikson, therefore, speaks of "an instinct for fidelity - meaning that when you reach a certain age you can and must learn to be faithful to some ideological view."[108] The adolescent, however, in his search for an ideology - a set of beliefs and values, a world view or vision of reality - to which he can commit himself, cannot stand alone and so looks to others for ideas to believe, ideals to pursue and idols to emulate. Hence the importance of adults in his life with values. Hence also the significance of religion which, as a source of beliefs and values, provides an object of fidelity and therefore, an institutional support for the formation of identity.

(iii) Time. A particular set of beliefs and values - religious or secular - may represent an object of temporary rather than lifelong fidelity and commitment. In this case, Erikson speaks of a psychosocial "moratorium" which societies may provide for young people - "a span of time after they have ceased being children but before their deeds and works count toward a future identity."[109] It is in this light that he interprets the religious commitment of Martin Luther as a young man to the monastic life. It was, he contends, a way of marking time until Martin could become clear as who he was and what his true mission in life was to be. Thus for some, in Luther's time, the monastic life was "one possible psychosocial moratorium, one possible way of postponing the decision as to what one is and is going to be."[110] This does not mean that a permanent commitment such as that to the monastic life with its perpetual vows is trivialized by *intentionally* treating it as a way of marking time. It means that any total and permanent commitment - religious, political, or social - may end in a crisis in which the young person "half - realizes that he is fatally overcommitted to what he is not."[111] In the developmental schema, what was thought to be a permanent object of fidelity and devotion turns out to be a psychosocial moratorium.

(2) *In adolescence a new type of relationship emerges which is based on mutuality and which becomes the pattern for a new type of religious relationship* (Faber).

As we have seen, Faber views the psychosocial stages in the light of the pattern of relatedness which emerges at each stage. Thus, in the first three stages, the child grows from a relationship of trust, participation and oneness, to a stage of striving for autonomy and emancipation from mother and finally into an "I - thou" relationship with the father which combines the features of the first two stages, i.e., a relationship in which trust and participation are established over a distance. In the case of the relationship with the father, there is the aspect of submission to authority or, as Faber puts it, there is "an above and below." What he sees as new in the adolescent relationships is the fact that, while they have the same quality as that to the father - a bond established over a distance or "cleft," - the aspect of "above and below" is replaced by mutuality based on equality.

> If I see the matter rightly, we could say that the aspects of cleft, call and bond, which are taken over from the third phase, continue in the structure of this relationship, though without an above and below.[112]

Though Faber does not emphasize it, I would suggest that this quality of mutuality or exchange between equals becomes evident in the changing relationship between adolescent and parent where question and answer and command and obedience give way to discussion and sharing of ideas. It is more evident in the relationship of the adolescent to her peers with whom she is a "companion in destiny." As equals they "are called towards the future together" and have "a common future which they have to realize with one another and for one another."[113]

Faber is of the opinion that Erikson, in speaking of adolescence, focuses on identity to the exclusion of this emerging pattern of relationship of mutuality. For Erikson, however, this very mutuality and togetherness especially in the case of heterosexual attachment is often "an attempt at arriving at a definition of one's identity by talking things over endlessly, by confessing what one feels like and what the other seems like, and by discussing plans wishes, and expectations."[114] James Fowler, in the same context, refers to the adolescent's relationship to a "chum" of either sex - "another person with time and parallel gifts and needs" - in whom she finds a "mirror" to see "the image of personality emerging and to get a bearing for new feelings, insights, anxieties and commitments that are forming and seeking expression."[115] He further suggest that where God is a factor in the young person's life, he becomes the God who "knows, accepts and confirms" the self which the adolescent is trying to discover.[116] It would seem, then, that the quest for identity and the relational aspect of adolescence are closely connected. In stressing the aspect of mutuality as prototype for a new type of religious relationship, Faber is suggesting , I believe, that the adolescent is beginning to relate to God less as an authority figure and more as a companion and confidant, with whom one is "on the way together." Faber suggests, furthermore, that this pattern of religious relationship seems to be the one that is emerging in our own contemporary culture in which we see ourselves not as living and working under a divinely established order ruled over by God but as working toward a new reality to which God is leading us.[117] This "exodus" model of reality is reflected in the theologies of hope and liberation where God is seen not as ruling from above but as leading us from ahead. In terms of experiential prototypes, this represents a transition from the oedipal to the adolescent pattern.

(3) *The basic elements of identity - self - knowledge and self - acceptance - are realized, on the spiritual level, in humility.* (Meissner).

We have seen that Erikson stresses the social dimension of identity, i.e., the idea that who I am must be confirmed by and have meaning for one's society. For Meissner this means that the self - awareness implied in the concept of identity includes an awareness of the other, the "non - ego reality," the self and the real, and the boundaries that separate them. This implies that a true sense of identity includes self - knowledge and self - acceptance, which, on the spiritual level, are realized in humility. On this level, awareness of the "non - ego reality" includes an awareness of the divine. A healthy sense of the boundaries between the self and reality - the opposite of "identity diffusion" - includes, therefore, an awareness and acceptance of one's creatureliness and dependence on God. This awareness is humility and is part of one's spiritual identity. Pride, on the other hand, represents a failure to achieve "that awareness and acceptance of self which perceives one's place before God as creature, as contingent, as dependent, as derivative in its own existence."[118] To put the matter simply, a clear sense of identity which is always in relation to "non - ego reality" and therefore implies a sense of what I am not, includes of necessity, a sense of humility. Meissner, therefore, sees identity as the natural foundation for humility and its absence as a hindrance to humility. Reciprocally, authentic humility - involving self - awareness and self - acceptance - is seen as a safeguard against identity diffusion.

(4) *The conflict of identity vs. role confusion is the experiential foundation for the religious/moral conflict of self - commitment vs. dissipation* (Evans).

The social aspect of identity (who I am in relation to others) leads Meissner to relate it to the psychospiritual quality of humility. For Evans, the same aspect of identity suggest the "attitude - virtue" of self - commitment. Each attitude - virtue, he maintains, represents a positive response to a particular human problem. As we have seen, trust is a positive response to the sources of mistrust (abandonment, dividedness, etc.) Humility is a response to the problem of shame which comes from the realization of one's limitations. Self - acceptance is the positive response to the problem of guilt and responsibility to the problem of inferiority. Self - commitment, as an attitude - virtue, is related to the problem of identity because, as Evans suggests, the psychosocial question of identity is "who am I in relation to the human community and the cosmos?"[119] This implies that my relationship to the community and its expectations of me are supposed to give me a sense of who I am and lead to the competent carrying out of the task assigned to me by society. In other words, a healthy sense of identity is linked to being good at something which is useful to society, i.e., to commitment to a meaningful role. As identity is the basis of such social commitment, so its opposite - role confusion - results in a sense of alienation from the community with no clear sense of one's role in that community. This results in dissipation - the opposite of self - commitment - whereby one's personal energies are scattered in the unfocused pursuit of some meaningful role.

6. *ADULTHOOD*

In an essay entitled "Psychotherapists or the Clergy" (1932), C.G. Jung expressed the opinion that, of all the patients "in the second half of life" who had consulted him, "there has not been one whose problem in the last resort was not that of finding a religious outlook on life."[120] This oft - quoted passage reflects Jung's conviction that the second half of life was, developmentally, a time of special religious significance; it was a time of introspective adaptation to unconscious archetypal patterns and the process of individuation which, for Jung, was a "religious" quest. It was a time for the discovery of one's soul as distinct from the adaptation to the external world which preoccupies us during the first half of life. This emphasis on the spiritual and religious significance of adulthood balanced the preoccupation of some of the early psychologists of religion with adolescent conversion (perhaps because of their interest in religious education). I would suggest that Erikson, in his delineation of the psychosocial stages of growth, has also helped to refocus our attention on the religious significance of adulthood. He does so, I believe, in at least three ways: first the ego - strengths or "virtues" associated with the three stages of adulthood are the natural foundation for basic features of the life of faith; secondly, the three adult stages reflect increasing degrees of that quality of self - transcendence which characterize the religious personality; thirdly, Erikson carries human development through to old age and describes the "ego - integrity" of old age in such a way as to suggest an openness to transcendence. We shall now look briefly at these three stages.

A) *Young adulthood: Intimacy vs. isolation* (Love).

We have seen that the intimate friendships of adolescence serve the developmental purpose of helping the partners to clarify their individual identities. As Erikson says, intimacy with another also involves becoming intimate with one's own inner resources.[121] This more or less clearly established sense of identity in adolescence provides a foundation for the development of intimacy with another in young adulthood. Intimacy, as an ego - strength is "the ability to fuse your identity with somebody else's without fear that you're going to lose something yourself."[122] This definition clearly indicates that the achieving of intimacy presupposes the prior achieving of identity. Since "no one gives what he does not have," it is the sense of identity which makes possible the self - commitment implied in intimacy. Erikson points out that where one fails to achieve true intimacy the result is isolation from human relationships or relationships which have a stilted and formal quality. Where intimacy, however, predominates over isolation, love - the psychosocial virtue of this stage - becomes possible. The ability to love in an intimate relationship is therefore based on the prior sense of individual identity. As Erich Fromm remarks: "Love is union with somebody, or something, outside oneself, under the condition of retaining the separateness and integrity of one's own self."[123] Mature love, then, involves fusing one's identity with another while retaining one's individual identity (what Fromm calls "productive relatedness"), and the capacity for it is one of the hallmarks of maturity. Erikson quotes Freud as remarking that a mature person should be able to do two things well: love and work.[124] If authentic prayer can be understood as an expression of one's love of God, then perhaps the motto of the medieval monks - *ora et labora* - could be taken as an expression of the same ideal of maturity.

I have suggested that there is an implicitly religious quality of self - transcendence in the stages of adulthood. In the young adult's achieving of intimacy and love we can note a transcending of the self - preoccupation which marks the adolescent search for identity. Evans explains that self - preoccupation means being "turned perpetually inward on myself and my own requirements."[125] It is the "attitude - vice" derived from the intimacy/isolation conflict and it poisons personal relationships for it leads me to either treat others as a function in my life (fulfillers of my needs) or keep others at a distance because they are seen as a threat. The opposite attitude - virtue is "friendliness" which is described as "a readiness and willingness to risk the self by entering into intimate `I - thou' relations of love, giving and receiving at a very deep personal level."[126] At first glance "friendliness" would seem to be a pale description of such deep human relatedness, but Evans chooses this word to denote a readiness for or openness to such intimate relationships. As a pervasive stance toward all of reality (including "moral" intimacy with people and "aesthetic" intimacy with things), friendliness is an implicitly religious attitude toward God as "the pervasive unifying reality which is immanent in all the particulars and transcends them all." It is implicitly, then, an openness to mutual friendship with God. Evans stresses that this kind of divine - human friendship is more like the friendship between two adult friends than the trusting dependency of the infant towards mother.[127] This distinction is reminiscent of Faber's discussion of the quality of mutuality in adolescent relationships as a prototype for a new type of religious relationship.

For William Meissner, the psychosocial capacity for intimacy is related to the religious virtue of charity or love of neighbour for which it provides the natural foundation. "On the psychospiritual level," he suggests, "the basic sense of intimacy seems to find its complement in the second great commandment of the law: love of neighbour." In achieving the capacity for intimacy and, therefore, love of neighbour, "the ego reaches a level of development in which its control of intrapsychic dynamisms permits diversion of its energies outside itself."[128] This is a reference to the self - transcending quality of this stage. On the psychosocial level, the gradual accumulation of ego - strengths culminating in a sense of personal identity provides the necessary foundation for the transcending of the ego in a loving, intimate relationship. In the same way, Meissner contends, on the psychospiritual level, the gradual accumulation of ego - strengths which culminated in a sense of spiritual identity provides the necessary foundation for a self - transcending love of one's neighbour. As we have noted earlier, the term *agape* - the Christian moral ideal - expresses the spontaneous, altruistic and self - transcending quality of love. For Meissner, then, the natural capacity for intimacy is the foundation for spiritual love of neighbour. Conversely, spiritual love of one's neighbour can have a healing influence on an ego which has failed to develop the capacity for intimacy.[129]

B) *Middle age: Generativity vs. stagnation* (Care).

Erikson proposes that the typical outcome of true intimacy is the desire on the part of sexual partners "to combine their personalities and energies in the production and care of common offspring." This desire is but one expression of a more fundamental and pervasive attitude which he calls "generativity" which refers to "the interest in establishing and guiding the next generation."[130] Though this interest is typically expressed through parenting, the term itself has a more general meaning of care for and contribution to others which might take the form of some kind of social service or artistic or intellectual creativity. In this respect it is akin to Alfred Adler's concept of "social interest." Generativity could be described, then, as a desire to live on in others, whether one's physical children or one's "brain children." It is clear that Erikson believes that the course of psychosocial development demands this expansion of interest and concern and contribution beyond the limits of the intimate relationship, thus again underlining the movement toward ever greater self - transcendence in adult growth. Erikson refers to this as an "enrichment" of intimacy and failure to achieve generativity in one form or another results in a state of apathy, egoism or an obsessive fixation on intimacy all of which result in developmental "stagnation." When generativity predominates over this tendency to stagnation one develops the psychosocial virtue of "care" which Erikson describes as including "`to care to do' something, `to care for' somebody or something, `to take care of' that which needs protection and attention, and `to take care not to' do something destructive."[131]

For Donald Evans, the conflict of generativity vs. stagnation is reflected in the conflict of the attitude - virtue of concern vs. the attitude - vice of self - indulgence. As generativity is an extension of and represents a greater degree of self - transcendence than intimacy, so concern is an extension of friendliness. While friendliness is an openness to mutually enriching human relationships, concern has a more altruistic quality, for it involves helping those in need - children, the helpless, the underprivileged, the oppressed etc., - who are not necessarily able to offer help in return.[132] Evans refers to concern as "pastoral" when it involves direct personal encounter with people who need help and as "prophetic" when it aims at the reform of social and political institutions which are the source of social injustice. Thus it is based on "a critical stance towards social institutions, passionately probing them in terms of their humanizing and dehumanizing effects on people, especially the needy and the powerless."[133] Like generativity, concern may be expressed in the care of one's own children or in the broader area of human concerns. In either case it is "passionate" because it is based more explicitly on empathy, an aspect of passion which is an element of trust, than is friendliness. The attitude - vice which opposes concern is self - indulgence which, like concern, takes two forms: a reversal of pastoral concern whereby I take my own self and my own needs as the objects of my concern or a reversal of prophetic concern whereby one's social position and privileges are taken for granted in such a way as to create an attitude of indifference to social injustice.

Meissner points out that generativity involves self - actualization since it has to do with "utilizing the individual's maximum creative capacities." Since however such realization of capacities is to some extent determined by a person's sense of identity and capacity for mature and cooperative interpersonal relations, generativity "depends closely on the satisfactory resolution of the two preceding phases of identity and intimacy."[134] For Meissner the psychospiritual counterpart of generativity is "zeal," understood here in the sense of service and not according to the unfortunate connotations with which that word has been burdened. Both generativity and zeal represent a social commitment based on the realization "that each individual has a responsibility to his fellow human beings," but while generativity is expressed either in parenting or in one's contribution to humanity's social, cultural or economic welfare, the term "zeal" is usually applied to a commitment to humanity's spiritual welfare and the attaining of what is perceived to be its ultimate goal.[135] According, therefore, to Meissner's principle of "reciprocal influence," generativity provides the natural foundation for the development of spiritual zeal because it calls for self - sacrifice and unselfishness which are basic ingredients of zeal. At the same time an authentic spiritual zeal can enable the ego which is deficient in generativity to develop those same attributes of self - sacrifice and generous service of others and thus "help to sanate the original failure of the ego."[136]

(c) *Old age: Ego - integrity vs. despair* (Wisdom)

Integrity here refers to the culminating point of psychosocial development which involves the preceding psychosocial crises and the integration of accumulated ego - strengths. Erikson offers no clear definition of ego - integrity but suggest that one of its attributes is "the acceptance of one's own and only life cycle and of the people who have become significant to it as something that had to be and that, by necessity, permitted of no substitutions."[137] Such an acceptance of what one's life has been forestalls self - recrimination over "what might have been" and facilitates the acceptance of death. Failure to achieve such ego - integrity can result in despair over one's life and fear of death which precludes the possibility of starting another life. Erikson is not precise in defining the meaning of integrity but the acceptance of one's life cycle to which he refers seems to be related to the recognition of it as "the accidental coincidence of but one life cycle with but one segment of history "[138] This suggest to me that integrity has to do with a sense of the continuity of one's life cycle with the past and the future, so that one's necessarily limited accomplishment are seen as building on the efforts of previous generations and subject to completion and extension by future generations. In this way the continuity of one's life cycle with past and future creates a meaningful whole which relates to the meaning of integrity. Despair, on the other hand, results from the sense of living in a rootless and disconnected present so that one's life is a series of unrelated events. The well known anxiety and despair of some existentialist writers seems to be rooted in this sense of life's events and experiences unconnected by any network of meaning.

The meaning of integrity, then, seems to be related to putting one's life into a larger context. This results in a new perspective which Erikson identifies as "wisdom," the psychosocial virtue of this stage. This new perspective derives from seeing one's life in the context of some universal, ultimate reality or destiny. In this respect it is similar to James Fowler's concept of "universalizing faith"[139] or Abraham Maslow's description of the kind of "god - like" perception of the "whole of Being" which characterizes peak experiences.[140] William Meissner relates this stage to the human search for ultimate meaning and notes that the religious person finds the answer to this human need in the resources of revelation and faith. In this case wisdom comes from "an understanding of the meaningfulness of existence in relation to a spiritual order governed and directed by God's will and loving providence."[141] Thus life is placed in a larger context of ultimate meaning and destiny by reason of its relation to a transcendent order of reality. For Meissner, then, the love of God (charity) in the psychospiritual analogue of wisdom. Both represent a new perspective which derives from placing one's life in a larger context of ultimate meaning and destiny and thus represent the last stage in the process of self - transcendence which characterizes adult growth. The self - absorption of the adolescent's search for identity is transcended first through an intimate human relationship, then through a self - sacrificing commitment to society at large and finally through a sense of universal and ultimate meaning and destiny.

Donald Evans describes this new ultimate perspective as a product of contemplation, an "attitude - virtue" which involves seeing each particular being - including myself - as "an expression of a loving creativity which pervades and unifies the universe."[142] Contemplation is a unitive kind of experience which involves a sense of oneness with the cosmos and sees all particular beings as rooted in a unifying ground of being. In language which suggest Jung's concept of the collective unconscious, Evans speaks of contemplation as coming to an awareness of the centre or core of my real self which "is also a part of universal reality."[143] Thus the self is put into a larger context and the self - absorption and the resulting anxiety is transcended. Without such self - trancendence, the result is a form of self - consciousness which is narcissistic in that all things are perceived not as aspects of a universal, pervasive reality but only in their relation to the needs of my isolated ego. From this isolation proceeds the despair of which Erikson speaks. For Evans, the attitude - virtues of the three stages of adulthood are three species of love which are successively wider and more inclusive in their scope and thus represent successive degrees of self - transcendence. Friendliness extends to one's personal circle of friends, concern to needy individuals and groups, and contemplation to universal reality.[144]

I have suggested that the forgoing reflections on the religious significance of the stages of psychosocial development are illustrative of the theological axiom that grace presupposes and builds on nature in that psychosocial development is seen as the natural foundation for religious and spiritual growth. However, the theological perception of the relationship between nature and grace is twofold: not only does grace presuppose a natural foundation, it also perfects nature, i.e. orients natural development towards its proper goal. Of the commentators we have received, only William Meissner seems to illustrate this second part of the theological axiom when be speaks of the "reciprocal" relationship between psychosocial and psychospiritual development. Thus, not only does spiritual identity presuppose a degree of personal psychosocial identity but spiritual identity is in some way perfective of personal identity. Meissner's stated objective is "to demonstrate that a psychological analysis of the process of spiritual growth under the influence of grace is feasible."[145] His purpose then is to analyze the psychological effects of grace or the effect of grace on psychological development and the attaining of psychological maturity.

This is precisely the aim of Part B of this study: to make a contribution to what Meissner would call a "psychology of grace" by analyzing the human experience implied in the Christian understanding of grace and faith. It will focus on the second question implied in the reciprocal relationship of nature and grace, or, as Meissner would put it, between psychosocial and psychospiritual development. That question is: In what way does grace perfect nature or, more specifically, in what way is spiritual identity perfective of personal identity? I believe that this aspect of the reciprocal relationship between human and religious development has been underdeveloped in the literature on the developmental psychology of religion. The focus has been largely on the development of moral reasoning (Piaget, Kohlberg) and on the development of faith (Fowler) which is seen as an autonomous and natural adjunct of cognitive, moral and psychosocial development and, therefore, independent of the influence of grace. Fowler's significant work in the area of faith development has been given scant attention in our reflections thus far. This is not to minimize its value and importance but because his focus is on "human faith" which is a consequence of human development, and which he clearly distinguishes from religion, while the focus of our study is a specifically religious (i.e. Christian) faith experience which is seen by the believer as the consequence of grace. This limitation of our focus is purely methodological and does not imply any normative status for Christian faith.

In reflecting on the effects of grace on psychological identity and maturity with reference to the Christian faith experience, I would like to extend the current discussion of human and religious development to include an examination of the question as to how grace is perfective of human nature i.e., of human growth and maturity. As I have noted, this seems to be a neglected question - a neglect which Meissner also seems to have noticed.

> The psychological preoccupations of our times have sometimes led us away from an appreciation of the meaningfulness and pertinence of God's grace for those very concerns.[146]

In the remaining chapters of this study I shall try to address this question of the meaningfulness of grace for the psychological concern for growth and maturity by examining the question: Is the experience of grace and faith, in itself, an experience of human growth and maturity? It is a variation of the question: does grace perfect nature? In studying this question it must be made clear that the principle that grace perfects nature refers to the *intrinsic* psychological effects of grace. Grace is not something "tacked on" to an already complete and self - sufficient human nature, like an admission ticket to heaven or an honorary membership in some higher (supernatural) level of existence. In the theological view, grace restores a fallen human nature and reintegrates a nature wounded by the disintegrating effects of sin. Grace, then, is seen as orienting human nature to its own proper goal which is the natural thrust of its growth. But the goal of full human growth and maturity is a transcendent goal, i.e., beyond the unaided capabilities of a fallen human nature.

To say, therefore that grace perfects nature is to say that grace orients the person toward the goal of human becoming, i.e., helps the person to become what he or she was meant to be *humanly*. Meissner explains this principle in terms of ego development.

> The basic principle is that grace works in and through the resources of the ego.... Its effect is to reinforce, support and energize the ego in the exercise of proper ego functions... Grace does not force the ego to act, nor does it replace the ego's proper function with a divine activity. Its healing effect is precisely to enable the ego to mobilize its own latent resources and direct then to purposeful action.[147]

A "psychology of grace" examines this psychological influence of grace on human development. The question it raises is "the question of human nature and of what changes may occur in it under the influence of grace.[148] Meissner insists that a psychology of grace must be a valid psychology. This means that the effects of grace must be described in the language of psychology and its conclusions related to "existing psychological theory." It must however dialogue with theology for an understanding of the experience it seeks to interpret.

> Nevertheless, while the methods and concepts are psychological, the validity of any conclusions may be established only by crosschecking with theological insights into the nature and operation of grace.[149]

Meissner remarks, in this regard, that, despite the wealth of theological reflection on grace and its effects, "we have not yet achieved a meaningful understanding of its action on the human psychic structure and functioning."[150]

In the remaining chapters of this study I want to pursue this question of the psychological effects of grace and thereby to suggest the possibility of a "psychology of grace" which would critically examine the theological assumptions that "the order of grace is perfective of the order of nature."[151] This will involve the construction of a dialogue in which theological descriptions of the experience of grace and faith are put into dialogue with psychological descriptions of human growth and maturity. The question posed by such a dialogue is: Do the two types of discourse in question - psychological and theological - describe the same type of experience and, therefore, can the experience of grace and faith be described in the psychological language of growth and maturity. An affirmative and answer to this question would support Meissner's contention that "man's elevation to the level of supernatural existence and function is more of a fulfilment and enrichment of his nature than an extrinsic accretion to that nature."[152]

ENDNOTES

1.   William W. Meissner, *Life and Faith: Psychological Perspectives on Religious Experience* (Washington D.C.: Georgetown University Press, 1987), p.82.

2.   Lawrence Kohlberg, *The Psychology of Moral Development: The Nature and Validity of Moral Stages* (San Francisco: Harper & Row, 1984) p.171.

3.   Lawrence Kohlberg, *The Philosophy of Moral Development: Moral Stages and the Idea of Justice* (San Francisco: Harper & Row, 1981), p.316.

4.   *Ibid.*, p.319.
5.   *Ibid.*, p.345.
6.   *Ibid.*, p.343.
7.   In part B of this work we shall see that theology also sees morality or ethical life as a necessary preamble to an authentic religious or faith orientation.
8.   *The Philosophy of Moral Development*, p.354.
9.   *Ibid.*, p.345.
10.   *Ibid.*, p.371.
11.   *The Psychology of Moral Development*, p.171.
12.   *Ibid.*, p.199.
13.   *Ibid.*, p.197.
14.   *Ibid.*, p.111.
15.   *Ibid.*, p.177 - 178.
16.   Richard Evans, *Dialogue with Erik Erikson* (New York: E.P. Dutton & Co., 1969), p.15.
17.   *Ibid.*, p.15.
18.   *Ibid.*, p.17.
19.   *Ibid.*, p.18.
20.   *Ibid.*, p.17.
21.   Erik Erikson, *Identity and the Life Cycle* (New York: W.W. Norton & Co., 1980), p.66.
22.   *Ibid.*, p.66.
23.   *Ibid.*, p.66 - 67.
24.   *Ibid.*, p.67.
25.   *Ibid.*, p.67.
26.   *Ibid.*, p.62 - 3.
27.   Heije Faber, *Psychology of Religion* (Philadelphia: Westminster Press, 1975), p.164.
28.   Paul Tillich, *The Courage to be* (London: Fontana, 1962), p.167 - 68.
29   Erik Erikson, *Identity and the Life Cycle*, pp. 53 - 7.
30.   Paul Tillich, *The Courage to be*, pp.89 - 93.
31.   Heije Faber, *Psychology of Religion*, p.166.
32.   *Ibid.*, p.172 - 73.
33.   Paul Tillich, *Theology of Culture* (New York: Oxford University Press, 1964).
34.   William W. Meissner, *Life and Faith*, p.66.
35.   *Ibid.*, p.66.
36.   *Ibid.*, p.67.
37.   *Ibid.*, p.67.
38.   *Ibid.*, pp.67 - 8.
39.   Donald Evans, *Struggle and Fulfillment: The Inner Dynamics of Religion and Morality* (New York: Collins, 1979), p.16.
40.   *Ibid.*, p.5.

41. *Ibid.*, p.23.

42. Sam Keen, *To a Dancing God* (New York: Harper and Row, 1970), p.131.

43. Donald Evans, *Struggle and Fulfillment*, pp.49 - 55.

44. Erich Fromm, *Man for Himself: An Inquiry into the Psychology of Ethics* (Greenwich Conn.: Fawcett Publications, 1965), pp.73 - 5.

45. Donald Evans, *Struggle and Fulfillment*, p.55 - 60.

46. *Ibid.*, p.63.

47. James Fowler, *Stages of Faith: The Psychology of Human Development and the Quest for Meaning* (San Francisco: Harper & Row, 1981) p.20.

48. *Ibid.*, p.19.

49. Donald Evans, *Struggle and Fulfillment*, p.71.

50. *Ibid.*, p.74.

51. *Ibid.*, p.75.

52. *Ibid.*, p.93.

53. *Ibid.*, p.93.

54. *Ibid.*, p.93 - 4.

55. Erik Erikson, *Identity and the Life Cycle*, pp.70 - 71.

56. *Ibid.*, p.72 - 73.

57. Heije Faber, *Psychology of Religion*, p.195.

58. *Ibid.*, p.197.

59. Richard Evans, *Dialogue With Erik Erikson*, p.19. It is worth noting that, in the past, authors of books on morality and spirituality routinely listed "Pudor" (Shame) among the virtues.

60. Heije Faber, *Psychology of Religion*, p.201

61. *Ibid.*, p.202.

62. *Ibid.*, p.205.

63. Max Weber, *The Protestant Ethic and the Spirit of Capitalism* (New York: Scribner's, 1958).

64. Heije Faber, *Psychology of Religion*, p.209.

65. *Ibid.*, p.210.

66. William Meissner, *Life and Faith*, p.209.

67. *Ibid.*, p.69.

68. *Ibid.*, p.69.

69. Donald Evans, *Struggle and Fulfillment*, p.111.

70. *Ibid.*, p.111.

71. Adrian Van Kaam, *Religion and Personality* (Englewood Cliffs, N.J.: Prentice - Hall, 1964), p.46.

72. Donald Evans, *Struggle and Fulfillment*, p.112.

73. *Ibid.*, p.112.

74. Jean Piaget, *Six Psychological Studies* (New York: Random House, 1967) p.23.

75. W.W. Meissner, *Life and Faith*, p.70.

76. Erik Erikson, *Identity and the Life Cycle*, p.84 - 85.

77.   Heije Faber, *Psychology of Religion*, p.242.
78.   *Ibid.*, p.246.
79.   *Ibid.*, p.247 - 248.
80.   Paul Tillich, *Theology of Culture*, Ch.2.
81.   Gordon Kaufman, *God the Problem* (Cambridge: Harvard University Press, 1972), Ch.4.
82.   Heije Faber, *Psychology of Religion*, Ch.12.
83.   W. W. Meissner, *Life and Faith*, p.71.
84.   *Ibid.*, p.71.
85.   *Ibid.*, p.72.
86.   *Ibid.*, p.72.
87.   *Ibid.*, p.72. One might question why Meissner does not relate the virtue of penance to a sense of purpose which is the developmental goal of this stage rather than to the more morally neutral concept of initiative.
88.   Donald Evans, *Struggle and Fulfillment*, p.117.
89.   Paul Tillich, *The Courage to be*, p.160.
90.   Donald Evans, *Struggle and Fulfillment*, p.118.
91.   *Ibid.*, p.118.
92.   *Ibid.*, p.119.
93.   Erik Erikson, *Identity and the Life Cycle*, p.91.
94.   *Ibid.*, p.92 - 93.
95.   Some recent biblical translations used the words "do not worry" instead of "do not be anxious," which suggests that the translators, though good linguists, were not very good psychologists!
96.   W. W. Meissner, *Life and Faith*, p.73 - 74.
97.   *Ibid.*, p.74.
98.   *Ibid.*, p.74.
99.   Donald Evans, *Struggle and Fulfillment*, p.121.
100.   *Ibid.*, p.121.
101.   Viktor Frankl, *The Doctor and the Soul* (New York: Bantam, 1967), p.47.
102.   Donald Evans, *Struggle and Fulfillment*, p.123.
103.   *Ibid.*, p.123.
104.   *Ibid.*, p.123.
105.   Erik Erikson, *Identity and the Life Cycle*, p.94.
106.   *Ibid.*, p.95.
107.   Jean Piaget, *Six Psychological Studies*, p.64.
108.   Richard Evans, *Dialogue with Erik Erikson*, p.30.
109.   Erik Erikson, *Young Man Luther* (New York: W.W. Norton, 1962), p.43.
110.   *Ibid.*, p.43.
111.   *Ibid.*, p.43.
112.   Heije Faber, *Psychology of Religion*, p.300.
113.   *Ibid.*, p.301.

114.   Erik Erikson, *Identity and the Life Cycle*, p.101.
115.   James Fowler, *Stages of Faith*, p.151.
116.   *Ibid.*, p.153.
117.   Heije Faber, *Psychology of Religion,* Ch.16.
118.   W. W. Meissner, *Life and Faith*, p.75.
119.   Donald Evans, *Struggle and Fulfillment*, p.125.
120.   C.G. Jung, *Modern Man in Search of a Soul* (New York: Harcourt, Brace & World, 1933), p.229.
121.   Erik Erikson, *Identity and the Life Cycle*, p.101.
122.   Richard Evans, *Dialogue with Erik Erikson* p.48.
123.   Erich Fromm, *The Sane Society* (Greenwich, Conn.: Fawcett Publications, 1965), p.37.
124.   Erik Erikson, *Identity and the Life Cycle*, p.102. It is interesting to note that Viktor Frankl adds a third dimension to adult maturity when he says that a mature person should actualize the values represented by work, love and suffering, in Viktor Frankl, *The Will to Meaning* (New York: New American Library, 1969), pp.69 - 70.
125.   Donald Evans, *Struggle and Fulfillment*, p.130.
126.   *Ibid.*, p.129.
127.   *Ibid.*, p.138 - 139.
128.   W. W. Meissner, *Life and Faith*, p.77.
129.   *Ibid.*, p.77.
130.   Erik Erikson, *Identity and the Life Cycle,* p 103
131.   Richard Evans, *Dialogue with Erik Erikson*, p.53.
132.   Donald Evans, *Struggle and Fulfillment*, p.141.
133.   *Ibid.*, p.142.
134.   W. W. Meissner, *Life and Faith*, p.78.
135.   *Ibid.*, p.78.
136.   *Ibid.*, p.78.
137.   Erik Erikson, *Identity and the Cycle*, p.104.
138.   *Ibid.*, p.104.
139.   James Fowler, *Stages of Faith*, pp.199 - 211.
140.   Abraham Maslow, *Toward a Psychology of Being* (New York: D. Van Nostrand, 1962), p.77.
141.   W. W. Meissner, *Life and Faith*, p.79.
142.   Donald Evans, *Struggle and Fulfillment,* p.148.
143.   *Ibid.*, p.149.
144.   *Ibid.*, p.152.
145.   W. W. Meissner, *Life and Faith*, p.82.
146.   *Ibid.*, p.83.
147.   *Ibid.*, p.23.
148.   *Ibid.*, p.5.
149.   *Ibid.*, p.6.
150.   *Ibid.*, p.8.
151.   *Ibid.*, p.8.

152.   *Ibid.*, p.8.

PART B

FAITH AS FOUNDATION OF HUMAN TRANSFORMATION

(GRATIA PERFICIT NATURAM)

CHAPTER II

Human Transformation: A Theological View

In speaking of the "dynamics of faith" a distinction should first be made. When this term is used, it might refer to the overall dynamics of the divine - human encounter which the bible generally describes as evolving in three stages: God's initiative (in revealing himself in some way); the human response of faith; and, the "covenant" or special relationship between God and the individual believer (as, for example, in the case of Abraham) or the believing community (as in the case of the Israelite community at Sinai). In reflecting on the dynamics of faith, however, in this and the following chapter, I want to focus on the second stage of that overall dynamic - the believer's response of faith - and to think of the dynamics of faith in the more restricted sense of what takes place within the person, who makes this response of faith, i.e., the psychological states the believer experiences in the process of growth towards religious maturity or faith. In each of the four theological descriptions of the faith experience to be examined we shall find that experience described as a radical act of trust (in divine acceptance and forgiveness) which is the basis of a radical transformation of motives - a transformation from self - justifying to self - transcending motives. It is precisely to the extent that the transforming and liberating quality of the faith experience can be called a transformation of motives that a psychological analysis of the experience becomes possible. Whatever differences there might be in the thoughts of the four theologians under review, they have this in common: They all point to the radical act of trust as the formal element in faith and the source of the transforming and self - transcending quality of faith. They are all likewise "existential" to the extent that they speak of faith in terms of its meaning for human existence and thereby provide us with a starting point for the development of a "psychology of faith."

Our four theologians share another similarity: each one can, I believe, be interpreted as speaking of the dynamics of faith in terms of a three stage dynamic or dialectic (though Kierkegaard is the only one who does so explicitly). In this they represent developments or elaborations of the three stages of religious development proposed by St. Paul. The most explicit New Testament description of the dynamics of faith is to be found in Romans V - VII. Here the apostle Paul speaks of the three stages of humanity's religious history as he understood it, i.e., from Adam to Moses, from Moses to Christ and the period after Christ. Translating these from historical to existential language they become respectively the stages living without the law, living under the law, and living under grace. It soon becomes evident, however, that Paul is speaking not just of the history of humanity but of his own personal odyssey towards faith and, by extension, of the stages that every believer passes through in arriving at faith. For Paul, faith - existence meant living "under grace," i.e., living a life based on faith (trust) in God's free gift of love, forgiveness, and acceptance. This in turn implied a transcending of that religious orientation which he called living "under the law" in which that same love, forgiveness, and acceptance must be earned through religious and moral observance, which Paul found to be an impossible, frustrating, and guilt - producing task. Faith, for Paul, meant the acceptance of God's freely given grace, and, therefore liberation, not from the law as such, but from the necessity of justifying oneself before God through observance of the law. The law may now be kept for reasons other than proving oneself worthy of God's favour, i.e., from self - transcending rather than self - justifying motives. Faith is then an experience involving a transformation of motives, a transformation which is liberating and self - transcending because it permits the believer to transcend the kind of self - preoccupation which characterizes the anxious striving for self - justification of one who lives "under the law."

Through faith, Paul was able to transcend the inner moral, religious, and psychological conflicts occasioned by his attempts to observe what was for him the law of God, i.e., the Mosaic law. But the Mosaic law represents only one means of self - justification. There are other types of "law" which, when we try to fulfil, we discover another frustrating law "in our members." The Mosaic law would seem to be a prototype for all human efforts to live a self - justifying or self - authenticating existence through reliance on our human resources. These include all forms of moralistic striving which represent the self -

consciously religious person's attempts at self - justification (by keeping "God's law") as well as all forms of self - actualization by which people generally - religious or non - religious - attempt to authenticate their existence (i.e., make it worthy, worthwhile, acceptable). In the thought of the theologians we are about to review, the notion of "law" is expanded in this way. Like the Mosaic law, all forms of religious and secular idealism are doomed to failure if they are used as means of self - justification through our human resources. It is "law" in this generalized sense which must be transcended in favour of "living under grace." Thus for Kierkegaard "law" becomes the ethical life in general; for Barth it becomes "religion", i.e., the human attempt to know and serve God; for Bultmann it becomes the pursuit of a philosophical vision of authentic human existence; for Tillich it becomes the pursuit of self - affirming autonomy. In chapter one, we shall link Kierkegaard and Barth as interpreting "law" in terms of religious idealism and look to the life of Martin Luther as a "case history" exemplifying faith as the transcending of "religion." In chapter two, we shall link Bultmann and Tillich as interpreting "law" in terms of secular idealism and St. Augustiné of Hippo will be our example of faith as transcending the human striving for self - actualization.

(1) FAITH AND RELIGION

(i) *Soren Kierkegaard: From Ethical to Religious Existence.*
The transformation which St. Paul describes as a transformation from living under the law to living under grace is, for Kierkegaard, a transformation from the ethical to the religious level of existence. In the Pauline understanding of faith, two characteristics are prominent. In the first place, it is existential: faith is not merely an assent of the mind to revealed truth, but a new mode of existence arrived at through trust, decision, and commitment. Secondly, it is dialectical, because the assent and decision of faith embraces and accepts the paradox of law and grace. Later Christian thinkers such as Luther, Kierkegaard, and Barth will speak more explicitly of this paradoxical element of Christian faith, but it is already there in St. Paul's thought since, for him, the one who is justified by God's free grace is not liberated from the law in any absolute sense but is still confronted by its still valid moral demands (though one's justifications no longer depends on their fulfillment). The law is still "holy and just and good," (Romans VII:12) and, therefore, one must still measure oneself

against it. In light of the law and its demands, the self justified by grace is seen as still being a sinner. The self, which stands under the unconditional acceptance of God's grace but at the same time under the unconditional demand of God's law, sees itself - in Luther's phrase - as *simul justus et peccator.* This is the paradox which faith must accept.

This same existential - dialectical thrust can be found in the thought of Soren Kierkegaard (1813 - 1855). He is both an existentialist philosopher and a dialectical theologian. For Kierkegaard the philosopher, reality cannot be reached by the manipulation of abstract concepts but by immediate experience. To exist is to is to be aware of one's unique, individual existence for which one is responsible. This awareness is most acute in moments of extreme tension and anxiety. It is at such times that one must decide to live or die. Existence, in this context, refers to that form of being which is proper to a human being; but it is not a "given," it is something to be achieved. In other words, we are not human simply by reason of our human birth; we achieve genuine human existence only through our free decisions and commitments. Such decisions and commitments transform possibilities into concrete realities. It is only by facing the anxiety and dread which accompany such freedom of choice and, therefore, responsibility that one can truly arrive at authentic human existence.

Kierkegaard's existentialism - his insistence that individual existence is the result of the individual's own personal decisions and commitments and not merely a stage in the dialectical unfolding of the absolute Idea or Concept - stands in opposition to the idealism of Hegel. The individual, he believed, is not merely the manifestation of a universal definition of human nature; on the contrary, the individual defines himself through his own existential decisions. At the same time, it is not the atheistic existentialism of some contemporary thinkers like Jean - Paul Sartre. Unlike Sartre, Kierkegaard did not believe that each individual "creates himself" in an absolute sense, but, through free choice and commitment, seeks the essence or objective pattern of his being established by God and rejected by humanity through sin and rebellion. Thus, for Kierkegaard, there is an objective meaning to existence (which Sartre denies) but that objective pattern or meaning is not a matter of necessity or natural unfolding (as Hegel had maintained) but is rather accepted or rejected by free human decisions.[1] This same idea appears in his religious thought in the insistence on "inwardness" or subjectivity. Truth may be stated n objective propositions but it becomes truth for the individual only when it is subjectively appropriated and acted upon.   What is important, therefore, is not to know the meaning of Christianity in itself but to understand how one can become a Christian.   Christianity is not a philosophy but an event which confronts us and challenges us to make an existential decision.   Thus one enters into or appropriates Christianity not by force of rational arguments but by one's own free decision.   Faith is not a rational conclusion but a free decision and commitment.

Kierkegaard the theologian found himself in a religious atmosphere which was, in some sense, similar to that which St. Paul had encountered. Paul has maintained the paradox of law and grace in opposition to the extremes of the legalism of those Christians who wanted to maintain Mosaic law (the Galatian Judaizers) and the libertinism of those who wanted to use that freedom under grace as "an opportunity for the flesh" (Galatians V:13).   In the same way, Kierkegaard tried to maintain the paradox of faith and works in opposition to what he considered to be the legalism and misplaced asceticism of the Catholic church on the one hand and, on the other, the "worldliness" of the Lutheran church of his native Denmark which he looked upon as having used Luther's doctrine of justification through faith as a means of avoiding the asceticism and suffering which accompanied any serious attempt to imitate Christ. The reason for this, in Kierkegaard's opinion, was the shift from subjectivity to objectivity.   What Luther had subjectively experience through his inner spiritual struggle (justification through faith) was turned into an objective doctrine or principle and applied to all Christians.[2]   Luther arrived at the experience of justification through faith by first personally experiencing the futility of earning God's grace through good works (in the from of monastic asceticism).   But succeeding generations simply applied Luther's hard won victory to themselves without going through the same inner struggle; they tried to imitate the faith of Luther without experiencing the anxiety and despair - producing conflict which is its necessary precondition.   Thus they "transformed the Lutheran passion into a doctrine, and with this they diminished the vital power of faith."[3]

Kierkegaard's existential view of faith probably results from the dialectal nature of his theology. Faith is described in terms of decision and commitment because God confronts us with a paradox which demands an existential response, a paradox which one must decide to accept or reject. This paradox originates in the Incarnation, in the

union of the eternal *Logos* and the temporal Jesus. Human existence
is made paradoxical because God has done the absurd and confronts us
with it. The absurdity with which God confronts humanity is the event
of the God - man; not a piece of pantheistic philosophy which speaks
of the union of the human and the divine, but the concrete absurdity of
a man who claims to be God. One can react to such a paradox not by
"mediating" it, by making it plausible through rational reflection; one
can only respond with faith or be "offended" by it.

> The God - man (and by this, as has been said, Christianity does not
> mean that fantastic speculation about the unity of God and man, but
> an individual man who is God) - the God - man exists only for faith;
> but the possibility of offence is just the repellent force by which
> faith comes into existence - if one does not choose instead to be
> offended.[4]

Thus both the deed of God in Christ and one's response of faith are
paradoxical. Faith accepts and lives with the paradox; it cannot
resolve the paradox through speculation.

Faith, in this view, is the inward grasping of the paradox with
which God confronts the believer.

> Faith is the objective uncertainty due to the repulsion of the absurd
> held fast by the passion of inwardness which, in this instance, is
> intensified to the utmost degree.[5]

It is precisely this "objective uncertainty" which makes faith necessary.
For Kierkegaard, faith is belief in one's eternal happiness. But there
is an infinite qualitative difference between the temporal and the
eternal and, therefore, one's assurance of eternal happiness cannot be
founded on anything temporal such as philosophical or historical
proofs. Faith does not rest on historical facts such as the life and
miracles of Jesus, no matter how certainly established, for no historical
fact can assure my eternal happiness. Faith results not from historical
fact but from the believer's free personal decision that this historical
fact means everything to him and he is willing to stake his eternal
happiness on it. Risk is of the essence of such faith.

> And so I say to myself: I choose; that historical fact means so much
> to me that I decide to stake my whole life upon that "if." Then he
> lives; lives entirely full of the idea, risking his life for it: and his life
> is the proof that he believes. He did not have a few proofs, and so

believed, and then began to live. No the very reverse. That is called risking; and without risk faith is an impossibility.[6]

In the context of Kierkegaard's existential thought, dialectical theology refers to the dialectic of existence involved in becoming a Christian. The path to faith is made up of what James Collins calls a series of "basic choices which confront the individual in his search for mature self - possession".[7] In this process, Kierkegaard identifies the principle stages or levels or spheres of existence through which one passes on the way to faith or religious maturity. These are the aesthetic, the ethical and the religious levels of existence and each one represents a philosophy or total orientation of one's life. Consequently, the transition from one level to the next takes place only when one has reached the limit and realized the futility of one's present mode of existence. Thus there is not a natural evolution from one level to the next; the aesthetic does not evolve naturally into the ethical, nor the ethical into the religious. The transition is accomplished only by a "leap" or free decision, and can be made only when the possibilities of the inferior mode of life have been exhausted and a new choice in the total orientation of one's life is made. If, therefore, the religious level is the level of genuine faith, then one may speak of the aesthetic and ethical levels as being necessary preconditions of faith - necessary for the development of a "readiness" for faith - and of the living out of the three stages as being a sort of psychological or existential preamble to the act of faith.

The Aesthetic Life: This level of existence is characterized by the fact that one looks for answers and fulfilment from a source outside of oneself. The aesthetic person is one at the mercy of external events, whose speculation about the meaning of life has not reached the point of ethical decision. Kierkegaard begins with the fact of human freedom which categorizes each unique individual existence. One must assume responsibility for one's existence by deciding what one will be and what will give life meaning, purpose and direction. Freedom means freedom to decide, to commit oneself. One who lives in the aesthetic level of life is precisely the one who has not made the decision or commitment. Reduced to its simplest terms, the difference between the aesthetic and the ethical life is the difference between the uncommitted and committed life. The aesthetic life is not the choice of evil over good; it is no choice at all. Thus, in volume II of Kierkegaard's *Either / Or,* Judge William, who is representative of the ethical way of life, pronounces the following judgement on the aesthetic.

> You will perceive also in what I have just been saying how essentially my view of choice differs from yours (if you can properly be said to have any view), for yours differs precisely in the fact that it prevents you from choosing....your choice is an aesthetic choice, but an aesthetic choice is no choice.[8]

The aesthetic tries to enjoy life as it comes, enjoying it either in a sensual way or in an intellectual way by speculating about it, by taking refuge in metaphysical abstractions. Both represent avenues of escape from existential commitment, and a shirking of responsibility to give meaning to one's individual existence. For Kierkegaard such evasion of responsibility results in mediocrity and a failure to actualize authentic human existence. The aesthetic sphere is a world of possibilities never actualized by decisiveness.

> It is therefore not existence, but an existential possibility tending toward existence, and brought so close to it that you feel how every movement is wasted as long as it has not yet come to a decision. But the existential possibility in the existing "A" refuses to become aware of this, and keeps existence away by the most subtle of all deceptions, by thinking; he has thought everything possible, and yet he has not yet existed at all.[9]

Almost 150 years later, it is easy for the contemporary reader to be deceived by the word "aesthetic" denoting, as it does for us, an enviable good taste and appreciation of what is beautiful. As Kierkegaard, however, used the word, it denotes something which is distressingly more prevalent in modern society than good taste and aesthetic sensitivity; it describes the existence of those who live lives of quiet desperation, lives which are morally uncommitted and socially uninvolved, lives without meaning and purpose, and who try to fill the existential vacuum by pursuing pleasure or retreating to an intellectual ivory tower. It is at the dead end of such existence that we are confronted with the necessity of ethical choice.

The Ethical life: Kierkegaard maintained that the aesthetic life was doomed to failure and ended in despair. One cannot continue to simply enjoy life or speculate about it without assuming the responsibility of structuring one's life through some kind of ethical commitment. Consequently, the aesthetic life ends in despair when the irony of one's situation is perceived, namely, that the pursuit of pleasure has brought unhappiness; that one's self - seeking is the very antithesis of that choosing of oneself which Kierkegaard identifies with ethical choice or decision. The aesthetic chooses himself only for the moment and "in his immediacy" and "as this fortuitous individual," while the ethical person "chooses himself in his eternal validity."[10] It is the very despair, however, in which the aesthetic life ends which makes possible a transition to a higher form of existence.

> So it appears that every aesthetic view of life is despair, and that every one who lives aesthetically is in despair, whether he knows it or not. But when one knows it, a higher form of existence is an imperative requirement.[11]

That higher form of existence is the ethical life in which one accepts the responsibility which accompanies freedom. Decisions about how life is to be lived, and accordingly commitment to ethical norms and principles, are made.

For Kierkegaard, this commitment is the first step on the road to authentic selfhood, for in structuring one's life in this way one chooses and finds oneself. To assume one's responsibility before God is to give expression in one's life to universal and eternal values and thus to choose one's eternal nature rather that one's temporal enjoyment. It is this kind of choice - the choosing of oneself in one's "eternal validity" - that Kierkegaard refers to in the following passage.

> The heavens part, as it were, and the I chooses itself - or rather receives itself....even the richest personality is nothing before he has chosen himself, and, on the other hand, even what we might call the poorest personality is everything when he has chosen himself; for the great thing is not to be this or that but to be oneself, and this everyone can be if he wills it.[12]

But the ethical life too ends in despair because of our inability to live up to the ethical ideals we set for ourselves. Kierkegaard held that what we perceive at the dead end of the ethical life is the essential humour of our pathetic attempts to achieve the good commanded by our ethical principles. Here Kierkegaard universalizes the experience of St. Paul. Paul came to an awareness of the reality of sin through his transgressions of the Mosaic law. In the same way, argues Kierkegaard, everyone's effort to organize life along ethical lines results in a greater awareness of one's lack of rectitude, lack of self -

sufficiency and need for forgiveness. The higher we aim, the greater our sense or failure.

Moreover, ethical existence does not meet the demands of individual existence (of "inwardness"), for it means that the universal takes precedence over the individual. Universal ethical norms reduce everyone to the same level and subject everyone to the same demands. While the ethical life gives expression to universal moral values and, therefore, to the meaning of life in general, it does not express the meaning of my individual existence. The despair, therefore, which is experienced at the dead end of ethical striving is based on a twofold realization. First, there is the realization of one's inability to live up to one's ethical ideals, a state which has been described as being "cognizant of the good which, however desired, cannot be personally grasped."[13]   Secondly, there is the realization that, even if ethical ideals were perfectly realizable, such realization would not satisfy the demands of authentic human selfhood. As David Roberts, interpreting Kierkegaard, remarks: "even the most exalted ethical heroism falls short of a religious relationship because it leaves the personal subordinate to the social and the legal."[14] The ethical life cannot fully meet the demands of individual existence because it expresses the meaning not of my unique existence but of everyone's. What is further required to give meaning to my individual existence is a sense of religious vocation or calling, and this is to be found in the personal relationship with God or the Absolute which is experienced in faith.

The Religious Life: When one fails to achieve fulfilment in either aesthetic enjoyment or in ethical effort, one faces, in Kierkegaard's view, an "either / or" situation. The choice is between radical despair and radical trust or faith. The decision of faith is the decision to accept salvation and forgiveness offered by God in Christ, and it is based on the realization that we cannot save ourselves or authenticate our own existence. For Kierkegaard, the religious level of existence is achieved through faith, i.e., through the freely made decision to accept the seeming paradox and absurdity of the event of the God - man and to stake one's eternal happiness on it. The following points should be noted about Kierkegaard's understanding of faith.

In the first place, he insists that faith begins with the consciousness of sin which occurs at the dead - end of ethical existence. Ethical striving seems to be a necessary pre - condition for faith; like the law for St. Paul, it is "our tutor unto Christ, that we might be justified by faith" (Galatians, III:24). Speaking of religious existence, Kierkegaard remarks that "it is an existential requirement that it should have passed through the ethical."[15] The "leap" of faith is a decision one makes to abandon of one's attempts at self - sufficiency; a decision to commit oneself to the transcendent source of human fulfilment. The despair in which the ethical life ends is a stepping - stone to that radical act of trust which is faith because it leads to repentance which involves the abandoning of reliance on human resources to achieve fulfilment and authentic selfhood. Kierkegaard speaks of the consciousness of sin as the only valid way to faith:

> For the terrible language of the law is so terrifying because it seems as if it were left to man to hold fast to Christ by his own power, whereas in the language of love it is Christ that holds him fast...only the consciousness of sin can force one into the dreadful situation - the power on the other side being grace...only through the consciousness of sin is there entrance to it, and the wish to enter in by any other way is the crime of *lèse - majesté* against Christianity.[16]

It is, therefore, only through "the torments of a contrite heart"[17] that one learns to accept as gift what one failed to earn thorough ethical effort, i.e., that one enters into the religious sphere of faith.

Secondly, the act of faith is a "leap" because it is not a natural and logical conclusion to one's ethical efforts. There is a radical discontinuity between ethical and religious existence. Faith is a radical act of trust which is made in the face of the futility of the ethical life, a radical reorientation of one's life after the possibilities of the ethical life have been exhausted. To speak of the act of faith then as a "leap" does not reduce it to the level of the compulsive or irrational; it merely emphasizes the fact that one does not naturally evolve from the ethical level to the religious but must do so by a free choice and decision which involves not the rejection of ethical values (which are still valid as universal norms) but a recognition of the insufficiency of ethical existence to achieve the desired religious relationship with the eternal. Religion is not the natural outcome of ethics but, in some real sense, an alternative to it.

Thirdly, since faith - existence transcends the ethical, it involves what Kierkegaard calls a "paradoxical suspension of the ethical." If religious existence means transcending the anxiety associated with self - sufficiency and moral effort, it also means taking on the risk and adventure of faith. While the universal ethical norms remain valid, the believer, within the context of the demands of the personal relationship of faith, must be prepared to suspend these ethical rules on any given occasion; to consider himself, on the grounds of faith, an exception to the universal rule. This is what St. Paul referred to as freedom from the law since faith puts one into a personal relationship with a higher authority than the law and thus relativizes universal moral laws as criteria for moral decision making. Kierkegaard sees an example of this in Abraham's willingness to sacrifice Isaac, an instance in which the obedience of faith demanded a suspension of the relevant ethical imperative. Abraham is commanded to do what, ethically, must be considered murder.

> The ethical expression of what Abraham did is, that he would murder Isaac; the religious expression is that he would sacrifice Isaac; but precisely in this contradiction consists the dread which can well make a man sleepless, and yet Abraham is not what he is without this dread.[18]

Kierkegaard's implication is that to have faith is to be willing to do what Abraham did - to transgress a universal ethical law by going beyond it in obedience to a higher obligation, the obligation arising out of the personal relationship of faith. In such terms did Kierkegaard describe the paradox of faith.

> The paradox of faith is this, that the individual is higher than the universal, that the individual...determines his relation to the universal by his relation to the absolute, not his relation to the absolute by his relationship to the universal,....From this however it does not follow that the ethical is to be abolished, but it acquires an entirely different expression, the paradoxical expression - that, for example, love to God may cause the knight of faith to give his love to his neighbour the opposite expression to that which, ethically speaking, is required by duty.[19]

In other words, The believer enjoys a personal, religious relationship with God (the absolute) which transcends and, therefore, is not mediated or determined by his relationship to the moral law (even when regarded as God's law). We do not forge a religious relationship with God through observance of moral laws (the universal); that desired relationship is a free gift of grace and it is a relationship whose demands take precedence over the demands of the law as criteria for moral decision making in concrete circumstances. Understood in this way, therefore, faith can be said to bring about a transformation in the personality of the believer since, through the relativizing (but not the abrogation) of the ethical, he transcends the conflict between the demands of the universal moral principles and the unique needs and responsibilities of his individual existence.   These needs and responsibilities are no longer subordinated to and frustrated by the universal norm but expressed in his unique and personal relationship to the absolute.   Kierkegaard sees the mature person as one who has been liberated from the necessity of self - justification through observance of religious and moral precepts.   But, as always, adult freedom requires the assuming of adult responsibilities.   In this case, freedom from the self - absorbing pursuit of justification demands a self - transcending commitment to the demands of one's personal relationship to the absolute - a commitment which Kierkegaard insists must sometimes be carried out with "fear and trembling."

(ii) *Karl Barth: From Religion To Faith.*
The dialectical theology of Kierkegaard reappears in the following century in the work of Karl Barth (1886 - 1968). Beginning with the same theological premise - the infinite qualitative difference between the human and the divine - Barth developed a dialectical theology which was a reaction against the liberal Protestant theology of his day, just as Kierkegaard had reacted against the rationalism of nineteenth century Christianity. In his first major publication, his commentary on the Epistle to the Romans, Barth abandoned what had been the preoccupation of liberal Protestantism up to that point, historical criticism of the Bible (the quest for the "historical Jesus") and the justification of religious experience and belief in a scientific age. He called instead for a return to the kind of orthodox Christian thought which begins with God and not with human experience. God, said Barth, could not be discovered through human reasoning or human experience or human history; the God discovered in this way would be a reflection of what is human, a God made in humanity's image. Moreover, because the intellect as well as the will is in bondage to sin, and therefore self - seeking, all our human efforts to discover God lead us not to the true God but to the God we want to discover.
    For Barth, there could be no question of any kind of continuity between the human and the divine which would make it possible for us to know God by knowing ourselves.   Thus he rejects the presuppositions of Catholic natural theology (an analogy of being between the human and the divine) which underlies the attempt to prove God's existence through objective reasoning.   On the same grounds, he rejects the foundation of the liberal theology of Schleiermacher (continuity from matter to life, from life to mind and

from mind to God) which would make possible the discovery of God in the human experience of dependence. "One cannot speak of God," Barth contended, "simply by speaking of man in a loud voice."[20] This denial of any analogy or continuity between the human and the divine - the insistence that God is "wholly other" - reflects Barth's desire to defend the absolute sovereignty of God and, therefore, his freedom and initiative in regard to human salvation. But the fact that neither human reason nor human experience can lead to the true knowledge of God does not mean that God is not immanent in human existence; it means that God's presence within human existence is not discoverable apart from God's gracious act of self - revelation. To think otherwise would be to make the human, not the divine, the measure of all things. In this regard, H.R. Mackintosh remarks that Barth's insistence on the sovereignty and transcendence of God is not in opposition to God's real immanence which is known through revelation, but rather to the "immanentism" of liberal theology which makes the human discovery of God's immanence "a product of the autonomous human reason untaught by revelation."[21]

In this view, the knowledge of God is impossible apart from God's self - revelation. For Barth, this means that there is no knowledge of God apart from the Christian revelation, i.e., the revelation of God in the person and work of Jesus Christ. But this revelation can only be given human expression in a series of dialectical statements: Jesus is both God and man; God is both hidden and revealed; God is both the God of wrath and the God of grace. In the same way, what revelation reveals about the human condition must be explained dialectically: we are both sinners and just; we stand under God's wrath and condemnation, but also under his grace and forgiveness (as Barth would say, under the No and Yes of God's judgement). This paradoxical juxtaposition of seemingly contradictory statements, of affirmation and negation, is the only way in which we can speak about God and about our relationship with God. The truth about God can only be approached by maintaining what appears, on the finite level, as the contradiction of affirmation and negation, for God is a Truth which cannot be humanly apprehended; the mystery in which affirmation and negation are reconciled.

This dialectical way of speaking about God and about human existence before God is necessary, as Mackintosh remarks, because we use finite terms to denote the infinite and, therefore, when we speak of our situation before God "every assertion of what we are must and does contain, as a constituent opposite, the thought of what we are not."[22]

It is faith which enables one to transcend this apparent contradiction, which makes it possible to see the opposites as belonging together. In faith one accepts God's YES as the final verdict. Barth sees the believer as one who has come to see the unworthiness and futility of all moral and religious attempts to justify oneself before God and has accepted God's election or acceptance in spite of that unworthiness. The believer who knows that in himself he is a sinner and has been rejected also knows that in Christ he is justified and accepted. Through faith in God's revelation the believer transcends the condition of sinner standing under God's condemnation by believing in the forgiveness and acceptance which are revealed in Christ. In the words of Barth, God deals with us "not with a natural 'therefore' but with a miraculous 'nevertheless'."[23] The natural and logical presupposition, "I am not worthy and therefore rejected" becomes, for the believer, the miraculous declaration, "I am unworthy (and remain so) but nevertheless elected."

If faith then means a belief in one's acceptance (election) by God in spite of the awareness of one's unworthiness, it follows that one must first become aware of that sinfulness or unworthiness, and this is the function of "religion."[24] It is precisely through religion, i.e., the human attempt to live a self - justifying life before God, that the reality of that unworthiness is made painfully obvious. This awareness is the stepping - stone to the act of faith in the grace of God which accomplishes what cannot be accomplished through any human resources. The same levels of existence by which Kierkegaard describes the stages of faith development can be discerned in Barth's treatment of faith and justification. Though he does not speak explicitly of stages, nevertheless, we can extract from his writings on this topic a description of three distinct existential states which correspond to Kierkegaard's aesthetic, ethical and religious levels of existence. For purposes of discussion these stages will be referred to as fallenness, religion, and faith.

Fallenness: This refers to the fallen or unredeemed condition of one who has not experienced a saving encounter with Christ. This unredeemed human condition, left to its own resources, is essentially self - centred and tends inevitably to make the self the center of reality, thus usurping the place of God. Barth describes this state in which sin, in the Pauline sense of the word, dominates human existence in these words:

> Sin is a robbing of God; a robbery which becomes apparent in our arrogant endeavour to cross the line of death by which we are bounded; in our drunken blurring of the distance which separates us from God; in our forgetfulness of his invisibility; in our investing of men with the form of God and of God with the form of man.[25]

For Barth, this unredeemed state, dominated by sin is the state of the "old Adam". This does not imply a literal interpretation of the biblical story whereby the fallen condition of humanity is attributed to one isolated historical act, a single transgression by the first man. Original sin is seen as the finite, helpless state of human nature which inevitably falls into sin apart from the saving encounter with Christ. The Adam of Scripture is a symbol of this condition, not its historical cause. Barth is anxious to defend the eternal, sovereign, predestining will of God against the relativities of human history. The human condition before God is not accounted for by any event in human history, but by the saving action of God. The focal point of that saving action is the reconciliation of God and humanity in Christ which creates in the believer a realization of his former fallen condition of which Adam is the symbol.

> The fall is not occasioned by the transgression of Adam; but the transgression was presumably its first manifest operation ....predestination unto rejection precedes the "historical fall." Only insofar as Adam first did what we all do, is it legitimate for us to call and define by his name the shadow in which we all stand. By the first Adam we mean the natural, earthy historical man; and it is this man who must be overcome.[26]

The recognition of our fallenness, our lack of self - sufficiency and authenticity, our incompleteness, and our estrangement from our essential humanity is the starting point of religion.

Religion: In understanding what Barth says about the function of religion in the dynamics of faith J.A. Veitch's distinction between "religion" and "religiosity" is helpful.[27] In its most positive sense, religion is the human response to God's revelation, the attempt (through observances, moral effort, ritual, etc.) to give expression to this encounter with the divine. As such, Barth describes it as the "human, historical, subjective side" of revelation and the resulting divine - human relationship. It is the "conscious and creative human actuality" which gives "visible expression to the transformation of the old into the new man."[28] Religion, understood in this positive sense, functions as a sign of the divine presence. It presupposes the divine - human relationship which God has established and revealed; it does not try to create or produce that relationship. In true religion, says Barth, the divine - human relationship "is presupposed by the concrete reality of religion."[29] True religion points to something beyond itself; it is the subjective impression of an objective revelation.

"Religiosity" attempts to elevate this human, subjective expression into an absolute and consequently leads to idolatry. Commenting on Romans I:23 - 24, Barth contends that when the qualitative difference between the human and the divine is ignored, we try to find and experience God in human creations and institutions. The result is that "the No - God is set up, idols are created and God, who dwells beyond all this, is 'given up'."[30] Religion becomes "religiosity," therefore, when it is changed from a way of responding to God's freely given grace and revelation to a way of trying to discover God and justify oneself through ethical effort and religious observance. Religiosity, therefore, is a distortion of true religion but even as such it functions as a preamble to faith since it represents the frontier, the high point of achievement in the human effort to discover God. And, for Barth, it is necessary to arrive at this frontier - to exhaust the possibilities of religion in this sense - in order to come to the realization of the infinite gap still separating that human achievement from God and divine possibility. Like the law for St. Paul and the ethical life for Kierkegaard, religion in this sense represents the high point of human achievement in the human attempt to justify oneself before God or earn God's acceptance. It is a sign of good will but ultimately it brings with it a realization of one's need for redemption; it reinforces the experience of oneself as sinner. The visible achievements of religion merely serve to make visible what was previously invisible - the fallen condition of humanity.

> The invisible possibility of religion operates and must operate as a visible possibility, in order that the fall of man be made visible, and the necessity of his turning unto righteousness may be manifest in his visible attainments. In the religious man we are able to perceive most clearly that men are flesh, sinful, hindrances to God, under his wrath, arrogant, restless, incapable of knowledge, and weak of will.[31]

Barth's language is strong, but the truth of his words finds its counterpart in a common human experience: it is precisely the pursuit of excellence that brings us to an awareness of our inadequacies, the pursuit of perfection to an awareness of our imperfection and the pursuit of knowledge to an awareness of our ignorance. Only those who do not pursue such goals can take comfort in the illusion " I could, if I wanted to." Only in those who try and fail do we observe human weakness and inadequacy, not in those who refuse to try for fear of failure. And, for Barth, it is only in those who are truly religious, i.e., those who genuinely strive to overcome the "natural man", that we observe the reality of sin and the need for redemption.

It is this "religious" effort at self - redemption which is the necessary precondition for faith, for only when the futility of this effort is experienced is one prepared to accept justification as a gift of God's grace, just as perhaps a person may be prepared to accept charity only when his own material resources have been used up. In Barth's language, it is only by arriving at the frontier of human possibility that we are prepared to accept the divine possibility of grace.

> Religion compels us to the perception that God is not to be found in religion. Religion makes us know that we are competent to advance no single step. Religion, as that final human possibility, commands us to halt. Religion brings us to the place where we must wait, in order that God may confront us - on the other side of the frontier of religion.[32]

Religion, for Barth, is what the law was for St. Paul; it is a crisis - producing agent, a frustrating and anxiety ridden human endeavour at the end of which one is faced with the critical decision to despair or to believe - to despair of the human possibility of religion or to believe in the divine possibility of grace.

Faith: It is through faith, therefore, that the gap between human and divine possibility is bridged.

> Faith is the incomparable and irrevocable step over the frontier separating the old from the new man and the old from the new world..... Faith is the possibility which belongs to men in God, in God himself, and only in God, when all human possibilities have been exhausted.[33]

The consequence of such faith in divine possibility, i.e., in the divine forgiveness and acceptance as revealed in Christ, is that one is relieved of the necessity of self - justification through one's own efforts. Grace means that one is rendered acceptable to God independently of one's efforts in that direction. This means, for Barth, that faith is essentially an act of trust in God's acceptance.

> "I believe" means "I trust." No more must I dream of trusting myself, and no longer require to justify myself, to excuse myself, to attempt to save and preserve myself. This most profound effort of man to trust himself, to see himself as in the right, has become pointless. I believe - not in myself - I believe in God the Father, Son, and the Holy Ghost.[34]

Again Barth's theological language reflects a homespun truth. Even those for whom words like "grace" and "justification" have lost all meaning   recognize   something   immature   and   unfulfilled (unredeemed?) in the person who has not somehow risen above the need to be always blameless and in the right and who has not learned to admit failures and laugh at his own foibles.

This kind of mature self - possession is not something we achieve on our own for our self - esteem is built on the foundation of the esteem we receive from others. This, I believe, is the general truth expressed in Barth's theological language. In faith the believer accepts the justifying verdict pronounced by God in Christ and thereby subjectively appropriates that reconciliation which was objectively achieved in the death and resurrection of Christ. In simpler terms, we might say the believer's sense of self - esteem and self - acceptance is based not on his own achievements but ultimately on God's unconditional acceptance of him, just as, in a general way, each person's self - acceptance is based on the experience of being accepted. This makes possible a new attitude to oneself and one's achievements in which the anxiety is replaced by a feeling of security. For Barth the result of faith is that:

> I can regard myself as secure in my heart. I can think my few thoughts in peace, say my few words in peace, do my few works in peace.[35]

This peace and security are the result of transcending the moralism of what Barth calls "religion."   What one is liberated from is the "distaste, negation, and the despair" of the legalistic effort to secure one's position with God on the basis of one's moral and religious achievements.   Such a self - justifying effort can only lead to despair over its inadequacy, but faith changes such despair over one's "works" into humility about them. Since justification (acceptance) is assured on other grounds, despair over the justifying power of one's works is pointless. The believer, therefore, can "do his few works in peace."

It is precisely at this point that one may speak of faith as an experience of self - transcendence. Faith is an act of trust in God's transcendent act of reconciliation, If, by this act of faith, one achieves assurance of justification as an accomplished fact independent of his own achievements, then the possibility is created of a radical transformation of motives. This transformation results from the fact that the believer's religious and moral achievements (his "works") are no longer burdened with the task of effecting his justification. Since these "works" are no longer directed towards the needs of the believer, they can be directed in a self - transcending or altruistic way towards the needs of others. Barth speaks of this transformation as permitting one's love to be what it should be - occupied with the object of one's love and not with one's own needs.

> It amounts to this, that in love man is occupied with something else, and he ought always to be so. It would completely destroy the essential character of Christian love as the freedom given to man and to be kept by man if we tried to burden it with the, in itself, impossible and superfluous task of accomplishing or actualizing or even completing the justification of man. No one can and will love God who does not believe....Christian love does not will anything from God. It starts from the point that there is nothing to will, which has not already been given....The love in which man thinks that he can justify himself before God is not, as such, a love which derives from faith. It is not a free and pure love, which loves God for His own sake, because He is God. It is rather a work of the old mercenary spirit, of the man who at bottom hates the grace of God instead of praising and honouring it.[36]

There is a place for moral effort, good works, sanctification, or what Barth calls the "obedience of love" in the Christian life; but its task is not to bring about our justification, but to respond to and confirm that justification which has not been earned but given freely. The relationship between faith and love in the Christian life seems to consist precisely in this: that the love of the Christian for God and neighbour is free, spontaneous and altruistic to the extent that one's life is based on faith. Love is given freely and disinterestedly - concerned with others and not with self - when justification before God is accepted on faith as a free gift. The obedience of love is an obedience to the command of Christ: "you have received without pay, give without pay" (Matthew X:8). Only one who has been loved unconditionally ("without pay") can love others in the same way. The Christian cannot separate faith and love since the freedom received through faith is ultimately the freedom to love.

(iii) *Martin Luther: Faith as Transcending Religion.*

For both Kierkegaard and Barth faith becomes possible only when one experiences the frustration and anxiety produced by one's attempts at self - justification. Faith appears as a divine possibility when the human possibilities of what Kierkegaard calls "ethical existence" and what Barth calls "religion" have been exhausted. In the context, therefore, of the dynamics of the faith experience, this frustration and anxiety appears as a necessary predisposition or psychological preamble to faith. The religious experience, therefore, of Martin Luther seems to me to be a singularly apt illustration of this dynamic. Luther was a scrupulously religious man who discovered his faith only in transcending the moralism and legalism of his attempts to justify himself before his God through moral and religious observances, especially those of the monastic life.

The decisive personal and intellectual breakthrough came for Luther with the insight that the Gospel, as the message of divine grace was to be clearly distinguished from God's law. Thereafter, the foundations of both his personal belief and of his theology was the fact that the paradox of Christian existence was to be stated in terms of the polarity of Law and Gospel. Because the Christian stands at one and the same time under the Law (God's unconditional demand) and the Gospel (God's unconditional acceptance or grace), his religious self - consciousness consists of a twofold awareness, and awareness that he is *simul justus et peccator*. Law and Gospel are sharply differentiated in Luther's thought; they cannot be synthesized by converting the unconditional grace of the Gospel into a gift which is conditional upon human achievement. The opposition of Law and Gospel corresponds to the opposition of despair and faith in the believer and if, for Luther, one is justified before God *sola fide* it is because only faith is capable of transcending this paradox; only faith is capable of believing in God's acceptance in opposition to the guilt and condemnation which the law reinforces in one's conscience. Luther describes his reaction to the gospel's message of grace in these words:

> Whose heart would not rejoice in its inmost core at hearing these things? Whose heart, on receiving so great a consolation, would not

become sweet with the love of Christ, a love which it can never attain by any laws or works.[37]

To maintain the full force of the paradox, however, it must be kept in mind that Luther finds in the message of the gospel an assurance and confidence he cannot find in his own moral achievements ("laws and works") even when those achievements are commanded by God. The same God who accepts and loves him unconditionally, also holds him liable for his failure to live up to the ideals proposed by the law. Thus Luther can say, "when I believe, God saves me in opposition to the law."[38] Luther believes not only in spite of his own human lack of self - sufficiency but in spite of God's own word (law).

The foundation of this teaching on the paradoxical nature of Christian faith and on justification through faith is to be found not only in Luther's exegesis of the Biblical text and theological reflection, but also in his subjective religious experience. In a person such as Luther was - one who is more prophet than theologian, more religious genius and leader than abstract religious thinker - there is a much more intimate connection between religious thought and personal religious experience. One may therefore speak of the great Lutheran doctrines of the bondage of the will, justification through faith and the paradox of law and gospel as having not only a theological and biblical foundation, but also a "psychological" foundation in the personal and religious experience of Luther's life and times. I want to suggest that it is possible to point to at least three aspects of Luther's experience of life and religion which may be seen as psychological roots of his theological doctrine: his childhood experience of religion; his adult experience of the divine - human encounter; and the tension in Luther's life between self - negation and self - affirmation which reflects the tension of his times between religious and humanistic ideals.

Childhood Experience: It seems to be agreed that Luther's childhood was characterized by harsh disciplines and severe religious upbringing. If there is disagreement among Luther's biographers and interpreters, it has to do with the possible continuing influence on his adult life and on his subsequent religious thought and experience, of the severe corporal punishment at home and school and the strict moral and religious training of his childhood years. Roland Bainton[39], Luther's well - known biographer, seems to minimize the long term effects of Luther's childhood experience. Those, however, whose interpretation has a more psychoanalytic bias will, not surprisingly, assign more significance to early childhood experience. One of the earliest of such interpretations[40] accounts for Luther's spiritual orientation in terms of a unresolved Oedipus complex and therefore an overdeveloped superego; this takes the form, in adult life, of an obsession with the devil and with concupiscence as obstacles to salvation and enemies to be crushed. Behind this harsh superego was the figure of a wrathful God - the transposed image of the harsh authoritarianism of Luther's father. Luther speaks of such a God as a cruel and capricious tyrant "who seemed to delight in the tortures of the wretched and to be more deserving of hatred than of love."[41]

Whatever the merits of such a psychological interpretation of Luther's religious formation, the accounts of his early upbringing (including his own) seem to substantiate Erik Erikson's conclusion that:

> ...when little Martin left the house of his parents, he was heavily weighed down by an overweening superego, which could give him the leeway of a sense of identity only in the obedient employment of his superior gifts and only as long as he was more Martin than Luther, more son than man, more follower than leader.[42]

For Erikson, the unresolved Oedipus complex with its accompanying ambivalent feelings of love and hate towards the father - feelings then transposed onto God, the surrogate father - resulted in a severe identity crisis for Luther which continued into adult life. If Luther could establish his identity only as an obedient son, it is not surprising that he retained in both his piety and his theology the image of a wrathful, demanding God and, therefore, the paradox of law and gospel.

Erikson links Luther's identity crisis to his ambivalent relationship to his father and offers the following evidence to substantiate both. In the first place, Luther, after consciously defying his father by choosing a way of life (the monastery) to which his father objected, still felt the need of obedience to and approval from his father. Thus, in Erikson's view, the famous incident of the "fit in the choir" in which Luther says of his monastic life "it isn't me," represents an "unconscious obedience to his father and implied rebellion against the monastery."[43] Again, the chance remark of his father after Martin's first mass casting doubt on the genuineness of Martin's religious vocation, throws Martin into a state of doubt and melancholy. The result was that Martin's monastic life which at first had been (in Erikson's view) "a life of obedience to God which would eventually come to count also as obedience to a reconciled father" became an "ambivalent form of overobedience." This overobedience took the form of the scrupulous observance of monastic rules which unconsciously was an attempt to make monastic life look absurd in agreement with his father's views.[44] Finally, when Martin leaves the monastery, he speaks of his marriage as something that would please his father.[45]

In addition to this continuing need for obedience and approval Erikson finds an unconscious hostility which cannot be expressed openly and directly. This hostility expresses itself in Luther's opposition to the Pope, and in his ability in his later life to "hate quickly and persistently, justifiably and unjustifiably, with pungent dignity and with utter vulgarity."[46]

There seems to be some justification, therefore, for interpreting the law - gospel paradox in Luther's teaching as being, at least in part, an expression of the ambivalence in his own life experience. The ambivalence finds its counterpart in the juxtaposition of the wrathful God of the law and the merciful God of the gospel. Luther the man, even as an adult, needed obedience to and approval from his father; Luther the Christian, even after reaching his theological conclusions about justification through faith, still saw himself as standing under the unconditional demand of God's law. The God of Luther's early school years was such a forbidding figure that "I would be terrified and grow pale at even the mention Christ's name, because I was persuaded that he was a judge."[47] In Erikson's view, because of such psychological conditioning, Luther never really succeeded in transcending this kind of moralistic and guilt - inducing religion.

> Luther all his life felt like some sort of criminal, and had to keep on justifying himself even after his revelation of the universal justification through faith had led him to strength, peace and leadership.[48]

What we might conclude from all of this is that Luther's case exemplifies the fact that depth of theological insight does not, of itself, produce perfect religious maturity. And Luther would certainly agree with the further conclusion that faith is a fragile possession; it is not a once - in - a - lifetime event but must be constantly reaffirmed in the face of the evidences of one's unworthiness which the law reinforces. Erikson's conclusion about Luther serves to highlight a truth of common human experience - that it is no easy matter to actually live according to one's beliefs. And if the core of one's belief is faith in God's total and unconditional acceptance, that faith must be maintained in spite of all the sources of self - rejection in one's temperament and upbringing. In the case of Luther, the seeds of self - rejection seem to be so deeply planted that his faith becomes a prototype of the "in spite of" quality of faith. If we identify with him it is because we recognize that he experienced to an intense degree what we all experience to some degree. It is the experience of the in - spite - of quality of one's less than perfect faith which reinforces for the believer the truth of Luther's teaching that the extent of one's freedom from the threatening character of the law corresponds to the depth and authenticity of one's faith. This is so because faith in an other than legal source of justification creates the possibility of observing the law and serving the needs of others from the kind of altruistic and self - transcending motives which are consistent with freedom. This is the basis of the paradoxical claim which Luther makes in his essay on Christian freedom: "A Christian man is the most free lord of all and subject to none; a Christian man is the most dutiful servant of all, and subject to everyone."[49] It would be difficult to find a more accurate description of religious and human maturity.

Experience of the Divine - Human Encounter: Another psychological foundation for Luther's teaching on the paradox of law and gospel is the problem of what John Dunne has called "unmediated existence."[50] The lack of spiritual mediation, it could be argued, was the spiritual problem of not only Martin Luther but of the whole period of religious history which he inaugurated. The religious life of the medieval world which preceded Luther was based on the premise of spiritual mediation. One did not stand alone before God; the path to God was facilitated by a whole system of mediation - church, priesthood and sacraments - which dispensed or mediated salvation in God's name.

Luther's attack was not only against the abuses of this system of mediation such as the selling of indulgences but ultimately an attack on the whole system of spiritual mediation as such. Luther was preoccupied with the question of the "justice" or "righteousness" of God, and his spiritual problem was precisely the problem of how an individual was to satisfy or appease the justice of God and thereby earn justification in God's eyes. Erikson remarks:

> To be justified became his stumbling block as a believer, his
> obsession as a neurotic sufferer, and his preoccupation as a
> theologian.[51]

The Catholic answer to this problem was to turn God's law into
something observable through the exercise of free will and the
sacramental aids of the church including sacramental forgiveness for
one's failure to measure up to the demands of the law. Luther saw this
system of spiritual mediation as putting limits on what he saw as the
demands of God's justice which were unconditional and impossible of
fulfilment by any human achievement. As Dunne remarks,

> For Luther, the wrath of God was the wrath of a demanding God
> who could not be satisfied no matter what man did, since everything
> a man did would inevitably lack the whole - heartedness, the whole -
> mindedness, and the whole - souledness that God demanded.[52]

In Luther's view, God's demands cannot be satisfied by any human
achievement; only God's unconditional acceptance (grace) could offset
the unconditional character of the law. This unconditional acceptance
or grace to which the gospel bears witness is the other side of the
Christian paradox and it too was seen as being limited and humanized
by the system of spiritual mediation. The unconditional character of
God's grace is destroyed when it is made conditional upon one's moral
and religious observance. Luther could not accept any system of
mediation which destroyed the unconditional character of God's
demand or God's acceptance, of either law or gospel. Dunne argues,
however, that the rejection of spiritual mediation put one in the
spiritual situation of being too close to God and at the same time too
remote from God. The situation of the believer is now similar to that
of Christ who had no mediator between himself and God, no
mediating system or agency which might mitigate the demands of God
or restrict his grace.

> Christ, the mediator between God and man, had no further mediator
> to stand between himself and God, and so was exposed to the naked
> wrath of God, as well as to the boundless graciousness of God.
> Ironically, therefore, as Luther saw, it could be that it is not by
> having a spiritual mediator, a lord spiritual, standing between
> himself and God that man comes into relation with Christ but rather
> by not having a mediator and by being exposed to the hell, the
> purgatory, and the heaven that Christ experienced.[53]

But again, Luther's thought on this question reflects not only his theological reflection but his personal experience as well. If he refused to place any limitation on either the demand or the acceptance of God, it was because, in his own life, he found it impossible to do so. Therefore, he rejected the system of spiritual mediation as reflecting a lack of trust in God, a desire to introduce a human element or agent between the believer and God.

As Dunne[54] also points out, however, Luther's spiritual odyssey begins with a lack of trust and confidence before his conversion. In his own attempt to satisfy the demands of God's justice he entered the monastery only to discover that these unconditional demands are impossible of human fulfillment even by the most scrupulous monastic observance. Luther's experience as a monk was the same kind of experience which Kierkegaard describes as the ethical life and Barth as "religion." Its essential component is the experience of guilt, anxiety and futility which is the necessary predisposition for the act of faith. In Luther's case the frustration was such that it issued in what he considered to be a blasphemous hatred of God.

> Through I lived as a monk without reproach, I felt that I was a sinner before God with an extremely disturbed conscience. I could not believe that he was placated by my satisfaction. I did not love, yes, I hated the righteous God who punishes sinners, and secretly, if not blasphemously, certainly murmuring greatly, I was angry with God.[55]

Luther's conversion, the spiritual insight which made possible a new mode of existence, was occasioned by his meditations on Romans I:17. Luther describes the experience in these words:

> At last, by the mercy of God, meditating day and night, I gave heed to the context of these words, namely, "In it the righteousness of God is revealed as it is written, 'He who through faith is righteous shall live'." Then I began to understand that the righteousness of God is that by which the righteous lives by a gift of God, namely by faith. And this is the meaning: the righteousness of God is revealed by the gospel, namely the passive righteousness with which the merciful God justifies us by faith as it is written, "He who through faith is righteous shall live." Here I felt that I was altogether born again and had entered paradise itself through open gates. There a totally other face of the entire scripture showed itself to me. Thereupon I ran through the scriptures from memory. I also found

> in other terms an analogy, as, the work of God, that is, what He does
> in us, the power of God, with which he makes us strong, the wisdom
> of God with which he makes us wise, the strength of God, the
> salvation of God, the glory of God.[56]

In this, biblical text, Luther believed that he had discovered the true
meaning of the "righteousness of God." The term no longer refers to
the righteous or just demands of God which we observe with the help
of divine grace and thereby achieve our own active righteousness; it is
rather the righteousness of God himself which is imputed to the
believer (passive righteousness). The righteousness of God and his
grace are identified.

This understanding of the righteousness of God as "passive
righteousness" permitted Luther to define the relationship between law
and gospel. If the righteousness by which one is justified is passive -
God's own righteousness imputed to the believer - the human response
is the acceptance in faith of the imputed righteousness of justification.
 This means that there is no need to turn God's absolute, unconditional
law into something observable since one's justification does not depend
on such observance. Nor is it possible to make God's unconditional
grace conditional upon moral and religious observance for grace is
identified with that imputation of righteousness which is a free gift
and not something to be earned. Hence law and gospel retain their
unconditional character and paradoxical relationship. But if law and
gospel are to be maintained in paradoxical opposition, they are also
intimately related. As for Kierkegaard ethical existence must precede
religious, and for Barth "religion" must precede faith, so for Luther
law must precede gospel. One is ready to accept justification as a free
gift only when the futility of trying to earn it through moral and
religious observance is recognized. Only by following the way of the
law is one prepared to receive the Gospel with faith. This, according
to Roland Bainton, is the meaning of Luther's monastic life.

> The meaning of Luther's entry into the monastery is simply this, that
> the great revolt against the medieval Church arose from a desperate
> attempt to follow the way by her prescribed. Just as Abraham
> overcame human sacrifice only through his willingness to lift the
> sacrificial knife against Isaac, just as Paul was emancipated from
> Jewish legalism only because as a Hebrew of the Hebrews he had
> sought to fulfil all righteousness, so Luther rebelled out of a more
> than ordinary devotion.[57]

Luther expresses this same truth in terms of law and gospel:

> The gospel...most beautifully follows the law. The law introduces
> us to sin and overwhelms us with knowledge of it. It does this so
> that we may seek to be freed and desire grace.[58]

The believer learns to accept God's free gift by learning from the
commandments "his inability to do good and may despair of his own
ability."[59]

The Tensions within Luther's Personality: A third psychological
foundation for Luther's teaching on the paradox of law and gospel
might be found in what Karl Hall[60] has referred to as the tension
within Luther's personality between self - negation and self -
affirmation.   In this respect Luther reflects the tension of his times
between the religious self - sacrifice of the monk and the humanistic
self - affirmation of the Renaissance. The same tension is to be found
in the paradox of law (self - affirming reliance on moral and religious
"works") and gospel (self - negating surrender in faith to God's
initiative).   In Hall's view it was precisely this tension within Luther
which permitted him to maintain both his self - confidence as a
reformer and religious leader (self - affirmation) and at the same time
his basic religious consciousness before God (self - negation). But for
Luther faith meant the transcending of this tension:

> Since he knew how to bind together self - negation and self -
> affirmation, Luther transcended the inner contradiction which
> dominated contemporary feelings of personality.   In the waning
> Middle Ages the ideals of humanity were either the absolute self -
> rejection of the monk or the equally absolute self - affirmation of the
> strong man of the Renaissance. There was no bridge between them.
> Luther was able to unite the truth of both because his faith in God
> encompassed them both. From his certainty of forgiveness came a
> self - confidence of the highest sort; but it was only a gift of which
> he did not feel worthy.[61]

And this, Hall concludes, is what faith is supposed to be for every
believer - a state in which one transcends the tension between
"humility before God and self - confidence in God."[62]

Thus the paradox of faith - if we may state it in yet another way -
consists in the fact that the believer finds the resources for self -
affirmation in the very act of surrender in which he discovers a
confidence not rooted in the autonomous self or its accomplishments
but in the forgiving and accepting initiative of God.   Hence Louis

Bouyer can state that the recognition of God's gift "in detaching us radically from ourselves, is at the same time the most personal act we could perform."[63] It is precisely, therefore, in the transcending of this tension that the transcending power of faith lies, for it creates the possibility of true freedom. For Luther, both self - affirmation and self - negation, taken separately, can represent different forms of the "bondage of the will," for both represent an enslaving type of response to God's law. To the will of God arbitrarily imposed from without, self - assertion reacts with rebellion; self - negation, on the other hand, obeys but in a calculating way, i.e., in order to receive a reward or to escape punishment.[64] Both are motivated by egoism and hence the resulting conduct is voluntary but not free, for true freedom means to act out of pure love rather than egoism. When Luther, therefore, speaks of "bondage of the will" he is in no way contradicting the philosophical arguments for freedom of choice. What he does maintain is that our "free" choices do not represent true freedom if they are motivated by egoism or self - seeking. True freedom is freedom from self, that is, from the allegedly autonomous ego in pursuit of its choices.

This same principle applies to one's moral and religious life. Even "good works" are not truly free if inspired by a self - seeking or self - justifying motive. The function of faith in regard to human personality is the transformation of motives; the transcending of the egoism of both moralistic striving for rewards (self - negation) and rebellious rejection of law (self - affirmation). In faith, one whose justification is a free gift of God is liberated from self - justifying motives and is free to act out of pure love and gratitude. Justification *sola fide* therefore does not imply a rejection of law or good works; it stresses the truth that love and good works, when not burdened with the task of earning one's justification (which rests solely on faith), can proceed from motives which are spontaneous and self - transcending.

> Hence the man of faith, without being driven, willingly and gladly seeks to do good to everyone, serve everyone, suffer all kinds of hardships, for the sake of love and the glory of God who has shown him such grace. It is impossible to separate works from faith, just as it is impossible to separate heat and light from fire.[65]

Thus Luther speaks of two kinds of righteousness in the believer. Besides the righteousness which is imputed to him and involves the forgiveness of sins ("the righteousness which faith is") there is also the creation of a new being by which the believer is made righteous in himself ("the righteousness which faith gives"). This latter, in so far as it may be described psychologically, refers to that transformation of motives by which one achieves a new obedience which - to the extent that it is rooted in faith - is free of self - seeking. What faith, in other words, is intended to achieve is at least a partial and fragmentary realization of the Christian moral ideal of *agape* (altruistic, self - transcending love). Such freedom, however, only becomes possible through the power of original forgiveness and acceptance appropriated by the believer's faith, that is, only in so far as it is based on and springs from "the righteousness which faith is," for one must first be liberated in order to act freely.[66]

In this section we have examined the theological descriptions of the Christian faith experience which are found in the writings of Kierkegaard and Barth with a view to understanding the human meaning of that experience, that is, the human dynamics underlying it and the type of human transformation it involves. We have also examined the religious experience of Martin Luther as an example of the living out of this dynamic. These theological descriptions of the faith experience have revealed that faith is a response of trusting confidence in the loving acceptance and forgiveness of God as it is expressed and proclaimed in the person and work of Jesus Christ. As such it liberates the believer from the necessity of justifying himself before God since justification, as a free gift of God, is no longer regarded as something to be earned but as something to be believed.

This understanding of faith has at least three implications for our discussion of human transformation. In the first place, faith radically alters the nature of the divine - human relationship. To have faith means to respond freely and trustingly to God's loving initiative and hence to enter into a personal relationship with God as opposed to the legal - if not legalistic - relationship of one who still sees himself as bound by the necessity of self - justification. The psychological and ethical consequences of such a change of status are obvious; for the difference between the obligations of a personal as opposed to a legal relationship is the difference between what I want to do for a loved one of whose love I am assured and what I have to do in order to earn the favour of one of whose love I am not at all certain. Secondly, faith involves what we have been calling a transformation of motives. It creates the possibility of a relationship with God to which one is freely committed from motives of love and gratitude rather than fear or coercion. It means, as I have suggested earlier, that one's whole moral and religious life is inspired by motives that are self - transcending rather than self - justifying which in turn makes possible a way of life which is beyond what is possible through sheer ethical effort. The reason for this refers to the third consequence of our understanding of faith, namely, that faith is essentially a liberating experience of self - transcendence. I have suggested that the believer's motives are self - transcending motives, i.e., free of self - seeking and the desire for self - justification. But this is so precisely because the liberating aspect of faith refers to freedom from self. One who genuinely believes in God's free gift of justification (acceptance) and finds in that the ultimate basis for his own sense of self - worth, is liberated from much of the self - preoccupation or self - absorption which characterizes one who lives constantly under the pressure of having to justify himself, prove himself, render himself worthy. And to the extent that one is free of self - preoccupation, to that extent one is free to occupy and concern oneself with the needs of others. As Barth has suggested, our love is now free to be concerned with others; it does not have to be concerned with earning something for us by loving others. This is "pure love," i.e., love which is free of self - seeking or ulterior motives - even ulterior motives of a highly "moral" kind. Perhaps this is why St. Paul ranks love as greater than faith or hope (I Corinthians, XIII:13); because perfect love is not a means to an end but an end in itself, having no further goal beyond itself. Faith, on the other hand, is the means by which that ideal of altruistic, self - transcending love is at least partially realized. If faith liberates us, it is to give us that freedom from self - preoccupation which makes love possible. This, I believe, is the sense of Ignatius of Antioch's statement on faith and love: "These are the beginning and goal of life: faith the beginning, love the goal."[67]

2.   FAITH AND SELF - ACTUALIZATION

I have suggested that the four theological descriptions of the faith experience we are examining share certain common features. First, each speaks of faith as something other than belief - intellectual assent to revealed truth; its formal element is seen rather as a radical act of trust which is the source of that transformation and self - transcendence which characterize the experience of faith. Secondly, they all represent an "existential" view of faith - one which reveals the meaning of faith for human existence - which, in the perspective of our present discussion, can be put into dialogue with a psychological view of human existence. Thirdly, each of the four theologians we are reviewing describes the process of faith development in terms of a three stage dynamic or dialectic. As we have already seen in the thought of Kierkegaard and Barth and in the life experience of Luther, faith, is here regarded as a total life orientation or level of existence which is a radical alternative to other life orientations which are nevertheless its necessary preconditions. The "readiness" for faith occurs only at the dead end of ethical existence (Kierkegaard) or of "religion" (Barth). For Luther, this meant at the dead end of monastic observance.

In the same vein faith was, for St. Paul, a radical alternative to living "under the law." But we have seen that it is not the law as such which is transcended in faith but a way of observing the law which is motivated by the need to justify oneself before God and earn his love, an effort which comes to be regarded as futile in the light of one's failure to measure up to the law's demands and unnecessary in the light of God's grace. We have also noted that the Mosaic law in Paul's thought is a prototype for any kind of law or ideal by the fulfilling of which one might attempt to justify one's existence. Thus we have seen that in the thought of Kierkegaard and Barth faith becomes a radical alternative not only to life under the Mosaic law but to all forms of religious moralism and idealism. In the thought of the two theologians to be described in the present section (Bultmann and Tillich) we find, I believe, a further expansion of the concept of "law." Faith is described as a radical alternative not only to religious idealism but to "secular" idealism, that is, to all human efforts towards self - actualization and self - authentication whether religiously inspired or not. It seems to me that in the thought of these two men there is an implicit claim about the value of faith for human existence, namely, the claim that faith, as the radical alternative to the human drive toward self - actualization, represents the transcendent goal of that drive. If this be true, then a correlation exists between the life of faith and the conditions of human existence.

(i)   *Rudolf Bultmann: From Idealism to Faith.*

For Kierkegaard the existential philosopher and Christian "prophet" the problem which preoccupied him was the question of how one is to become a Christian; for Barth, the Christian preacher, the problem was how the word of God was to be preached; for Rudolf Bultmann (1884 - 1976), the biblical exegete, the problem is the interpretation of the word of God. In carrying out the task of interpreting the biblical text Bultmann makes use of the philosophical categories of the existentialist philosophy of Martin Heidegger. It was Heidegger's book *Sein und Zeit* which, by Bultmann's own admission, was most influential in the development of his "existential hermeneutic."

> Instructed by this book, I attained a deeper understanding of the historical character of human existence, and thereby at the same time the conceptual framework in which theology too can operate in order to bring faith to appropriate expression as an existential attitude.[68]

When Bultmann speaks of Christian faith as an "existential attitude" he refers to the fact that for him the essence of faith is the new understanding of one's existence which the believer derives from the message of the New Testament. Every interpretation of scripture, he maintains, is based on philosophical or psychological presuppositions. The reader of the biblical text has his own relationship to the subject matter of the text which prompts the questions he brings to the text and elicits the answers to be obtained from it.[69] But the basic question which the reader brings to the biblical text is the religious question which, for Bultmann, is the question of human existence. The reader brings to the bible the question: How is human existence, that is, my existence, understood in the bible?[70] Therefore if one is going to interpret the bible correctly, that is, in terms what it says about human existence, one must do so by using philosophical concepts and categories which adequately describe human existence; and in Bultmann's view, this means using the concepts of existentialist philosophy since it is this philosophical school which makes human existence "directly the object of attention."[71]

Bultmann agrees with the existentialists that human existence is different from all other worldly existence in that human becoming is not determined by fate or nature but by free human decision; and this freedom implies a responsibility for one's existence which each one must face individually and in loneliness.

> Always his present comes out of his past and leads into his future. He realizes his existence if he is aware that each "now" is the moment of free decision....No one can take anther's place, since every man must die his own death. In his loneliness every man realizes his existence.[72]

Such an existentialist view, in Bultmann's opinion, helps the reader of the Biblical text to properly frame the most fundamental question he brings to the biblical text. By insisting that the individual take responsibility for his own existence, it helps him to be open to the word of the bible, a word which reveals to him a new understanding of his existence and challenges him to live according to that self - understanding.

For the Christian believer, Jesus is the bearer of this word which confronts him with a new understanding of himself, places him under decision and opens up to him the possibility of authentic existence. For this reason faith can be thought of as knowledge since "ultimately 'faith' and 'knowledge' are identical as a new understanding of one's self."[73] When the believer is confronted with the word of Jesus, that word is not merely the report of historical events; it is the kerygma, the personal "address, demand and promise" to which he must respond with "obedience, acknowledgement and confession."[74] What is important for Bultmann is not so much the historical event of Jesus but the word of Jesus which confronts us and challenges us to a decision about our existence here and now.

> It [the kerygma] is not teaching about external matters which could simply be regarded as true without any transformation of the hearer's own existence.[75]

Besides knowledge, faith requires surrender and trust for the hearer of the word is enjoined to surrender the previous understanding he had of himself including the security he saw himself as having in the tangible, visible world of things, and to find security in that which is invisible and beyond one's control, that is, the grace and the promise of God. It involves

> ...accepting completely different standards as to what is to be called death and what [is to be called] life. It means accepting the life that Jesus gives and is - a life that, to the world's point of view, cannot be proved to exist.[76]

What the new testament offers the reader is "an understanding of himself which will challenge him to a genuine existential decision;"[77] and that decision involves the "surrender of his previous understanding of himself" and "the reversal of the direction his will had previously had."[78]

It is just this existential understanding of faith which leads Bultmann to the method of "demythologizing" so closely associated with his biblical scholarship. To make such an existential response to the message of the New Testament, one must first discover what that message is; and to do this it is necessary to separate the essential kerygma which is proclaimed in the New Testament from the first century world view, mythological in character, in the context of which that kerygma is expressed. It is this mythological element in the New Testament (e.g., the three - tiered world view - heaven, earth, hell; the existence of supra - human angelic and demonic beings; miracles, etc.) which moderns cannot accept and which are not specifically Christian. To make the New Testament intelligible to the modern reader, whose world view is not mythical but scientific, these mythological elements must be removed from having any necessary connection with the essential Christian message.

By demythologizing, however, Bultmann does not mean to eliminate the mythology but to interpret it existentially, that is, not in terms of what it says about the cosmos or about history but in terms of what it says about human existence and its possibilities. Nor does he mean simply to replace a mythological world view with a scientific one. What he means to do is to make faith self - authenticating, that is, relying on nothing but God, and independent of all external security. Faith must not depend for its validation on any world view, mythological or scientific nor on any philosophical, scientific or historical arguments for faith "calls man out of all man - made security."[79] Thus in removing the mythical world view as a stumbling block, the real stumbling block is revealed - the human tendency to find security in human resources and therefore to base one's faith on some kind of objective historical or scientific evidence. But to have faith is, for Bultmann, to place one's security in that which is not scientifically demonstrable, historical or objective. Faith does not rest on empirical evidence or an empirical world view for "nothing of God or of his action is visible or can be visible to men who seek security in the world."[80]

If it is true that faith is the acceptance of the kerygma, not in a purely rational way but as "that genuine obedience to it which includes a new understanding of oneself,"[81] then we may perhaps speak of a "psychology" of faith to be found in the various forms of human self - understanding which mark the stages of faith development. In this connection Bultmann speaks of three types of human self - understanding: the self - understanding of one "enslaved" to the world of things; of one who pursues an ideal of authentic existence achieved through philosophical reflection; and finally of one who has achieved the self - understanding of faith.   These three forms of self - understanding may be regarded as the stages of faith development.

Enslavement: In the New Testament, enslavement to the world is attributed to supra - human demonic forces, "to principalities and powers" (Romans VIII: 38; Ephesians VI: 12; Colossians II: 15) which control human destiny.   It is just such a mythological view of the world and of our place in it which Bultmann believes makes the Christian message unintelligible to the modern mind whose world view is scientific and historical.   One "solution" to this problem is to simply reject these mythological elements as Gnostic corruptions of the New Testament kerygma.   Bultmann himself sees the influences of Gnostic dualism in much of the New Testament thought and imagery such as: the differentiation between this age or world and the age or world to come; the designation of Satan as "the ruler of the world" (John XII: 31; XIV: 30; XVI: 11); the "principalities and powers" against which Christians must struggle (Romans VIII: 38; Ephesians VI: 12; Colossians II: 15); the idea of Christ as a cosmic figure, a pre - existent divine being who descended from heaven and is exalted again to heavenly glory and wrests sovereignty over demonic forces to himself (Philippians II: 15; Ephesians IV: 8 - 10; Colossians II: 15); the corresponding notion of redemption as the emancipation of the believer from demonic world rulers, from sin and death and a personal ascent after the manner of Christ; the description of the conversion to Christ as a coming "to the knowledge of the truth" (Galatians IV: 9; John VIII: 32).   All these are, in Bultmann's opinion, evidence that "to express convincingly to Hellenistic ears his (Christ's) eschatological meaning....Gnosticism and its myths offered a stock of terms that were intelligible to great numbers of people."[82]

Bultmann, however, does not simply accept or reject the Gnostic myth; he interprets it, as he claims St. Paul does, existentially, by introducing the element of human will and decision.   St. Paul considered the world as God's creation; it becomes the rival of God ("this world"), and therefore demonic when one chooses to worship the creation rather than the creator.   Such an existential interpretation is suggested by the basic differences which Bultmann sees between Gnosticism and Christianity.   Both recognize what he calls "the utter difference of human existence from all worldly existence" and that the world is "foreign soil to the human self."[83]   For both systems, therefore, the human condition is one of bondage or enslavement which seeks liberation; but whereas Christianity offers liberty within one's actual existence in the world, Gnosticism views salvation as an escape from one's real worldly existence.[84]   While the Gnostic sees himself as a "man of the spirit" through a quality of nature (*the pneuma*), the Christian is a "man of the spirit" only through a decision of faith, a decision which must be continually repeated and renewed because of the ever - present danger of becoming a "man of the flesh."[85]

For the Christian, both bondage and freedom involves free will and decision. It is ultimately from this free decision that the demonic beings derive their power. The tragedy of the human situation derives from the fact that the demonic powers, having been given their power by human will and decision, then proceed to enslave that same human will. Loss of control over one's own self and alienation from one's true self are the result.   Bultmann, using the categories of Martin Heidegger's existential philosophy, would describe this enslaved or "fallen" state as an absorbtion in the world of things and in immediate concerns in which the possibilities for our existence are decided for us. The result is an "inauthentic existence" since the self cannot choose among the various possibilities for its existence.[86]

In Bultmann's view, therefore, the state of the enslavement to the world of which the New Testament speaks is real but it is brought about not by demonic forces but by human decision, the decision to live for this world and to find one's security in it; in St. Paul's words, to "live after the flesh." The essential quality of this level of existence is the pursuit of one's security through some human creation or achievement. For the Galatian Judaizers it was the fulfilment of the law; for Martin Luther it was the monastic observance. But whatever form it takes Bultmann concludes:

> Such a pursuit is, however, incongruous with man's real situation, for the fact is that he is not secure at all. Indeed, this is the way in which he loses his true life and becomes the slave of that very sphere which he had hoped to master, and which he hoped would give him security. Whereas hitherto he might have enjoyed the world as God's creation, it has now become "this world," the world in revolt against God. This is the way in which the "powers" which dominate human life come into being, and as such they acquire the character of mythical entities. Since the visible and tangible sphere is essentially transitory, the man who bases his life on it becomes the prisoner and slave of corruption.[87]

To be enslaved, therefore, is to be caught in the trap of trying to find one's ultimate security in the sphere of "the visible and tangible," that is, through one's human achievements, creations, or possessions. While this is obviously true of the gross pursuit of pleasure or power, it is equally true of those who try to find their security in moral or religious achievements, that is, in the "works of the law" or in what Barth calls the human possibility of "religion." These too are ways of "living after the flesh." But as Bultmann maintains, such a pursuit of security through human resources is the antithesis of faith:

> To believe in the word of God means to abandon all merely human security and thus to overcome the despair which arises from the attempt to find security, an attempt which is always in vain.[88]

Deliverance from enslavement comes when one decides to find his security not in material things or in his own human achievements, but in the salvation which God gives him in Christ. Surely it was from such a perspective of faith that St. Paul was able to write to the Philippians about his reappraisal of those things which he "used to consider gain," namely, the righteousness he thought he had achieved through his observance of the law. Now "in the light of Christ" he considers all his previous achievements in which he found security as "loss" and "rubbish." The security he now experiences "comes through faith in Christ" and is not "based on observance of the law." (Philippians III: 7 - 9).

Idealism: To be "fallen" - enslaved to the world - means to be not living the life for which one was originally created. What is required, therefore, is a new understanding of one's existence. But how do we arrive at this new understanding? Are we dependent on an enlightenment that comes with divine revelation? Bultmann maintains that an understanding of what constitutes authentic human existence does not necessarily require New Testament revelation; it is possible to arrive at it through unaided human reason. The philosopher, for example, is capable of arriving at the realization that authentic human existence consists in self - commitment rather than egocentric self - affirmation. The study of human nature can reach conclusions as to what is necessary in order to fulfil and realize that nature. Some philosophers, he points out have arrived at what is basically a Christian understanding of the human condition. In this connection, he refers to Martin Heidegger who speaks of the security of recovering one's true but lost selfhood through unreserved self -

commitment as an alternative to immersing oneself in the concrete world of nature. To exist authentically means to be open to and responsibly choose among the possibilities of existence which confronts us in the world.

Among these possibilities is that which is offered in the New Testament kerygma. Thus Bultmann is able to find in the biblical text those concepts and images which correlate with Heidegger's concepts of inauthentic existence ("natural man," "the flesh," "sin") and authentic existence ("man of the spirit," "faith"). Authentic existence implies that one chooses to exist. Likewise, authentic faith means that one chooses to accept the existence offered by God in Christ. As John Macquarrie puts it:

> The resoluteness which, in Heidegger's view, brings a man into authentic existence, has its counterpart in the New Testament concept of "faith." Here Bultmann stresses the elements of decision for and commitment to the view of life which God offers to men in Christ.[89]

Does this mean that the Christian revelation merely repeats an ideal of human existence which could otherwise be known through philosophical reflection? Or, as Bultmann phrases the question, "Can we have a Christian understanding of being without Christ?"[90] To this question Bultmann answers in the affirmative. Yes, the demands of authentic existence - the vision of what life should be - can be known through philosophical reflection. But for the theologian this is not really the critical question.

> The question is not whether the nature of man can be discovered apart from the New Testament....No, the question is whether the nature of man is realizable. Is it enough to show man what he ought to be? Can he achieve his authentic being by a mere act of reflection?[91]

Bultmann's point is, quite simply, that knowledge is not virtue; that philosophy can point out the ideal of authentic existence, can show us what we ought to be and encourage us to become what we essentially are, but cannot give us the ability to realize this ideal. There is, nevertheless, a correlation between reason and faith, in that the self - understanding achieved through philosophy helps one understand what the New Testament kerygma is about. It leads one to the kerygma which addresses human existence but comes from beyond it, in that it proposes an ideal which is impossible to fulfil except through faith. Bultmann, therefore, assigns to philosophy in particular or what we might call human idealism in general the same preliminary or propaedeutic function in regard to faith as Kierkegaard assigned to the ethical life and Barth to religion.   And again we may note the expansion of the concept of "law" as preliminary to faith.   The necessary precondition of faith is the failure of idealism, whether that idealism takes the from of religious observance or not.

Faith: Release from one's fallen state, the realization of authentic existence, must come as a gift of God.   That existence which the philosopher analyses and sees as desirable becomes possible only when God offers it freely in Christ.   In Bultmann's view, philosophy must be content with this "propaedeutic function."[92]   If it attempts to go beyond this preliminary function, philosophy (idealism) becomes the sin of self - sufficiency and, in the obedience of faith, all such self - sufficiency is renounced.   We might recall here that, for Kierkegaard, the ethical life ended not only in the consciousness of sin but also in the awareness of the insufficiency of even the best of one's ethical efforts.   In the same way Bultmann sees the self - understanding of philosophy as ending   not only in repentance for sin but in the renunciation of human accomplishment, "the sacrifice of all that has been his pride and gain in 'existence under the law'."[93]   In faith the self - assertion of human accomplishment is given up and one lives in "obedient submission to the God - determined way of salvation."[94] For the realization of authentic existence, one must look beyond the resources of human nature and human idealism.

> For [the New Testament] affirms the total incapacity of man to release himself from his fallen state, that deliverance can come only by an act of God. The New Testament does not give us...a doctrine of the authentic nature of man; it proclaims the event of redemption which was wrought in Christ.[95]

What then does faith add to the insights of philosophy? Over and above the vision of authentic existence it offers the possibility of attaining that existence, no through one's human efforts but through the grace of God. In this regard the New Testament tells the reader two things: First, that he is a "self - assertive rebel" who knows from bitter experience that the life he actually lives is not his authentic life, and that he is totally incapable of achieving that life by his own efforts.[96] Secondly, that God accepts him in spite of this. Bultmann speaks of God as "a power which embraces and sustains man even in his fallen self - assertive state."[97]   Liberation from this fallen, self - assertive state, is the result of being treated by God as other than what we perceive ourselves to be.

It is the experience of this loving acceptance of God as revealed in Christ which liberates the believer to be his true self and to live a life of generous self - commitment. To receive love from another releases in us the capacity to love others.   Thus what faith believes in is the love of God as revealed in Christ.

> The event of Jesus Christ is therefore the revelation of the love of God. It makes a man free from himself and free to be himself, free to live a life of self - commitment in faith and love....Only those who are loved are capable of loving.[98]

For Bultmann, therefore, the transformation of the believer is a transformation from inauthentic to authentic existence, freedom from one's (inauthentic) self and freedom to be one's (authentic) self. In Bultmann's thought the experience of faith appears as the transcending not only of all religious attempts at self - justification but also as the transcending of all human attempts at self - actualization (and therefore self - justification) through philosophical self - understanding, that is, of all forms of humanistic idealism.

A word should be said here about the question of "stages." Bultmann does not present these existential states or modes of self - understanding (enslavement, idealism, faith) as successive stages in a developmental process. Rather, he speaks of idealism and faith as alternative ways of transcending the fallen state of enslavement, as alternative ways of achieving the transformation from inauthentic to authentic existence, from self - affirmation to self - commitment.

What I am suggesting, however, it that these three existential states can be taken as a description of what I have been proposing as the three stages of faith development. If we take Kierkegaard's discussion of the levels of existence as descriptive of that three - stage development, then it seems to me that there is a clear analogy between what Bultmann calls the state of enslavement and what Kierkegaard describes as uncommitted "aesthetic" existence, as there is also between philosophical idealism and ethical existence and between faith and religious existence.

As a way of clarifying the meaning of the three stages of religious faith development - and before considering any of the specific psychological theories of human development to be discussed in the next chapter - it might be helpful to reflect in a general way on the three basic stages of human or psychological development, childhood, adolescence and adulthood. In the most general terms we might say that infancy and early childhood are characterized by a state of "unselfconsciousness." As we know, it takes the infant some time to differentiate himself or herself from the mother; and this is only the beginning of a long process of developing full self - consciousness, a mature sense of individuality and uniqueness and independence. In this first stage, the child is completely occupied with things external to the self; he is busy discovering the world around him. The child is unreflective, outward looking and outer - directed. This is the stage before the development of conscience and the experience of guilt along with the kind of reflective self - consciousness which those words suggest. This first stage of human growth is paralleled, I believe, by that first stage of faith development which we have described as aesthetic existence or enslavement; for these terms carry the idea of a state of absorption in and control by the world of things which precludes the self - conscious commitment of one's life to moral and ethical values.

The development of conscience in childhood, the psychological foundation of which is the child's growing self - consciousness, is the beginning of a process and a stage of introspective self - consciousness which reaches its peak in adolescence. The self - consciousness of the adolescent refers not only to an observable awkwardness in behaviour and concern with dress and appearance but more fundamentally to a set of inner attitudes that have to do with concern about one's identity, one's future role in society and about how one appears not only to others but to oneself. In the end it is a concern about one's fundamental worth as a human being. Thus the well known idealism of the adolescent, though it is the raw material of a productive adult life, is not yet a sign of maturity as it springs from a preoccupation with one's self and a desire to prove oneself worthy, acceptable, worthwhile which is analogous to the religious striving for self - justification. The adolescent tries to live up to self - imposed ideals as a means of proving his worth and acceptability to himself and to others. In St. Paul's language, he lives "under the law."

The maturity of adulthood lies beyond adolescent idealism for the hallmark of the mature adult would seem to be neither unselfconsciousness nor self - consciousness but a kind of "self - forgetfulness" which allows the adult to go beyond the inward -

looking self - preoccupation of adolescence and to commit himself to what is beyond the self - his role in society, the job to be done, the people to be loved, the trials to endure. In some way the adolescent needs to arrive at a sufficiently strong sense of identity and individual worth that he is able to outgrow his adolescent self - preoccupation, his concern about proving himself and earning acceptance, including self - acceptance. To do so requires an experience not unlike the religious experience of grace, of unconditional acceptance. The adolescent, striving to live up to a self - imposed ideal of self - worth and inevitably realizing his inability to live up to his ideals perfectly needs the assurance of the unconditional love of the important people in his life, a love which is independent of his success or lack of success in living up to the ideals which they themselves impose on him or which he imposes on himself. This kind of love - this "grace" - is what liberates the adolescent from his self - preoccupation and makes a life of adult self - commitment possible. To the extent that one is free of self - preoccupation, to that extent is one free to occupy himself with others and their needs. Adult maturity, therefore, requires a kind of faith (trust) in the unconditional love of the significant others in one's life which replaces reliance on one's human resources in the pursuit of an ideal of human existence. Faith in the religious sense is an extension of this since it looks to a transcendent God as the ultimate source of security and assurance and the ultimate object of trust. To cast all of this into Bultmannian terms, we might say that the adolescent passes into adulthood by accepting a "new understanding of his existence," that is, by seeing his existence as rooted in a new source of security and assurance which makes possible a new kind of self - transcending motivation. As Bultmann has reminded us, faith in both the human and the religious sense requires the abandoning not of ideals but of the self - sufficiency of idealism.

(ii) *Paul Tillich: From Autonomy to Theonomy.*

The understanding of faith which emerges from the writings of Paul Tillich (1886 - 1965) is rooted in his understanding of God and in the challenge he set for himself as a theologian and philosopher of religion. Tillich began his theological and philosophical enterprise in a world dominated by the spirit of science and scientific philosophy which increasingly restricted the word "truth" to that which could be discovered through the scientific method of observation of measurable data and phenomena. In such a world what possible basis or foundation could there be for religious belief? For Christian faith had been traditionally grounded in revelation and reason; Christians understood themselves to believe in God because God had revealed himself by intervening in the course of human history, a faith which was supported by the rational arguments for God's existence. In a world in which human reason was increasingly rejected as a foundation for religious belief, the Christian apologist was left with two alternatives: to emphasize revelation as the only source for the knowledge of God (as Barth did) or to find other grounds for belief, to establish faith on a kind of "truth" which was not the same kind of truth which science and philosophy dealt with. This attempt to give faith a subjective basis, to make it self - authenticating and independent of objective, rational evidence or arguments characterises, as we have seen, the work of Kierkegaard and Bultmann.

For Tillich also Christian faith is not grounded in scientific or rational argument, for God is not the supreme being whose existence is known by rational argument. Such arguments can only give us knowledge of "objects" distinct from the knowing subject. God, however, is not an object among others, not a being among others (however "supreme"), but the Ground or Power of being which is presupposed in every question about being, and in whom every particular being participates. Thus there can be no argument for or against the existence of God since such arguments can only be about particular beings. Such arguments, Tillich maintains, would make no sense unless the existence of "being as such" were not presupposed, just as an argument about whether a lily or a rose is more beautiful is pointless unless the existence of beauty as such is presupposed. Tillich then identifies God, the religious absolute, with "being," the philosophical absolute. One may argue about the existence of a particular being - even a supreme being - but not about the existence of being as such. Knowledge of being as such or what Tillich calls the "ground of being" is not therefore the result of rational argument but of immediate, direct awareness. This immediate awareness is what Tillich calls "ultimate concern;" it is the awareness of something unconditional or ultimate in one's scale of values. This, to Tillich, amounts to an existential awareness of God.

In speaking of God as the ground of being and thus putting God beyond the category of a particular being whose existence could be debated, Tillich was not only making faith self - authenticating; he was also giving a new meaning to the traditional Christian concept of God's transcendence. In speaking of God, he maintained, it was necessary to go "beyond naturalism and supranaturalism."[99] For Tillich, the God of traditional theism had become the God of supranaturalism, the God who, in J.A.T. Robinson's phrase, was "up there" or "out there."[100] Such a God, dwelling infinitely beyond his creation in transcendent glory, no longer had meaning for human existence. In the religious imagination such a God is divorced from human life and its concerns. Nor is the God of naturalism - the God who is merely a symbol for what is best in human nature and experience - an adequate substitute; for such a God has no separate reality apart from human existence.

In going beyond naturalism and supranaturalism, Tillich wanted to find a way of speaking of God which would neither reduce God to a symbol of the human nor divorce him completely from human experience; to preserve the transcendent reality of God without excluding him from human life. The solution to this problem was to be found in the use of the terms "depth" and "self - transcendence." This latter term refers to the fact that the finite world of human experience transcends or points beyond itself. Consequently, God is not discovered by looking away from the world and human existence; on the contrary, god is discovered precisely as the ultimate depth dimension of human existence. God is not transcendent in the sense of being "above" the finite; he is the transcendent depth or ground of all human existence.

> To call God transcendent in this sense does not mean that one must establish a "superworld" of divine objects. It does mean that, within itself, the finite world points beyond itself. In other words, it is self - transcendent.[101]

That to which reality or being points is its ultimate depth or ground. God is discovered not by looking up and away from reality but by looking into the depths of reality and of human experience. In doing so, one discovers his or her own finitude; and only by discovering the boundary or limit of one's own finitude can the unconditional or infinite be discovered. As Barth would say, only at the boundary of human possibility does one discover divine possibility.

This point at which one discovers the infinite in the depths of finite being, at which the infinite touches the finite, is what Tillich calls the "boundary situation." What is first discovered at this boundary point is what some have called the "abyss," the nothingness which threatens finite existence. It is at this point, where one realizes the finite, limited nature of all human activity and fulfilment, that the "threat of non - being" is experienced. For Tillich, it is also at this point that genuine faith becomes possible; for to have faith means "to be grasped by the power of being itself."[102] Faith "happens" when the experience of absolute being replaces the experience of absolute nothingness. As a result the believer experiences the "courage to be," the ability to affirm one's existence because at the depths of that existence one has encountered the ground of being in which all particular beings participate; and that ground of being is the power that sustains, the "YES" which contradicts the "NO" one experiences as a result of the limitations of one's finite being. But the affirmation can be experienced only by experiencing the negation; the reality only by experiencing the nothingness; the unconditional only by experiencing the conditional; the YES only by experiencing the NO:

> Religion is an experience of the unconditional and that means an experience of absolute reality on the ground of the experience of absolute nothingness; it will experience the nothingness of all existing things, the nothingness of values, the nothingness of the personal life; where this experience has led to the absolute, radical NO, there it shifts into an equally absolute experience of reality, into a radical YES.[103]

This passage illustrates Tillich's "method of correlation," a theological method based on the premise that there must be a correlation between the questions we ask about human existence and the answers given by theology.[104] Thus if human anxiety is seen as resulting from the threat of non - being, which is implied in human existence, then theology will speak of God as the infinite power of being which resists non - being.

To speak of faith in this way, as "being grasped by that toward which self - transcendence aspires, the ultimate in being and meaning,"[105] is to establish a correlation between faith and human existence as such. Tillich does not speak of faith as the answer to the dead end experienced by the religious person in the attempt at religious self - justification but, in a more general way, as the answer to the anxiety and nothingness experienced by anyone, religious or non - religious, in the striving for self - transcendence, the ultimate in being and meaning. Faith is perceived, therefore, as relevant to human existence itself and not just as an alternative to a certain type of religious striving, for the striving for self - transcendence ("ultimate concern") is a universal human trait. In the context of our discussion, the notion of "law," understood as that which is transcended in the life of faith, is expanded to include the universal aspiration toward self - transcendence.

This allows Tillich to maintain that everyone has faith precisely to the extent that one is human, that is, to the extent that one is driven to transcend oneself through concern for that which is ultimate and unconditional for "he who is not able to perceive something ultimate, something infinitely significant, is not a man."[106] In this way Tillich is able to apply the principle of justification through faith not only to the religious person who sees himself or herself as a sinner but also to the "irreligious" person who sees himself or herself as a doubter as far as material faith (the content of Christian faith) is concerned; for even one's doubt and despair reflect concern for the meaning of life. This kind of concern is what Tillich calls "unconditional seriousness" and he sees it as an "expression of the presence of the divine in the experience of utter separation from it."[107] Thus in Tillich's view, the necessary precondition for faith includes not just moral and religious striving but also the concern for the ultimate meaning of life of the supposedly irreligious person, for "there is faith in every serious doubt, namely, the faith in the truth as such, even if the only truth we can express is our lack of truth."[108]

The ultimate concern of the "non - believer" is seen to be a form of faith or at least the raw material of faith in the light of what Tillich calls the "Protestant principle." This is the principle "which gives God alone absoluteness and sanctity and denies every claim of human pride."[109] Only God can be considered absolute and of ultimate concern. Every symbol of ultimate concern including religion and the church must therefore negate itself, that is, proclaim its non - ultimacy.[110] The "non - believer" fulfils this condition when he passes beyond the surface concerns of life to concern for what is truly ultimate and unconditional; and this may involve a denial of the God presented to him in his upbringing on the grounds of its non - ultimacy.

Faith therefore, in Tillich's view, is not belief in the existence of a supreme being, but belief in the reality of something ultimate and unconditional, of an ultimate ground of being and meaning. No particular being - even a supreme being - can claim this kind of ultimacy. It is necessary to go beyond this supreme being to discover the ground of all being, the "God beyond God." Atheism, in this view, is not equated with the rejection of God as the supreme being but with the lack of ultimate concern, that is, a total indifference to the ultimate meaning of one's existence. To experience faith - to experience one's individual self as participating in this ground of all being - is, on the existential level, to experience a certain type of courage. Tillich calls this courage the "courage of confidence." In his book *The Courage to Be* Tillich contrasts this type of courage, the courage which is faith, with other types of courage by which human beings seek to cope with the threat of non - being which besets human existence. These are "the courage to be as part" and "the courage to be as oneself.' Life is characterized by the tension between these two ways of finding the courage to be: by subordinating our individual selves to some greater personality or collectivity, or by affirming the autonomy of the individual self. I believe we can discover the characteristics of the three stages of faith development in Tillich's discussion of the three types of courage.

The Courage to be as Part: Tillich uses the word "courage" in an ontological sense. Courage is the "ethical act in which man affirms his own being in spite of those elements of his existence which conflict with his essential self - affirmation."[111] Courage in this sense is the "courage to be" because the most basic human anxiety is an existential anxiety, that is, "the anxiety of a finite being about the threat of non - being."[112] The courage to be as part is derived from the security which comes from identifying with and submitting to a strong authority figure; but it is a security purchased at the price of one's own identity and individuality. As Erich Fromm[113] has pointed out, in this type of abject submission one hopes to overcome one's own sense of isolation and powerlessness by identifying with the strength of the authority figure. The conformist seeks the same kind of courage to be as part by submerging his individuality in the greater collectivity of which he is part.

In the same vein, Tillich speaks of the courage to be as part as the courage of participation since the individual finds the courage to be not in his inner resources as an individual but in the vicarious way of participating in the strength of the authority figure or the collectivity. This kind of courage, therefore, is the courage which is fostered in an authoritarian or what Tillich calls a "heteronomous" situation. Heteronomy, for Tillich, represents one possible mode of relationship between religion, the area of ultimate concern, and culture, the area of preliminary concern (the conditional, finite concerns of art, science, politics, etc.). The heteronomous relationship of religion and culture is one in which preliminary concerns are made absolute and thereby usurp the place of ultimate concern and in this way become demonic.

In a heteronomous situation an institution or personality arrogates to itself "the claim to speak in the name of the ground of being and therefore in an unconditional and ultimate way."[114]

This is clearly the case in a dictator state in which individual autonomy is subordinated to the absolute power of the state and the absolute truth of political ideology. But Tillich points out what we can also observe for ourselves, that religion too can be a heteronomous force. This happens when religion loses sight of its proper identity, when it no longer sees itself as the medium of that which is unconditional and ultimate but rather claims ultimacy for itself. When this happens religion first reduces itself to the status of a primary concern - a section of culture rather than the substance which informs all of culture - and as such seeks to dominate all other sections of culture. In a heteronomous religion which emphasizes obedience and orthodoxy, the individual is ruled not by his autonomous reason from within, but, as in secular forms of heteronomy, by a law imposed from without. In a heteronomous situation, religious or secular, an individual finds the courage to affirm his own existence only by making that existence part of something or someone greater than himself through abject submission, submerging one's individuality in some kind of collectivity, or through social conformity. The price is alienation from one's own autonomous self.

The Courage to be as Oneself: This kind of courage is what Tillich describes as the affirmation of the self as a self and it derives from an "autonomous" situation. In the context of the relationship of religion and culture, autonomy refers to a "secular" culture which for Tillich is a culture which lives without reference to a transcendent depth or substance. It is a culture in which preliminary concerns are in a relationship of "mutual indifference" to ultimate concern, that is, a self - sufficient culture which lives on its own resources and by its own values rather than being expressive in its cultural forms of a transcendent ground of meaning and value. An autonomous culture "profanizes" life because it denies and resists the self - transcending quality of finite reality, its ability to point beyond itself to its ultimate ground of meaning.[115]

In terms of individual life, autonomy is "the obedience of the individual to the law of reason which he finds in himself as a rational being."[116] This is the courage to be as oneself, the courage to be which one finds in oneself and not in a source external to the self. For Tillich, this type of courage exists in a dialectical relationship with the courage to be as part and the tension between these two types of courage reveals the human existential condition. Both are aspects of human self - affirmation but the existential split in human existence is revealed by the fact that we cannot seem to include both kinds of courage in one single act of self - affirmation. The courage to be as part (participation) leads to alienation from one's individual self, while the courage to be as oneself (autonomy) leads to alienation from the world apart from which one's selfhood cannot be realized.

> The courage to be as a part is an integral element of the courage to be as oneself, and the courage to be as oneself is an integral element of the courage to be as a part. But under the conditions of human finitude and estrangement that which is essentially united becomes existentially split. The courage to be as a part separates itself from unity with the courage to be as oneself, and conversely; and both disintegrate in their isolation. The anxiety they had taken into themselves is unloosed and becomes destructive.[117]

Because of this split between individuality (autonomy) and participation(heteronomy) an individual loses the essential unity between self - affirmation as an individual and self - affirmation as a part, and one's self - affirmation oscillates between the courage to be as oneself and the courage to be as part. This loss of unity leads to anxiety. What is needed is a kind of courage which unites both kinds of self - affirmation and a source of courage which transcends both the source of individuality (oneself) and the source of participation (one's world). This, in Tillich's view, is the courage of confidence or the "courage to accept acceptance" which derives from faith.

The Courage of Confidence: In view of the inadequacy of either the courage to be as part and the courage to be as oneself, of either one's world or one's self, to overcome the existential split in one's self - affirmation, it is necessary to discover a courage which is "rooted in a power of being that is greater than the power of oneself and the power of one's world."[118] For Tillich this is the courage of faith which is the courage "to accept acceptance." Faith is confidence in the divine acceptance and forgiveness; therefore, the courage which results from faith is based neither on oneself nor one's world. Faith involves the renunciation of all such finite sources of ultimate security. And here too the "in spite of" quality of faith is evident since the inability to find resources for self - affirmation in oneself is based on the awareness of the existential split in one's being. For Tillich, this amounts to an existential awareness of sin or unacceptability before the divine. To have faith is to believe in a transcendent source of acceptance in spite of this awareness of unacceptability and lack of self sufficiency. Tillich, therefore, defines faith as "the courage to accept oneself as accepted in spite of being unacceptable."[119]

The source of this forgiveness is the ground and power of being itself and, therefore, it permits the believer to affirm his own being in a way that transcends individualization and participation, oneself and one's world.

> Faith is not an opinion but a state. It is the state of being grasped by the power of being which transcends everything that is and in which everything that is participates. He who is grasped by this power is able to affirm himself because he knows that he is affirmed by the power of being itself.[120]

It is because faith relates the believer not to an alien power, remote and divorced from one's human existence, but to the depth dimension - the ultimate ground - of one's own being, that Tillich is able to describe authentic faith as a "theonomous" relationship. Again, this is a term which appears in the context of his discussion of the relationship of religion and culture.

A theonomous culture rejects both the imposition of divine law by an outside authority (heteronomy) and the self - sufficiency of reason divorced from its depth (autonomy). Theonomy implies a relationship between religion and culture in which "religion is the substance of culture and culture is the form of religion;"[121] cultural forms or creations (preliminary concerns) give expression to ultimate concern and the transcendent meaning of culture "not as something strange but as its own spiritual ground."[122] In this ideal situation culture perceives religion not as an alien force thwarting its human aspirations and contradicting its human, aesthetic and political values, but as giving expression to that ultimate concern and the ultimate value which undergirds all cultural life. Therefore religion is perceived as a call for culture to be true to its essential nature and its deepest ideals.

In individual life, theonomy means that one is recalled to his true and essential nature from which he has been estranged.[123] Tillich maintains that we always move towards theonomy because in our essential nature we are one with the infinite, but the achievement of theonomy is always incomplete because of our existential estrangement from the infinite.[124] In a theonomous situation, one's life is directed not by an alien law or by one's autonomous reason, but be a reason which is united with its own ground and depth. This means that obedience to God is obedience to a God who is seen as the ground of one's own reason and being, so that the law imposed is at the same time the law of one's own being and therefore of one's own growth and fulfilment.[125]   Disobedience to a law perceived in this way is experienced as a lack of integrity, a failure to be true to oneself. This unity of reason with its own depth and ground is experienced culturally as the unity of substance (religion) and form (culture), and psychologically as the unity of obedience and freedom.

Theonomy, therefore, refers to a divine - human relationship in which God's law is recognized as the law of one's own being. In submitting to that law one is submitting neither to an alien law (heteronomy) nor to a superficial law (autonomy). In the same way the courage to affirm one's own existence is derived neither from an alien source (one's world) nor from a shallow source(oneself) but from a source that transcends both, but transcends them as their ultimate depth and meaning. In this self - transcendence it to be found the transforming power of faith.

Again it must be pointed out that Tillich does not speak of the three types of courage as "stages" in a process of faith development. The courage of faith appears rather as a radical alternative to the tension between the courage to be as part and the courage to be as oneself. It is true, nevertheless, that the courage to be as a part could be taken as a description of that existential state which is characterized by outer - directed unselfconsciousness, while the courage to be as oneself is descriptive of that inner - directed, self - conscious striving for self - sufficiency which characterize the second stage of human and religious development and which has been described variously in this study as living "under the law," the ethical life, religion and idealism. All of these terms denote the attempt to find one's security and self - authentication in one's own inner rational , moral and religious resources, everything that Tillich implies in the word "autonomy." The way to faith, therefore, and its necessary precondition is the courage to be as oneself, the courage of autonomy, which comes into tension with the courage to be as part and thereby reveals the existential split in our existence, our lack of self - sufficiency - the inadequacy of both self and world to provide ultimate security and a ground for self - affirmation - the awareness of which is the necessary precondition of faith.

(iii) *St. Augustine: Faith as Transcending Self - Actualization.*

For Bultmann, as we have seen, faith involves the transcending of the self - knowledge acquired through philosophical reflection because it means accepting the understanding of one's existence which the New Testament offers; this makes possible the realization of authentic human existence to a degree that is not possible through mere philosophical reflection. For Tillich, on the other hand, self - transcendence means the transcending of the dichotomy between heteronomy and autonomy, between the courage to be as part and the courage to be as oneself, by finding the "courage to be" not in oneself or in one's world, not in individuality or participation but in the infinite ground of being (God) which transcends oneself and one's world. I believe that both these modes of self - transcendence can be found in the faith experience of Augustine of Hippo (354 - 430). Augustine's religious conversion represents the culmination of this search for both truth and freedom. As an experience of self - transcendence, it represents the transcending of both the self - knowledge he achieved through Neo - Platonic philosophy and the conflict within his own personality between dependency (heteronomy) and autonomy.

The Search for Truth: In the *Confessions* Augustine tells us that as a young student at Carthage he read Cicero's *Hortensius* and, as a result, decided to dedicate himself to the pursuit of wisdom. All other pursuits were deemed worthless "and with an incredible intensity of desire, I longed after immortal wisdom."[126]   This reading of Cicero gave to Augustine's life its most fundamental orientation which was to "love and seek and win and hold and embrace" not any particular school or position "but wisdom itself, whatever it might be."[127]   The pursuit of wisdom, therefore, is the philosophical context in which Augustine's religious conversion takes place. In retrospect Augustine himself sees his youthful commitment to the pursuit of wisdom as the beginning of his journey towards God, "I had begun" he says "that journey upwards by which I was to return to you."[128]

For Augustine the search for truth is identical with the search for Christ, not only for him but for everyone. As Father Coppleston remarks, Augustine interpreted his search for truth "as a search for Christ and Christian wisdom, as the attraction of the divine beauty, and this experience he universalized."[129]   In retrospect Augustine sees his life as a series of what we might call existential states, a series of successive changes in the orientation of his life rather than a mere succession of deeds and events. John Dunne has identified these existential states as childhood Christianity, manicheeism, skepticism, neo - platonism, philosophical Christianity and ecclesiastical Christianity. Each of these transitions is seen in Augustine as a "conversion," that is, one phase in the general movement of conversion toward the God of Christianity which began with his determination to pursue wisdom as a young student. Indeed, in Dunne's view, it was only many years later, when he wrote the *Confessions*, that Augustine saw his conversion to Christianity as something transcending his philosophical quest.[130]

Anyone's search for truth and wisdom takes place within the philosophical context of one's times; hence the critical role of Neo - Platonism in the life of Augustine. Tillich[131] sees Augustine's position in the history of philosophy as being part of the Neo - Platonic movement; this movement was a response to the skepticism which followed the collapse of the attempt by classical Greek philosophy to build an objectively rational world. The skepticism which followed this collapse denied the possibility of attaining objective philosophical certainty. As a reaction against scepticism, Neo - Platonism proposed a new epistemology. The basis for truth was not to be found by looking at external reality but by looking within oneself and through the elevation of one's soul to the ultimate and universal truth. This means that in his religious orientation Augustine countered the skepticism about attaining objective knowledge of God with the Neo - Platonic notion of the immediate inner - awareness of God. Platonic idealism had identified the truth with the impersonal, immaterial, universal essences. With Neo - Platonism this ancient philosophy, in the words of R.L. Ottley, "virtually passed over into theology."[132] The eternal ideas of Platonism became, for Neo - Platonism, the *Nous* or divine mind which emanates from "the One." All creatures are seen as manifestations of the *Nous* as archetypical form and therefore emanations of the One. This implies the pre - existence of the human soul within the divine. The soul, therefore, has direct knowledge of universal forms or essences; knowledge, accordingly, comes from within. Though Augustine, as a Christian, eventually rejected this Neo - Platonic version of the structure of the universe in favour of the Christian doctrine of creation, he nevertheless believed that the way to truth and therefore to God was away from visible creation and into the depths of one's soul. God is not to be found in the world of objective reality but as the ultimate depth of existence.

As we have already seen, this approach to the question of God is one which dominates Tillich's thought. God, for Tillich, is discovered as the ultimate ground of one's being and existence; he is not an object apprehended by the knowing subject but that which precedes every distinction between subject and object, the absolute which is presupposed in every relativity. Thus Augustine expresses his search for truth in the words *"Noverim me, noverim Te."* Augustine wanted to know himself and thereby know God; to find God in the depths of his own soul. Tillich explains Augustine's statement in the following words.

> This means that the soul is the place where God appears to men. He wants to know the soul because only there can he know God, and in no other place. This implies, of course, that God is not an object beside other objects. God is seen in the soul. He is in the center of man, before the split into subjectivity and objectivity....God is given to the subject as nearer to itself than it is to itself. In the Augustinian tradition the source of all philosophy of religion is the immediacy of the presence of God in the soul....This is the *prius* of everything.[133]

In Tillch's language, Augustine's approach to the question of God is "ontological" rather than "cosmological;" based on the immediate awareness of God as the ground of all being, as opposed to the inference of God's existence as a supreme being on the objective evidence supplied by the material universe.

Augustine himself describes this inner search for God in the *Confessions:*

> Being admonished by all this to return to myself, I entered into my own depths, with you as guide; and I was able to do it because you were my helper. I entered, and with the eye of my soul, such as it was, I saw your unchangeable light shining over that same eye of my soul, over my mind.[134]

In another passage[135] Augustine speaks of his passing from the knowledge of sensible things to the knowing faculty, the soul. and from the knowing and reasoning power which is mutable to that which is immutable, that is, God whom he describes as "That which is." By this process the mind arrives at an intuition or direct awareness of that which is being. God is being (*esse*); all other things merely have being. When the mind becomes aware of necessary and eternal truths, it thereby has an awareness of an eternal and changeless standard which is the ground of that truth. In Augustine's view, the mind at that moment encounters the Immutable Truth because it is illuminated by Truth Itself ("your unchangeable Light") in recognizing necessary and eternal truths.[136]

By entering into the depths of his soul Augustine heard his God speak to him "as one hears in the heart"[137] and the God he discovered was the ground of all beauty and truth and being so that "there was from that moment no ground of doubt in me; I would more easily have doubted my own life than have doubted that truth is...."[138] Augustine's intellectual "conversion" might be said to have taken place when he abandoned his manichean dualism and no longer doubted the existence of "an incorruptible substance from which every substance has its being."[139] And if God is the being of that which exists and the truth of that which is true he is also the beauty of that which is beautiful. To discover this God Augustine believed that one must look beyond the beauty of the visible creation to the immutable ground of beauty in the depths of one's own being.

> Late have I loved Thee, O Beauty so ancient and so new; late have I loved Thee! For behold Thou wert within me, and I outside; and I sought Thee outside and in my loneliness fell upon those lovely things that Thou hast made. Thou wert with me and I was not with Thee, I was kept from Thee by those things, yet had they not been in Thee, they would not have been at all.[140]

Ottley, commenting on Book 7 of the *Confessions* points out that Augustine discovered God not by the contemplation of the universe but by "penetrating into the recesses of his own personality" and concludes:

> Thus his own experience harmonized with the doctrine of Platonism in suggesting that human nature by its very constitution bears testimony to the true light, and that only by searching into his soul can man attain to belief in a transcendent spiritual being akin to himself: a being who is at once the immutable light of reason...the fountain of the soul's life...the supreme good towards which human nature aspires, and the final cause of its upward movement.[141]

The God Augustine discovered was not the "One" of Neo - Platonic philosophy but he was discovered in the same way, in the depths of one's own being.

Thus the philosophical tenets of Neo - Platonism served for Augustine the preliminary or propaedeutic function which Bultmann assigns to philosophy in general in the process of faith development. It also means however that Augustine's "philosophical" conversion was not sufficient in itself for the self - understanding it brought was not yet the self - understanding of faith by which authentic existence becomes realizable. For Augustine, the self - understanding of faith was to be found in the authority of the Church and its message of salvation, particularly as that message was proclaimed in the sermons of St. Ambrose. Augustine himself indicates in retrospect that his philosophical conversion was only a preliminary and incomplete step. In Neo - Platonism he found a doctrine similar to the Christian doctrine of *Logos* but not the message that the Word became flesh, that he emptied himself, took the form of a servant, and became obedient to death on a cross for humanity's redemption.[142]

It was necessary, therefore, for Augustine to go beyond his philosophical discovery of the God who is the immutable ground of being and truth. This further step occurs in the famous conversion experience in the garden which is described in Book 7 of the *Confessions:*

> So was I speaking, and weeping in the most bitter contrition of my heart, when, lo! I heard from a neighbouring house a voice as of boy or girl, I know not, chanting and oft repeating, "Take up and read; Take up and read"...So checking the torrent of my tears, I rose; interpreting it to be no other than a command from God, to open the book, and read the first chapter I should find....Eagerly then I returned to the place where Alypius was sitting; for there had I laid the volume of the apostle, when I arose thence. I seized, opened, and in silence read that section on which my eyes first fell: "Not in rioting and drunkenness, not in chambering and wantonness, not in strife and envying: but put ye on the Lord Jesus Christ and make no provision for the flesh." No further would I read; nor needed I: for instantly, at the end of this sentence, by a light, as it were, of serenity infused into my heart, all the darkness of doubt vanished away.[143]

What does this conversion experience add to Augustine's philosophical discovery of God? How are the two experiences related?

Coppleston[144] distinguishes between an intellectual conversion and a moral conversion. R. J. O'Connell, however, rejects the idea that Book 7 of the *Confessions* describes the intellectual phase of Augustine's conversion while Book 8 describes the moral phase or the conversion to Christianity proper.

> Such a view forgets that he very likely considered himself an enlightened sort of "Christian" while a Manichee....He now

considers himself as having returned to a specific type of Christianity, as a "Catholic" Christian.[145]

John Dunne attempts to avoid the difficulties inherent in the words "intellectual" and "moral" by describing the relationship of the two experiences as a transition from philosophical to ecclesiastical Christianity.[146] This distinction takes two important aspects into consideration: the importance of Neo - Platonism as the philosophical preamble to Augustine's faith and the importance to Augustine's faith of the church and its authority. For Augustine the church and submission to its authority was the forerunner of wisdom and just as much the answer to skepticism as was Neo - Platonic philosophy. Authority, he believed, cures one of pride and is one of the earthly realities through which the soul is admonished to return to God and pass from belief to vision.[147]

However the transition is described, it is possible to see in Augustine's passing from philosophical to ecclesiastical Christianity an illustration of what we have been referring as the transformation from philosophical self - understanding to the self - understanding of faith. In this transition, philosophy, like the law or religion or ethics serves to reinforce one's sense of insufficiency and the need for redemption. Positively it fosters humility and a readiness for the experience of grace. Jean - Marie Le Blond speaks of the humility that Augustine learned as making him aware of the impotence of thought. It made him aware that enlightenment (self - knowledge) without the transformation wrought by grace merely heightens one's frustrations.[148] Bultmann would describe Augustine the Neo - Platonist, the philosophical Christian, as one whose self - understanding is derived from philosophical reflection. Augustine, the ecclesiastical Christian, was one whose self - understanding was derived from his faith in the event of redemption accomplished in Christ.

The Search for Freedom: If on the level of conscious, rational reflection Augustine's conversion took place within the context of his search for truth, on the unconscious and affective level it took place within the context of the struggle between the two conflicting tendencies within his personality: the tendency towards submission (heteronomy) and the thrust towards autonomy. Augustine's faith therefore can be interpreted perhaps as a way of resolving this conflict which we all experience between dependency strivings and autonomy strivings; in terms of Tillich's understanding of faith, it may be seen as the achieving of a kind of courage which transcends self and world, individuality and participation, the courage to be as oneself and the courage to be as part.

Psychological interpretations of Augustine's life and conversion seem to agree on the presence of a strong oedipal element in his personality. Philip Woolcott Jr. remarks:

> There is evidence in the *Confessions* that Augustine did not succeed in resolving his "oedipal complex" satisfactorily. He was extremely close to his mother, idealizing her as the "handmaiden of God," and seemed to identify her with God and the church.[149]

The *Confessions* offer ample evidence of the dominant place of and attachment to Monica in Augustine's life, together with a certain repudiation of the father. This Christian mother is praised, the pagan father tolerated (1:xi); the mother sabotages the son's wedding plans with no protest from Augustine (2:iii; 6:xv); Augustine's mistress is driven from his home by Monica, and Augustine's resultant preoccupation with his own feelings of deprivation and apparent lack of concern for the dismissed woman reveals the narcissism characteristic of a mother fixation (6:xv).

But if there is evidence of dependency on Monica and alienation from the father, there is also evidence of displaced and disguised hostility and rebellion against Monica. There is bitterness towards teachers and adults generally in his childhood (1: ix), as well as rebellion against Monica in his early manhood by the adoption of a philosophy (Manicheeism) and a life style (sensual indulgence) which were contrary to her preferences.[150] The same rebellion is evident, according to Charles Kligerman, in Augustine's sudden departure from Carthage to Rome which was in fact a flight from Monica who wished to detain him and which Kligerman sees as "almost a direct re - enactment of the Aeneas and Dido legend,"[151] a legend which seems to have had a continuing fascination for Augustine during his boyhood.

The conflict within Augustine's personality, therefore, seems to have been the basic oedipal conflict between attachment to the mother and a repudiation of the father on the one hand, and rebellion against the mother's dominance and identification with the masculine father image on the other. Kligerman sees the mother and father as symbolic: Monica represents the "feminine," passivity, Africa, the mother country and the submission demanded by Christianity; the masculine, pagan father represents Rome, power, masculine aggressiveness, paganism and instinctual heterosexual strivings. In its most fundamental terms this was a conflict between heteronomy and autonomy. Woolcott describes the conflict as "a conflict between the urge to dominate and the urge to submit,"[152] and James Dittes sees it as the source of an identity crisis for Augustine. How was he to find an identity which was true to the conflicting tendencies within himself, the tendency "to submit passively to the comfortable authority" and the tendency "to fight submission and insist on autonomy?"[153] In this view Augustine was torn between submission to Monica and, by extension, to the authority of the Church and identification with the father and, therefore, with the masculine autonomy of Roman paganism. Both the above mentioned authors see Augustine's conversion in terms of a surrender and submission to the church after the failure of his attempts to assert his autonomy.

Dittes, for example, sees in most of Augustine's strivings towards autonomy secondary strivings towards submission and dependence and his conversion takes place when the secondary strivings become dominant. In Augustine's sexual indulgences, for example, there is an attempt "to deny the passive, feminine, dependent element of his nature and to assert his identity as a vigorous, assertive, active male."[154] But his failure to marry is seen as a failure to fully assume the active, masculine role of a husband and father. Again, his attachment to Manicheeism is a form of rebellion against Monica, but the "affiliative nature of the sect" satisfied his need to belong and submit.[155] With his conversion, Augustine's dependency strivings become dominant: he surrenders to his mother and to the church; he abandons masculine sexuality in favour of a life of celibacy; he abandons the efforts to become a father and becomes and obedient son. The victory of Augustine's dependency strivings is reflected in his theological teachings. Dittes sees his defense of the faith as reactions against threatening autonomy strivings inherent in the three heresies against which Augustine fought and which assert the relative independence of the human agent in the economy of salvation. These are: Pelagianism which emphasized the freedom of the human will; Donatism which emphasized the necessity of worthiness in the human ministers of the sacraments; and Manicheeism which emphasized the dualism of good and evil and therefore the importance of human choice. Kligerman agrees substantially with Dittes when he asserts his belief that the end result of Augustine's conversion experience was "an identification with the mother and a passive feminine attitude to the father displaced to God."[156]

In these interpretations Augustine's conversion appears to be a victory of heteronomy over autonomy because, as Dittes suggests, "this assertion of autonomy proved too precarious to maintain."[157] Woolcolt, however, is more disposed to see the conversion as a transcending of the conflict of dependency and autonomy. The inner tension of the conflict is replaced by unity, harmony and certitude, a liberation and release of energy made possible by the abandoning of the preoccupation with self implied in this type of inner conflict.

> Following his conversion a sense of inner unity and certainty coupled with a greater ethical sensitivity and diminished self - concern were evident in Augustine. His thoughts became more directed outwardly towards others.[158]

In other words, Augustine's post - conversion state is seen here not as a return to the dependency of childhood but as the achieving of that state of outer - directed self - forgetfulness which we have associated with adulthood.

This latter description of Augustine's conversion experience agrees with that of Tillch who maintains that "he did not experience it as heteronomy but as theonomy,"[159] that is, as an experience in which the inner conflict is transcended and his self - affirmation is grounded in a source of courage which transcends both heteronomy (submission) and autonomy. In this kind of experience one does not feel that any part of one's nature or any of one's legitimate strivings are denied but rather fulfilled in the obedience of faith. The law to which one submits is the law of one's own nature and the call to which one responds is a call to one's own human fulfilment. Augustine[160] himself, I believe, in commenting on the words of Christ, "No one comes to me unless the father draws him," describes faith as a theonomous experience. He considers the objection of those who "have not the slightest understanding of divine things" (perhaps referring to those who think that every act of surrender is a forfeiting of one's autonomy). Their objection is, "How can I freely believe if I am drawn?" and Augustine's answer is, "You are drawn by your own will indeed, but by delight as well." He then argues that everyone is drawn by what delights him. Therefore one is drawn to Christ "by his own delight in truth, beatitude, holiness, and eternal life, all of which Christ is." Perhaps we could paraphrase Augustine's words to read: The obedience of faith is not the grudging acceptance of an alien law imposed against our will but a response to a call which correlates with the deepest aspirations of the human heart, with what Tillich calls one's "ultimate concern." "Give me a lover," Augustine says, "he will know what I mean;" for one who is in love knows that in the act of surrender he finds his greatest freedom. And if it is the Father, the creator, who draws the believer, the implication is that we are created in such a way - the conditions of human nature are such - that we "delight" in the Father's self revelation in Christ. There is a correlation between the life of faith and the conditions of human existence. "If delights draw me," asks Augustine, "will Christ not draw us - he who is the revelation of the Father."

If Augustine's conversion was not a heteronomous but a theonomous experience it is perhaps because his submission to the church constituted a transition from philosophical Christianity to ecclesiastical Christianity. If this is the case, then Augustine's discovery of God within the contemporary Neo - Platonic philosophy served as the preamble and precondition for his discovery of the God of salvation in the teachings of the Church. One may therefore legitimately ask whether Augustine experienced the authority of the Church as theonomy because the God presented to him by the church was the God he had discovered within himself in his philosophical speculations. For Augustine, the authority of the Church was a means to the vision of that God of whom he was already aware as the ground of his own being. In Tillich's terminology, the theological absolute, the God of revelation, was identified with the philosophical absolute, being itself as the object of his "ultimate concern."

It is legitimate, therefore, to suggest that Augustine's conversion experience was an act of faith by which he transcended the existential split between individualization (the courage to be as oneself) and participation (the courage to be as part). But such an experience of self - transcendence occurs in what Tillich calls a "boundary situation;" that is, a situation in which all human possibility and all human resources are exhausted and one is confronted by the finitude of human existence. It is in such a situation that the awareness of the dichotomy in one's existence becomes most acute and the necessity of grounding one's self - affirmation in what is ultimate and unconditional is most evident. For Augustine it was the Christian doctrine of creation from nothing which enabled him to reject the Neo - Platonic belief in an existence prior to his present life in a world of forms and ideas. This enabled him reach that boundary situation which is the precondition of faith by confronting his own nothingness. It meant that in recollecting his life, as he did in the *Confessions*, he would reach a point at which he did not exist. Dunne points out that when Augustine overcame the Neo - Platonic illusion of pre - existence, he was able to confront the nothingness from which he came, experience freely the contingency of his human condition and encounter God as a creative power. The nothingness out of which he came was the same nothingness out of which the world came and in this kind of reflection "he found himself in some real sense contemporaneous with the beginning of time."[161] When Augustine confronted the nothingness out of which both he and his world came, he was able to transcend both himself and his world and ground his existence and his self - affirmation in him who created both out of nothing.

In this chapter, I have tried to focus on the human experience conveyed by the word "faith." This experience, I have suggested, is an experience of transformation which, as far as it can be analyzed psychologically, can best be described as a transformation of motives, from self - justifying to self - transcending motives. This seems to be the common element in the four theological descriptions of faith we have examined, though each theologian describes the transformation in his own way. What for Kierkegaard is a "leap" from the ethical to the religious level of existence is for Barth a bridging of the gap between the human possibility of "religion" and the divine possibility of grace. What for Bultmann is a transition from the frustrating self - knowledge of philosophy to the realization of authentic existence made possible by the self - understanding of faith is for Tillich a movement from a false sense of autonomy to the self - transcending state of theonomy.

We have seen, further, that in the transformation of motives which characterizes the faith experience there is a radical discontinuity between the two types of motivation. Self - justifying motivation in all its forms (ethics, religion, idealism, autonomy) does not lead of itself or develop into self - transcending motivation but must be abandoned in favour of self - transcending motives; and, in the Christian view, this transformation requires an experience of grace. In the transformation of faith we do not become more of what we are but something "different" or "new." But the "new being" of the believer is also perceived as at least a partial restoration of what Tillich would call his "essential being." The New Testament language of salvation, therefore, uses both images; salvation is the realization of the "new being" or "new creation," but it is also the "restoration" of something lost, that is, the restoration of the believer's essential being from which he had been estranged.

Because of the radical discontinuity between self - justifying and self - transcending motives, the faith experience can rightly be called an experience of self - transcendence. We have seen that what is common to all four theological descriptions of faith is the understanding of faith as the act by which one transcends all anxiety - producing efforts to live a self - justifying or authentic existence through one's human resources. Thus what is transcended in faith is that anxiety - producing preoccupation with self - both in the form of religious moralism and human idealism - which is the necessary precondition of faith. Faith, therefore, in the Christian view, represents religious adulthood since it makes possible some degree of that state of self - transcending self - forgetfulness which we have associated with adulthood. In examining the psychological theories to be reviewed in chapter III we shall be asking the question: does the achieving of human maturity and adulthood involve the same self - transcending transformation of motives?

ENDNOTES

1. For a discussion of Kierkegaard's existentialism, see B.E. and G.B. Arbaugh, *Kierkegaard's Authorship* (Rock Island, Illinois: Augusta College Library, 1967).
2. Soren Kierkegaard, *The Last Years: Journals 1853 - 1855.* Edited and translated by R.G. Smith (London: Collins, 1965), pp. 318 - 20.
3. Soren Kierkegaard, *Judge For Yourselves.* Translated by Walter Lowrie (Princeton: Princeton University Press, 1944), p. 202.
4. *Training in Christianity.* Translated by Walter Lowrie (Princeton: Princeton University Press, 1944), p. 122. See also *Concluding Unscientific Postscript.* Translated by D.F. Swenson and Walter Lowrie (Princeton: Princeton University Press, 1941), p. 188.
5. *Concluding Unscientific Postscript*, p. 540.
6. *The Journals of Soren Kierkegaard: A Selection.* Edited and translated by Alexander Dru. (London: Fontana, 1958), p. 185.
7. James Collins, *The Mind of Kierkegaard.* (Chicago: Regnery, 1965), pp. 42 - 43.
8. *Either/Or.* Vol. II, translated by Walter Lowrie (Garden City, N.Y.: Doubleday, 1959), pp. 168 & 170.
9. *Concluding Unscientific Postscript*, p. 226. "The existing A" is an allusion to the pseudonymous author of *Either/Or*, Vol. I, who represents the aesthetic mode of existence.
10. *Either/Or*, Vol. II, p. 215.

11.   *Ibid.*, p. 162.
12.   *Ibid.*, p. 181.
13.   Arbaugh and Arbaugh, *Kierkegaard's Authorship*, p. 85.
14.   David Roberts, *Existentialism and Religious Belief.* (New York: Oxford University Press, 1959), p. 70.
15.   *Concluding Unscientific Postscript*, p. 347.
16.   *Training in Christianity*, p. 71.
17.   *Ibid.*, p. 72.
18.   *Fear and Trembling.* Translated by Walter Lowrie (Garden City, N.Y.: Doubleday, 1954), p. 41.
19.   *Ibid.*, p. 80.
20.   *The Word of God and the Word of Man.* Translated by Douglas Horton (London: Hodder and Stoughton, 1935), p. 196.
21.   H.R. Mackintosh, *Types of Modern Theology.* (London: Fontana, 1964), p. 287.
22.   *Ibid.*, p. 255.
23.   *Church Dogmatics*, II, 2 (Edinburgh: T. & T. Clark, 1957), p. 315.
24.   The use of the word "religion" in this sense, differentiates it from Kierkegaard's use of the words "religion" and "religious." Kierkegaard equates the religious level of existence with faith. For Barth, religion refers to the necessary preamble to faith, to what Kierkegaard calls the ethical stage of existence.
25.   *Epistle to the Romans.* Translated by Edwyn C. Hoskyns (London: Oxford University Press, 1933), p. 168.
26.   *Ibid.*, p. 172.
27.   J.A. Veitch, "Revelation and Religion in the Theology of Karl Barth," *Scottish Journal of Theology*, 24:1, 1971, pp. 1 - 22.
28.   *Epistle to the Romans*, pp. 183 - 184.
29.   *Ibid.*, p. 19.
30.   *Ibid.*, pp. 50 - 51.
31.   *Ibid.*, p. 185.
32.   *Ibid.*, p. 242.
33.   *Ibid.*, pp. 201 - 202.
34.   *Dogmatics in Outline.* (New York: Harper Torchbook, 1959), p. 18.
35.   *Church Dogmatics*, IV, 1, p. 774.
36.   *Ibid.*, p. 105.
37.   "Concerning Christian Liberty" in *Luther's Primary Works.* Edited by Henry Wall and C.A. Buckheim (London: Hodder and Stoughton, 1896, pp. 245 - 293), p. 271.
38.   *Martin Luther's Werke, Kritische Gesamtausgabe*, Weimar ed., 39 - 1, p. 219. English translation quoted in Paul Althaus, *The Theology of Martin Luther.* Translated by Robert C. Schultz (Philadelphia: Fortress Press, 1966), p. 58.
39.   Roland Bainton, *Here I Stand: A Life of Martin Luther.* (New York: New American Library, 1950), p. 17.

40.   Preserved Smith, "Luther's Early Development in the Light of Psychoanalysis" in *American Journal of Psychology*, Vol. 24, 1913, p. 370.

41.   M. Luther, *The Bondage of the Will* quoted in P. Smith, *op cit.*, p. 373.

42.   Erik Erikson, *Young Man Luther.* (New York: Norton and Co., 1962), p. 77.

43.   *Ibid.*, p. 38.

44.   *Ibid.*, pp. 154 - 155.

45.   *Ibid.*, p. 91.

46.   *Ibid.*, p. 65.

47.   Martin Luther, "Lectures on Galatians," in *Luther's Works,* vol. 26. (St. Louis: Concordia Publishing House, 1963), p. 178.

48.   E. Erikson, *Young Man Luther*, p. 68.

49.   "Concerning Christian Liberty," in *Luther's Primary Works*, p. 256.

50.   John Dunne, *A Search for God in Time and Memory.* (London: MacMillian, 1967), pp. 76 - 83.

51.   *Young Man Luther*, p. 145.

52.   *A Search for God in Time and Memory*, p. 86.

53.   *Ibid.*, pp. 80 - 81.

54.   *Ibid.*, p. 79.

55.   M. Luther, "Preface to Latin Writings," in *Martin Luther: Selections from his Writings.* Edited by John Dillenberger (Garden City, N.Y.: Doubleday, 1961), p. 11.

56.   "Preface to Latin Writings," p. 11.

57.   R. Bainton, *Here I Stand: A Life of Martin Luther,* pp. 57 - 58.

58.   M Luther, "Against Latomus" in *Luther's Works*, vol. 32, pp. 226 - 227.

59.   M. Luther, "The Freedom of a Christian," in *Martin Luther: Selections from His Writings,* pp. 57 - 58.

60.   Karl Hall, "Martin Luther on Luther," in *Interpreters of Luther.* Edited by Jaroslav Pelikan (Philadelphia: Fortress Press, 1968), pp. 9 - 34.

61.   K. Hall, "Martin Luther on Luther," p. 30.

62.   *Ibid.*, p. 31.

63.   Louis Bouyer, *The Spirit and Forms of Protestantism.* Translated by A.V. Littledale (London: Harvil Press, 1956), p. 101.

64.   Philip Watson, "Erasmus, Luther and Aquinas," in *Concordia Theological Monthly*, XL: 11, pp. 747 - 758.

65.   M. Luther, "Preface to Romans," in *Martin Luther: Selections from his Writings*, p. 24.

66.   P. Althaus, *The Theology of Martin Luther*, p. 235.

67.   Ignatius of Antioch, *Letter to the Ephesians.*

68.   R. Bultmann, "Milestones in Books," in *The Expository Times*, LXX: 125.

69.   R. Bultmann, *Jesus Christ and Mythology* (London: S.C.M. Press, 1960), p. 51.
70.   *Ibid.*, p. 53.
71.   *Ibid.*, p. 55.
72.   *Ibid.*, p. 56.
73.   R. Bultmann, *Theology of the New Testament.* Translated by Kendrick Grobel, Vol. 1 (New York: Scribners, 1951), p. 318.
74.   *Ibid.*, p. 319.
75.   *Ibid.*, p. 319.
76.   R. Bultmann, *Theology of the New Testament*, vol. 2 (New York: Scribners, 1955), p. 75.
77.   R. Bultmann, "The New Testament and Mythology," in *Kerygma and Myth: A Theological Debate.* Translated by R.H. Fuller and edited by Hans Werner Bartsch. (New York: Harper Tourchbook, 1961), p. 16.
78.   R. Bultmann, *Theology of the New Testament*, vol. I, p. 315.
79.   R. Bultmann, *Jesus Christ and Mythology*, p. 39.
80.   *Ibid.*, p. 41.
81.   R. Bultmann, *The Theology of the New Testament*, vol. I, p. 324.
82.   *Ibid.*, p. 164.
83.   *Ibid.*, p. 165.
84.   *Ibid.*, p. 182.
85.   *Ibid.*, p. 182.
86.   John Macquarrie, "Philosophy and Theology in Bultmann's Thought" in *The Theology of Rudolf Bultmann*, edited by C.W. Kegley (New York: Harper and Row, 1966), pp. 127 - 143.
87.   R. Bultmann, "The New Testament and Mythology," pp. 18 - 19.
88.   R. Bultmann, *Jesus Christ and Mythology*, p. 40.
89.   J. Macquarrie, "Philosophy and Theology in Bultmann's Thought," p. 134.
90.   R. Bultmann, "The New Testament and Mythology," p. 23.
91.   *Ibid.*, pp. 26 - 27.
92.   J. Macquarrie, "Philosophy and Theology in Bultmann's Thought," p. 139.
93.   R. Bultmann, *Theology of the New Testament*, vol. I, p. 317.
94.   *Ibid.*, p. 316.
95.   R. Bultmann, "The New Testament and Mythology," p. 27.
96.   *Ibid.*, p. 30.
97.   *Ibid.*, p. 31.
98.   *Ibid.*, p. 32.
99.   P. Tillich, *Systematic Theology*, vol. 2, (Chicago: University of Chicago Press, 1957), p. 5.
100.   J.A.T. Robinson, *Honest to God* (London: S.C.M. Press, 1963), chapter 3.
101.   P. Tillich, *Systematic Theology*, vol. 2, p. 7.

102.   P. Tillich, *The Courage to Be* (London: Fontana, 1962), p. 153.
103.   P. Tillich, *Uber die Idee einer Theologie der Kultur.* (Berlin: Reither and Reichard, 1919), p. 35. Quoted in James Luther Adams, *Paul Tillich's Philosophy of Culture, Science and Religion* (New York: Harper and Row, 1965), p. 43.
104.   P. Tillich, *Systematic Theology*, vol. 1 (Chicago: University of Chicago Press, 1951), p. 60.
105.   P. Tillich, *Systematic Theology*, vol. 3 (Chicago: University of Chicago Press, 1963), p. 130.
106.   P. Tillich, *The New Being* (New York: Scribners, 1955), p. 121.
107.   P. Tillich, *The Protestant Era*, Translated by James Luther Adams (Chicago: University of Chicago Press, 1957), p. xi.
108.   P. Tillich, *The Protestant Era*, p. x.
109.   *Ibid.*, p. 226.
110.   Carl Armbruster, S.J., *The Vision of Paul Tillich* (New York: Sheed and Ward, 1967), pp. 59 - 60.
111.   P. Tillich, *The Courage to Be*, p. 15.
112.   *Ibid.*, p. 48.
113.   Erich Fromm, *Man for Himself*, (Greenwich, Conn.: Fawcett Publications, 1965), pp. 148ff.
114.   P. Tillich, *Systematic Theology*, vol. 1, p. 84.
115.   P. Tillich, *Systematic Theology*, vol. 3, p. 87.
116.   P. Tillich, *Systematic Theology*, vol. 1, p. 84.
117.   P. Tillich, *The Courage to Be*, pp. 92 - 93.
118.   *Ibid.*, p. 152.
119.   *Ibid.*, p. 160.
120.   *Ibid.*, p. 168.
121.   P. Tillich, *The Protestant Era*, p. 57.
122.   *Ibid.*
123.   P. Tillich, *Love, Power and Justice,* (New York: Oxford University Press, 1960), pp. 76 - 77.
124.   Cf. P. Tillich, *Systematic Theology*, vol. 3, p. 250.
125.   P. Tillich, *Systematic Theology*, vol. 1, p. 85.
126.   Augustine, *Confessions*, 3, iv. This and all subsequent citations are from the translation of F.J. Sheed (London: Sheed and Ward, 1948).
127.   *Ibid.*, 3, iv.
128.   *Ibid.*, 3, iv.
129.   Frederick Coppleston, S.J., *A History of Philosophy*, vol. II, part 1 (Garden City, N.Y.: Doubleday, 1962), p. 67.
130.   John Dunne, *A Search for God in Time and Memory*, (London: MacMillian: 1967), pp. 45 - 57.
131.   Paul Tillich, *A History of Christian Thought*, Edited by Carl E. Braaten (London: S.C.M. Press, 1968), pp. 103 - 133.
132.   R.L. Ottley, *Studies in the Confessions of St. Augustine*, (London: Robert Scott, 1919), p. 56.

133. P. Tillich, *A History of Christian Thought*, pp. 111 - 112.
134. Augustine, *Confessions*, 7, x.
135. *Ibid.*, 7, xvii.
136. F. Coppleston, *A History of Philosophy*, vol. II, part I, p. 80.
137. Augustine, *Confessions*, 7, xvii.
138. *Ibid.*, 7,x.
139. *Ibid.*, 8, i.
140. *Ibid.*, 10, xxvii.
141. R.L. Ottley, *Studies in the Confessions of St. Augustine*, pp. 94 - 95.
142. Augustine, *Confessions*, 7, ix.
143. *Ibid.*, 8, xii.
144. F. Coppleston, *A History of Philosophy*, vol. II, part 2, p. 538.
145. R. J. O'Connell, *St. Augustine's Confessions: The Odyssey of a Soul*, (Cambridge, Mass.: Harvard University Press, 1969), p. 91.
146. J. Dunne, *A Search for God in Time and Memory*, p. 53.
147. R. J. O'Connell, *St. Augustine's Confessions: The Odyssey of a Soul*, pp. 24ff.
148. J.M. Le Blond, *Les Conversions de St. Augustin,* (Paris: Aubier, 1950), p. 151.
149. Philip Woolcott Jr., "Some Considerations of Creativity and Religious Experience in Saint Augustine of Hippo," in *Journal for the Scientific Study of Religion*, V:2. Fall, 1965, p. 276.
150. James Dittes, "Continuities Between the Life and Thought of Augustine," in *Journal for the Scientific Study of Religion*, V:1. Fall 1965, p. 135.
151. Charles Kligerman, "A Psychoanalytic Study of the Confessions of St. Augustine," in *Journal of the American Psychoanalytic Association*, V:3, July 1957, p. 478.
152. P. Woolcott, "Some Considerations of Creativity and Religious Experience in St. Augustine of Hippo," p. 275.
153. J.E. Dittes, "Continuities between the Life and Thought of Augustine," p. 135.
154. *Ibid.*, p. 136.
155. *Ibid.*, p. 137.
156. C. Kligerman, "A Psychoanalytic Study of the Confessions of St. Augustine," p. 483.
157. J.E. Dittes, "Continuities between the Life and Thought of Augustine," p. 136.
158. P. WoolCott Jr., *op. cit.*, p. 280.
159. P. Tillich, *A History of Christian Thought*, p. 109.
160. Augustine, *Commentary on John*, Treatise 26.
161. J. Dunne, *A Search for God in Time and Memory*, pp. 56 - 57.

CHAPTER III

Human Transformation: A Psychological View.

1.   HUMAN EXISTENCE AS TRANSFORMATION.

In chapter II, I have already suggested that if faith is experienced authentically, it is, according to the theological descriptions of faith that we have examined, a "theonomous" experience, a religious experience which is at the same time an expression of authentic human growth and maturity. If this is true it is because the faith experience, as we have seen, involves the kind of self - transcending transformation of motives which we have posited as an essential element of psychological adulthood and maturity.   In the end, of course, the truth of the assertion that faith existence by its very nature involves growth towards human maturity and fulfilment can only be verified by the empirical evidence of individual believers for whom faith has been an experience of greater freedom, responsibility and self - transcendence.   The individual believer knows perhaps in an experiential way about the connection between the life of faith and the experience of one's full humanity.

But is it possible to abstract from the experience of individual believers and to assert this connection between faith and human growth in a more general way? Christian believers customarily do so and the grounds for their assertion seem to be twofold. First, there is the empirical evidence supplied by those whose lives are outstanding examples of faith. The life of a Mother Teresa or a Martin Luther King gives evidence not only of a deep faith relationship with God but also a self - transcending commitment to the service of humanity. Secondly, the assertion that the call to faith is a call to human growth and fulfilment may be made as a claim of faith itself; one's image of God is such that it is unthinkable that one's response to him would constitute a denial of one's humanity. Hence the claim of St. Irenaeus that "the glory of God is man fully alive," and the words of Jesus himself: "I have come so that they might have life and have it to the full." (John X: 10) In a published interview several years ago Gregory Baum,[1] in answer to a question about his understanding of God, spoke of the immanence of the divine in human life. God, he maintained, was a mystery present in human life "summoning men to self - knowledge and growth" who calls people (through his word) and graces them (through his spirit) "to become more fully human."

It would be difficult to find a more explicit faith - statement of the connection between faith and human growth than Baum's. It would be difficult also to find a theologian or a mature believer who would not, upon reflection, agree substantially with this statement. The belief that the call to faith is a call to the realization of one's full humanity seems to be a conviction and assumption of faith. Whatever his personal convictions might be, the psychologist of religion approaches this question with a view to asking methodologically whether there is a scientific basis to this faith conviction. He may do so by pragmatically applying psychological criteria of growth and maturity to the life of faith as it is actually lived. In *The Varieties of Religious Experience* William James, using this type of pragmatic "by their fruits you shall know them" approach, found the lives of some canonized Christian saints to be badly lacking in terms of human maturity and fulfilment. Unfortunately in the hands of some others who do not share James' caution about generalizing, this "Is religion healthy?" approach can become sadly reductive.

In this work I am also looking at the question of faith and human growth from the point of view of the psychology of religion but using a method which is more comparative and dialogical. What we want to know is whether the human dynamics underlying the experience of faith are the same as those underlying the experience of human growth. The word "transformation" has been chosen to describe the dynamics at work in both cases. If the life of faith is experienced by the believer as authentic human existence and human self - realization, it is because faith involves the same transformation of personality as does human growth. Such a comparative study is based on the premise that the two realities to be compared share a common ground. In this case the premise is that faith (whatever else it might be) and human growth are both human experiences, and it is only as human experiences that they can be compared. We cannot say that faith and human growth are the same reality but we can hypothesize that they are experienced in the same way, that each involves the same experience of transformation. This kind of comparison requires a dialogical approach in which both psychology and theology are allowed to speak within their own areas of competence and are taken seriously.

Thus far in this study we have allowed theology to instruct us on the meaning of faith and we have seen that, experientially, faith involves a self - transcending transformation of motives.   In this chapter I want to review four well - known psychologists of personality and what they reveal to us about the meaning of human growth.   I believe that these psychological theories reveal that human growth, like faith, is a process of self - transcendence involving a radical transformation of motives and a radical discontinuity between immature and mature human motivation.   The four theories to be examined are those of Alfred Adler, Erich Fromm, Gordon Allport and Victor Frankl.   In the chronological span represented by the four theorists there has been an increasing emphasis on the element of transformation and self - transcendence in the growth of personality. The inference I wish to draw from this is that in this area of human knowledge which is directly concerned with human self - understanding there has been a growing awareness of the fact that the fullness of human life demands a kind of self - transformation or self - transcendence which is analogous to the Christian experience of redemption.

(i) *Alfred Adler: From Self - Enhancement to Social Interest.*

A theory of personality is, at its most fundamental level, a theory of motivation; it seeks to identify the most basic motivating force in human personality.   In this respect those who comment on the individual psychology of Alfred Adler (1870 - 1937) often refer to "the will to power" as its most basic concept.   Victor Frankl, for example, identifies the most fundamental source of human motivation as the "will to meaning" and contrasts this concept with the "will to pleasure" of Freudian psychoanalysis and the "will to power" of Adlerian theory.

This makes for a neat distinction but it fails to do justice to Adler, for, in the final formulation of his theory, personality growth has little to do with the pursuit of raw power except in the case of the neurotic. In the normal personality Adler believed that the primary motivating force was the striving for superiority or perfection but with a social dimension.   The mature personality strives not for purely personal perfection, unrelated to others, but for the perfection of society; one's maturity is proportionate to the degree of such "social interest" present in the conduct of one's life.   The key concept therefore in Adlerian psychology is not the "will to power" but "social interest."   It is important for our purposes to trace the development of this idea in Adler's thought.

Freudian psychoanalysis had proposed that personality was the result of our being driven by physiological drives. Adlerian theory is a more "subjective" psychology in that it makes personality more of a creation of the individual in pursuit of goals. It was not just over the question of the primacy of the sex drive that Adler broke ranks with Freud; it was a more fundamental rejection of the primacy of the physiological drives as such. This switch in emphasis from the "physiological" to the "psychological" first occurred to Adler in his early studies of "organ inferiority" and the theory of compensation according to which an individual tries to compensate for physical inferiority by directly strengthening the inferior organ as in the case of one who tries to correct a speech defect or by strengthening another organ by way of compensation as a blind person might develop a highly sensitive sense of hearing. But Adler was led to the further conclusion that compensation can take place on a psychological level when nature fails to compensate or the possibilities of physical compensation are exhausted. In this case compensation takes place in the "psychological superstructure" of the organ. If the drive associated with the organ is frustrated it may lead to some kind of pathological compensation. Inferiority in the digestive tract for instance which frustrates the drive for food may lead to overcompensation by way of some other incorporative mode such as avarice.

Adler further noticed that drives are not isolated from each other. Several drives may seek the same object. Thus hunger is the result of such "confluence" of drives; the drive to eat (the primary or dominant drive) also includes the drives to see and smell. These observations led Adler to postulate the existence of one "superordinated" drive which would direct the confluence of all other drives and thus become the main driving or dynamic force of the personality. The development of his theory may thus be linked to the progressive refining of the meaning of this central drive. At first Adler identified it as aggression; This becomes a psychological force directing and connecting the primary drives. At this point in the development of Adler's theory aggression assumes that dominant role in personality which Freud had assigned to the sex instinct. In neurotics the aggressive drive finds expression in temper tantrums, defiance, paranoia, etc. It may also be turned against oneself as in hypochondria or suicide.

Eventually Adler recognized the aggressive drive as itself a neurotic form of a more general striving to overcome inferiority which now became the basic dynamic force in personality growth. Here aggression remains as the pathological or neurotic form of striving and results when a child's sense of inferiority is heightened by any denial of his need for affection.   Aggression then is the result of a combination of two things: the child's sense of inferiority and the frustration of his need for affection:

> Every unsatisfied drive ultimately orients the organism towards aggression against the environment. The rough characters and the unbridled, incorrigible children can instruct us in the way the continuously unsatisfied drive for affection stimulates the paths of aggression.[2]

In this latter formulation the physiological drives become subordinated to a more subjective factor, the feelings of inferiority. The striving to overcome feelings of inferiority becomes the prime motivating force in one's personality. This striving was originally formulated by Adler as the "masculine protest," that is, the striving to be strong and powerful as compensation for feeling unmanly Adler sees something neurotic in the man who has an exaggerated need to repress his so called "feminine" traits through what he calls "hypertrophical masculine wishes and efforts" (or what today we might call "macho" behaviour), "because the feminine tendency is evaluated negatively."[3] In women this neurosis takes the form of a denial and devaluation of one's gender. C.G. Jung of course has had much to say about this kind of sexual one - sidedness and feminist thinkers would have us reflect on the historical and sociological roots of this neurosis.

The concept of the masculine protest is however a negative and incomplete idea. It identifies the individual's most basic desire as the desire to escape from feelings of inferiority. But is there a positive goal to this striving? Adler's answer is that the positive goal of human becoming is the goal of superiority or perfection. Each individual is motivated (subjectively or unconsciously) by a goal of superiority. This is not an objective goal which determines his life in some fatalistic way; it is a subjective goal created by the individual as compensation for feelings of inferiority. Moreover, it is a largely unconscious goal and can be detected only by observation of a person's style of life. This goal is for Adler the root of the individuality and unity of the personality.

> Thus the aim of the mental life of man becomes its governing principle, its *causa finalis*.... Here we have the root of the unity of the personality, the individuality. It matters not what may have been the source of its energies: not their origin but their end, constitutes their individual character.[4]

Each person is unique because each has his own goal of superiority which compensates for the particular way in which he feels inferior. It is the thought of this goal, says Adler, the thought of this future success, which makes present difficulties bearable. Through the pursuit of the compensating goal of superiority "the individual mitigates his sense of weakness in the anticipation of his redemption."[5]

Put this way, it becomes questionable whether the striving for superiority is really the most basic motivating force; it appears rather to be a means to an end, to the more ultimate goal of overcoming feelings of inferiority. It would seem to become more basic and fundamental than the need to overcome inferiority only by acquiring, to use Allport's phrase, a kind of "functional autonomy," by becoming an end in itself rather than a means to an end. That this is what happens in the mature personality is implied, I believe, in Adler's concept of "social interest." With this term Adler attempted to distinguish the normal striving for superiority from those that were neurotic. The striving for superiority is neurotic or immature to the extent that it is self - centred, without social feeling, and gives to a person's life a purely "private meaning." This kind of striving which produces a life which has no meaning for others is what Adler calls "self - enhancement." The mature striving for superiority includes social interest, the desire to contribute to the welfare of one's group, one's world, one's fellow human beings. Self enhancement, on the other hand, is ego - centred; it is the desire to avoid defeat and the loss of self - esteem. In one who pursues the goal of self - enhancement the feelings of inferiority have become so great that he is afraid to pursue a goal of superiority in some socially useful way. One's concern is not for others but for oneself. The desire to be superior through real social accomplishment and contribution - a desire which carries with it a fear of failure or rejection - gives way to the desire to bolster one's ego by merely feeling superior.

His goal is still "to be superior to difficulties," but instead of overcoming obstacles he will try to hypnotize himself, to auto - intoxicate himself, into feeling superior. Meanwhile his feelings of inferiority will accumulate, because the situation which produces them remains unaltered... He does not train to be stronger, to be more adequate; he trains to appear stronger in his own eyes.[6]

The various forms of defense mechanisms, gamesmanship, role - playing, and downright bullying by which one attempts to appear superior "in his own eyes" represent for Adler neurotic solutions to the problem of inferiority.

Feelings of inferiority however are in themselves not abnormal. Adler sees the feeling of inferiority as the necessary starting point in a process of development whose goal is the achieving of social interest and therefore as the starting point for all human, cultural achievement. We have seen that Adler, in the development of his theory, gradually refined his concept of the goal of personality growth. At first this goal was the satisfaction of physiological drives; then it was an ego - centred state of self - enhancement; finally it was the goal of perfection which, because of the presence of social feeling, becomes the perfection of society. Not only do these represent stages in Adler's thought; they may also be considered as the stages of personality growth. Normal development means to pass from drive satisfaction to self - enhancement to social interest. Maladjustment means that one's growth towards social interest is blocked so that one remains fixated at the level of ego - centred striving for security and self - enhancement.

What is the measure of the mature personality? It is the degree of social interest in one's striving for perfection or superiority. The mature personality strives for a perfection or superiority which is useful to society. For Adler, social interest is an "innate potentiality" which must be consciously developed. Everyone must arrive at some idea of what life means. The meaning given to life will be either a private or a social meaning and this will be reflected in one's striving for superiority by the absence or presence of social interest. He adds further that the meaning one gives to life is indicated in the response one makes to the three social ties which make demands on each one of us - the occupational, the social and the sexual.

These three ties, therefore, set the problem: how to find an occupation that enables us to survive under the limitations set by the nature of the earth; how to find a position among our fellows, so that

we may cooperate and share the benefits of cooperation; how to
accommodate ourselves to the fact that we live in two sexes and that
the continuance and furtherance of mankind depends upon our love
life.
Individual psychology has found no problem in life which cannot be
grouped under these three main problems - occupational, social and
sexual. It is in his response to these three problems that every
individual human being unfailingly reveals his own deep sense of
the meaning of life.[7]

The ultimate reason for striving for superiority is to respond
adequately to these social demands which life imposes on us, to equip
oneself to make some meaningful contribution to society. Without this
social goal superiority is meaningless. If we try to develop personality
"in vacuo," says Adler, without reference to the social goal of that
development, "we shall merely make ourselves domineering and
unpleasant."[8]

Normal feelings of inferiority, therefore, lead to normal
adjustment because they act as a spur to the striving for superiority
which becomes, in optimal development, the desire to contribute to
society. If however the feelings of inferiority are too great or if they
are aggravated by environmental factors (Adler mentions as examples
neglected, pampered and handicapped children) then one's striving for
superiority is deflected away from a social goal and towards the
"useless" side of life because of the fear of failure on the useful side.

Those who have the courage to commit themselves to a social goal,
Adler maintains, are those "who consider themselves part of the
whole, who are at home on this earth and in this mankind."[9]

Individual psychology therefore sees human growth as a
transformation from drive satisfaction to self - enhancement and
finally to social interest. All growth, in Adler's view, begins with and
compensates for original feelings of inferiority. But if the growing
child is to overcome inferiority, she cannot do so by concentrating on
the goal of personal superiority in a self - absorbed way. True
superiority is achieved by concentrating on a goal outside of oneself.

If a child is to draw together his powers and overcome his
difficulties, there must be a goal for his movements outside of
himself, a goal based on interest in reality, interest in others and
interest in co - operation.[10]

In this view, personal superiority or perfection becomes a by - product of some other self - transcending goal, not an objective to be pursued for its own sake. Self - conscious preoccupation with one's own personality is self - defeating. On the other hand, commitment to a life of contribution and cooperation provides the motive power one needs to achieve some degree of personal perfection.

> If an individual, in the meaning he gives to life, wishes to make a contribution, and if his emotions are all directed to this goal, he will naturally be bound to bring himself into the best shape. He will begin to equip himself to solve the problems of life (behaviour towards others, occupation and love) and to develop his abilities.[11]

The mature person, in Adler's view, is no longer motivated by the egocentric desire to feel superior, to protect her self - esteem, but rather by the self - transcending desire to perfect and develop oneself in order to contribute to the welfare of the human community.

> The neurotic strives toward personal superiority and, in doing so, expects a contribution from the group in which he lives, while the normal individual strives toward the perfection which benefits all.[12]

The kind of superiority which is thus compatible with social interest might best be described as "competence." It replaces, in normal development, the desire for self - enhancement, the "will to power" and the uselessness of giving life a private meaning. This is the transformation inherent in the normal thrust of human growth which demands, in Adler's words, "the unconditional reduction of striving for power and the development of social interest."[13] Social interest then represents the goal of normal growth, the normal compensation for the feeling of inferiority. It is when the feeling of inferiority is exaggerated, that is, when it becomes an inferiority complex that a child's growth is deflected towards the useless side of life. As long as the feeling of inferiority is not exaggerated "a child will always strive to be worthwhile and on the useful side of life."[14]

How can the term "discontinuity" and therefore "transformation" be applied to Adler's description of human growth? What is clear is that Adler sees the human condition as a conflict between the striving for personal superiority and the striving towards social interest. The latter is innate and represents the goal of normal growth and true human self - hood; the former is something learned, the product of educational , environmental and social factors which deflect one's growth towards the useless side of life and the egocentric striving for self - enhancement. Together they represent the abnormal and normal paths taken by that striving which is innate, the striving to overcome inferiority. The transition from self - enhancement to social interest is not automatic or accounted for merely in terms of the innate capacity for growth. The development of social interest, while it is an innate capacity, depends on an external, environmental factor, the satisfaction of one's need for affection. The child's desire for self - enhancement becomes social interest only when his need for affection is satisfied in a healthy way. If it is frustrated by pampering or neglect the feelings of inferiority become an inferiority complex and the child continues to be motivated by the desire to escape from his feelings of inferiority, that is, by the desire for self - enhancement.

Neglect prevents the child from developing an attitude of trust towards the world and others. Pampering keeps the child at the level of self - enhancement for all difficulties are   solved by making demands on others and exercising power over them. It was for this reason that Adler, like Freud, saw the oedipal stage of growth as critical; his interpretation of the oedipal complex, however, is more in terms of the "will to power" than the will to pleasure or the sex instinct. For Adler, the child at this point in life takes a decisive step in the direction of either self - enhancement or social interest. The Oedipus complex was, in Adler's view, the result of pampering. It is the conflict within the child who does not want to give up his mother, not as an object of the sex instinct but as one over whom he has power or, more accurately, over whom he has been given power through pampering. In such a case mother becomes the one at whose expense the child escapes all feelings of inferiority and satisfies his need for self - esteem.

> ...the complex characterizes a pampered child who does no want to give up his mother. According to Freud the Oedipus Complex is supposed to be the foundation of the development of mental life, but Individual Psychology has shown that it is an error of upbringing.[15]

But in clinging to mother and power over mother the pampered child is seeking to overcome inferiority and achieve self esteem in an unhealthy way, a way of seeking the illusion of superiority rather than superiority itself. If the child's striving for superiority is restricted in this way then his sexual drive will also be restricted to the family circle. Thus Adler saw Freud's sexual interpretation of the complex as only one aspect of a much more fundamental drive, the striving to overcome inferiority.   On the other hand, to resolve the complex successfully means to give up not only sexual desire for mother but also, and more fundamentally, the will to power over mother. This in turn creates the possibility of openness to others as objects of love. Thus the oedipal situation becomes a paradigm of the basic choice one must make, the choice between the useless side of life and the useful side of life, between giving a private or social meaning to life, between self - enhancement and social interest; a paradigm also of the transformation that must take place if one is to achieve the fullness of growth and maturity.

(ii) *Erich Fromm: From Regression to Progression.*

Both Adler and Erich Fromm (1900 - 1980) describe human existence in terms of what Tillich would describe as the conflict between individualization and participation, the tendency to affirm one's individuality and to protect it against incursions from the environment versus the tendency to merge one's identity with the environment. For Adler, the threat to mature selfhood consists of an exaggerated sense of individuality in the form of self - enhancement which cripples the thrust towards that kind of social feeling and social commitment which is essential to human maturity. For Fromm, on the other hand, authentic selfhood is threatened by an exaggerated kind of involvement with one's environment, by the kind of submission or conformity in which a sense of belonging and relatedness is purchased at the price of one's individuality and integrity.

The starting point for Fromm's reflections on the human condition is the contradiction which he sees as inherent in human existence. Human existence is characterized by a fundamental existential dichotomy which is implied in the fact that the human person is, like the rest of animal life, a part of nature and yet, because of his capacity for reason and self - determination, he transcends nature.

> Man transcends all other life because he is, for the first time, life aware of itself. Man is in nature, subject to its dictates and accidents, yet he transcends nature because he lacks the unawareness which makes the animal a part of nature - as one with it. Man is confronted with the frightening conflict of being the prisoner of nature, yet being free in his thoughts; being part of nature, and yet to be, as it were a freak of nature; being neither here nor there. Human self - awareness has made man a stranger in the world, separate, lonely and frightened.[16]

Thus the distinguishing feature of human existence consists in the fact that it is less instinctively determined than animal existence. Whereas the animal is tied instinctively to nature and adapts to changes in the natural environment by changing itself, humans are less instinctively adaptable, and more helpless from the instinctual point of view. But the less complete the human being's instinctual equipment, the more developed is his brain, his ability to learn. To be capable of reason and self - awareness is to transcend, to some extent, and be separated from nature; to lose the animal's instinctual tie and harmony with nature.

Human self - awareness means that human adaptation is not instinctively determined. Human relatedness is the result of the human powers of reason and love. Since the animal's primary tie and harmony with nature has been broken, human relatedness to one's environment is something that must be learned. The human agent adapts to the environment by thinking rather than being determined by instinct, by choosing between different courses of action. He does not adapt passively to nature but masters it and uses it. To be thus a part of nature and yet self - determining means for Fromm that human existence is a problem to be solved.

> Man is the only animal for whom his own existence is a problem which he has to solve and from which he cannot escape. He cannot go back to the prehuman state of harmony with nature; he must proceed to develop his reason until he becomes the master of nature and of himself.[17]

This basic dichotomy - the tension arising from the fact of being at one and the same time a part of nature and yet transcending nature by reason of the specifically human faculties of reason and love - gives rise to the need to consciously relate oneself to the environment, to nature and to one's fellow human beings. The primary instinctive ties with nature have been broken and a new way of relating to the world must be consciously learned. There is an existential awareness of this need because the breaking of the primary ties with nature produces self - awareness.

But self - awareness is, as it were, a two - sided coin. On the one hand it means awareness of oneself as a unique and self - determining individual; on the other hand it carries with it an awareness of one's aloneness and separation from one's fellow human beings. To be human means to be a unique individual, but it also means to feel powerless and helpless in relation to the universe as a whole. This is a source of anxiety and, in Fromm's view, the need to overcome this sense of isolation and to achieve a human type of relatedness to one's world is the greatest human need. As with feelings of inferiority in Adlerian theory, it is also the starting point of human growth. In *The Art of Loving,* Fromm interprets the biblical story of Adam and Eve in this way. The eating of the fruit of the "tree of knowledge of good and evil" is seen as representing the dawn of human self - awareness, and the shame of Adam and Eve at each other's nakedness represents the fact that they are now aware of themselves as being separate individuals but remaining strangers because they have not yet learned to love each other and thus they are ashamed. This "awareness of human separation, without reunion by love" is for Fromm the source of shame, guilt and anxiety.[18] So great is the need for human relatedness that Fromm describes it as "an imperative need on the fulfillment of which man's sanity depends."[19]

This deep seated need for relatedness accounts for the fact that human beings seem to be capable of adapting to almost any kind of society or religion. Any kind of relatedness is better than none.

> The kind of relatedness to the world may be noble or trivial, but even being related to the basest kind of pattern is immensely preferable to being alone. Religion and nationalism as well as any custom and any belief, however absurd and degrading, if it only connects the individual with others, are refuges from what man most dreads; isolation.[20]

The goal therefore of authentic human growth is what Fromm calls "productive relatedness." This refers to that form of relatedness in which the individual preserves the sense of his own individuality, identity and integrity; a relatedness in which the individual not only contributes to the welfare of his fellow human beings (Adler's "social interest") but, in doing so, actualizes his own potential as a human person. So great however is the need to overcome isolation, that the relatedness is often purchased at the price of one's freedom and individuality. This is what Fromm calls "non - productive relatedness." This happens when the freedom which accompanies growing self - awareness is experienced as unbearable because of the isolation and fear it produces and so freedom and integrity are traded for the security of a sense of belonging.[21]

All non - productive forms of relatedness (Fromm mentions authoritarian relationships - both sadistic and masochistic -

destructiveness, and social conformity) have one thing in common; they achieve relatedness at the expense of individuality and integrity and therefore at the expense of genuine human growth which is in the direction of self - awareness, transcendence (of the "primary ties" with nature) and the development of the human capacity for reason and love. Fromm accepts the principle of self - preservation as the first principle of existence but, following Spinoza, he believes that the natural desire is not just to live but to live productively, that is, to actualize one's essential nature, to come nearer and nearer to the model of human nature, to become as fully human as possible. This productiveness must be achieved in all areas of human relatedness, in thought, action and feeling.

Productive thought refers to the power to grasp the world by reason, to understand the meaning of things and their relation to oneself, to see hidden relationships and hidden meanings. Thought is not an isolated, subjective activity; it is a way of relating oneself intellectually to one's world. Productive thought results in what Fromm calls a rational "frame of orientation;" a fundamental view of one's world and one's place in it which is consistent with the available evidence. Productive thought thus breaks down the barriers between oneself and the material world. According to Fromm, productive thinking must be both concerned and objective. It is not, in the first place, coldly detached and indifferent to the object of study (a distorted view of "objectivity"). Something becomes an object of thought because it is first an object of interest and concern The physician, the psychologist, the philosopher and the theologian all direct their thought toward some aspect of human existence, but to be productive thought (in the sense of promoting self - realization) it must be motivated by genuine concern for the human condition.[22] In this light, objectivity does not refer to a state of aloof detachment from the object of thought but rather to the ability not to distort or falsify reality. Objectivity sees things as they are in themselves; it is opposed to prejudice, wishful thinking and fantasy.

In the area of human activity, productiveness has little in common with the quantitative term "productivity." It refers rather to the self - actualizing aspect of human work. Productive work is that type of work by which a person realizes his creative potential, work which the individual plans, produces and of which he sees the result.

Finally, in the area of feeling, the human need for relatedness is expressed by love. Love, Fromm asserts, "is the only passion which satisfies man's need to unite himself with the world and to acquire at the same time a sense of integrity and individuality."[23] The passion thus described might be called "productive love" which Fromm defines as "union with somebody or something outside of oneself, under the condition of retaining the separateness and integrity of oneself." Love, he maintains is a paradoxical experience in which "two people become one, and remain two at the same time."[24]

Productive love is characterized first by "care and responsibility." Love is the "active concern for the life and growth of that which we love."[25] To love is to labour for something and make it grow. To love means to be my brother's keeper, to feel responsible for the growth and welfare of the other. Responsibility is not a duty imposed from without; it is my response to something I feel to be my concern. Fromm states that to love productively "is incompatible with being passive, with being an onlooker at the beloved person's life; it implies labour and care and the responsibility for his growth."[26] Secondly, love implies "respect and knowledge," without which love can degenerate into domination and possessiveness. Care and responsibility would be blind if not guided by knowledge of and respect for anther's individuality. These four qualities - care, responsibility, respect and knowledge - denote that love is an activity and an achievement; it is not just something that "happens" to us. They denote that love is active not passive because it consists essentially in giving rather than receiving and, as Fromm says "in the act of giving lies the expression of my aliveness."[27]

To summarize, each human person is a unique individual aware if his separateness but unable to bear being unrelated to his world and his fellow human beings. He can try to escape this contradiction by losing himself in submission, dependence, destructiveness or conformity, but there is only one solution which is:

> ...to face the truth, to acknowledge his fundamental aloneness and solitude in a universe indifferent to his fate, to recognize that there is no power transcending him which can solve his problem for him. Man must accept the responsibility for himself and the fact that only by using his own powers can he give meaning to his life. But meaning does not imply certainty; indeed, the quest for certainty blocks the search for meaning... there is no meaning to life except the meaning man gives his life by the unfolding of his powers, by living productively.[28]

It is against the background of this basic dichotomy inherent in human existence (awareness of both individuality and isolation) and the corresponding need for relatedness that we must examine Fromm's view of human growth; for growth, like relatedness, will be either productive or non - productive, either conducive to or destructive of human integrity and individuality, the realization of human potential and the development of our specifically human powers.

Fromm sees non - productive development as regression in the direction of an infantile orientation to reality and to a type of existence which represents a withdrawal or retreat from the free development of human self - awareness, which is seen as a threat. Productive growth, on the other hand, is a progression in the direction of the full development of self - awareness. The thrust of genuine growth is towards the development of "transcendence" in the sense of that transcending of the animal's instinctive ties with nature which characterizes human existence. It is experienced as growing self - awareness and the development of one's specifically human powers of reason and love. Thus, in Fromm's view, the question is the question of whether an individual will become fully human by continuing to progress in the way of transcendence, "until he becomes the master of nature and of himself;" or will he retreat from his humanity - escape from his freedom - and regress to the "pre - human state of harmony with nature."[29]

Fromm identifies the "symptoms" of progression and, therefore, of human maturity as biophilia (the love of life), relatedness, and independence or freedom. These three characteristics combine to produce what Fromm calls the "syndrome of growth." Regression, on the other hand, is revealed in the three opposite symptoms: necrophilia (the love of death), narcissism and incestuous fixation. These negative symptoms, taken together, form the "syndrome of decay." In reference then to human growth the basic dichotomy of human existence may be seen as manifesting itself existentially in a threefold polarity: necrophilia vs. biophilia; narcissism vs. relatedness; incestuous fixation vs. freedom and independence.[30] A brief examination of what Fromm has to say about each of these existential dichotomies may help us to understand his view of the conditions of human growth.

Necrophilia vs. Biophilia: Fromm believes that the most fundamental distinction to be made between human beings is the distinction between those who love death (necrophilia) and those who love life (biophilia). Necrophilia is used here to refer not only to the sexual perversion the word denotes, but to a much more general orientation of character. Such an orientation is seen in those who are preoccupied with sickness and death; in those who live in the past, rather than the present or future; in those whose personalities are cold and distant, who are lovers of "law and order" and force. The necrophile wants to make life certain, orderly and mechanical; to make life inorganic rather than organic, a matter of predictably repeated operations rather than unpredictable growth and unfolding. These symptoms represent an attempt to reverse the process of transcendence initiated by the development of human self - awareness and to return to the pre - human state of instinctual harmony with nature. As such it is rightly called the "love of death" since it is a retreat from the uncertainty and adventure which characterize human life. In Fromm's view the necrophile,

> ...wants to return to the darkness of the womb, and to the past of inorganic or animal existence. He is essentially oriented to the past, not to the future which he hates and is afraid of. Related to this is his craving for certainty. But life is never certain, never predictable, never controllable; in order to make it controllable, it must be transformed into death; death, indeed, is the only certainty in life.[31]

The necrophile wants to make life certain, predictable, mechanical and controllable; in doing so he turns life into death. Biophilia, on the other hand, represents an orientation towards life, an accepting of one's humanity with all that implies: self - awareness, transcendence of animal existence and the adventure, risk, responsibility and uncertainty of life which is organic - subject to open - ended growth and development - rather than inorganic and mechanical.

> The person who fully loves life is attracted by the process of life and growth in all spheres. He prefers to construct rather than retain. He is capable of wondering, and he prefers to see something new to the security of finding confirmation of the old. He loves the adventure of living more than he does certainty. His approach to life is functional rather than mechanical. He sees the whole rather than only the parts, structures rather than summations. He wants to mold and influence by love, reason, by his example; not by force, by cutting things apart, by the bureaucratic manner of administering people as if they were things. He enjoys life in all its manifestations, rather than mere excitement.[32]

For both Adler and Fromm a hallmark of maturity is the ability to live with risk and uncertainty, for this is what it means to love life (Fromm) and to live on its "useful side" (Adler).

Narcissism vs. Relatedness: If necrophilia can be regarded as an orientation towards death, or as a return to a condition which is inorganic and "pre - human," it is related to narcissism which represents a regression to an infantile state. The narcissistic person is recognized by the characteristics of self - satisfaction, sensitivity to any form of criticism and a lack of growing interest in the outside world. The term was used by Freud to describe the person whose "libido" or power of love was turned toward his own ego as an object whereas normal development demands the turning of the libido towards others as love objects.

Fromm finds no essential difference between the narcissism of the infant for whom the outside world has not yet emerged as real and the psychotic for whom the outside world has ceased to be real (with the exception of course that infantile narcissism is regarded as developmentally normal). Between these two extremes, however, we find intermediate levels of narcissism which are either "benign" (normal) or "malignant" (neurotic). The benign form of narcissism is that which results from the individual's efforts such as the satisfaction derived from one's work as an artist, scientist , artisan, etc. It is thus self - correcting since pre - occupation with oneself is balanced by interest in the work itself. In its malignant form, however, narcissism is the result not of what one does but of what one has (body, appearance, wealth, etc.) and thus represents a more total preoccupation with oneself and a correspondingly greater divorce from reality. If my self - esteem, Fromm argues, is based on some natural quality I have and not on any personal achievement then "I do not need to be related to anybody or anything; I need not make any effort. In maintaining the picture of my greatness, I remove myself more and more from reality."[33]

Narcissism is an obstacle to growth since it restricts the growth of both reason and love. It impedes the objectivity which should characterize reason since the narcissistic person is oriented toward seeing and judging reality only in reference to or as part of his own ego. It restricts love since the narcissist loves another only as an extension of his own ego and not as a distinct and separate personality. For the narcissistic person, the other is never a person in his or her own right but "exists only as a shadow of the partner's narcissistically inflated ego."[34] Narcissism thus becomes the antithesis of that kind of "productive relatedness" which, as we have seen, is characterized by objective and concerned thinking and the kind of love which is characterized by care, responsibility, respect and knowledge.

Incestuous Fixation vs. Independence: Fromm's views on this polarity represent a development of Freud's original discovery of the phenomenon of "mother fixation." In Freud's view the male child tends to be fixated in his attachment to mother and restricts his affective life to her love because she is the object of his sexual libido. For Fromm, what lies behind the child's fixation to mother is not the sex instinct but the human condition itself, that is, the basic human desire for security, warmth, protection and unconditional love which the child, male or female, finds in the attachment to mother. It is related, therefore, to both narcissism, which it nourishes and satisfies, and to necrophilia which also represents a return to the womb and to the pre - human condition and a reversal of the process of self - awareness and transcendence.

The clinical grounds for this interpretation if the oedipal theory is found primarily in the presence of the mother attachment of the pre - oedipal phase in girls as well as boys, which led Fromm to see in it something more that a "genital" impulse. Correspondingly, renunciation of the mother attachment is attributed to something more than the presence of the father - rival; the attachment is given up (in normal growth) because it is inconsistent with the main thrust of human growth which is a movement away from security and dependence and in the direction of independence and the risk, responsibility and insecurity which accompany freedom. Incestuous fixation is the clinging to a dependent relationship with mother, a relationship which represents a paradise which has been lost and must be given up if one is to achieve genuine freedom and independence. But while the demands of human growth impel us towards independence and the insecurity which accompanies freedom, there remains in us a tendency towards the warmth and security of our former condition. It is the basic dichotomy of each one's existence to be,

> ...torn between two tendencies since the moment of his birth; one, to emerge to the light and the other to regress to the womb; one for adventure and the other for certainty; one for the risk of independence and the other for protection and dependence.[35]

To grow, therefore, means to trade the security of dependence for the risk and insecurity of independence. A mother fixation represents the clinging to a state of dependency for the sake of the security and certainty it affords. And when this fixation persists into adult life it may become a fixation to a mother substitute such as one's spouse, church, political party, clan, family race, etc. From these mother substitutes one will expect the same reassurance, warmth, security and unconditional love as the infant expects from his mother. This kind of mother - fixation represents, as does narcissism, an obstacle to reason and love. One can only approve of what "mother" approves and love only those whom "mother" loves, that is, those who share the same fixation.

The question now becomes: In the context of the symptoms of progressive development, is it possible to speak of personality growth as a transformation from the symptoms of regression to the symptoms of progression; from necrophilia to biophilia; from narcissism to relatedness; from incest to independence? Fromm has related his concepts of biophilia and necrophilia to the concepts of the life instinct and the death instinct in Freudian theory, with this difference: unlike Eros and the death instinct, biophilia and necrophilia are not biologically rooted instincts; they are "character orientations," what we learn to be through environmental influences. Moreover, biophilia is a "primary potentiality," representing the normal thrust of human growth while necrophilia is a "secondary potentiality" and comes into play only if the appropriate conditions for life are not present. It is possible, therefore, (if necrophilia is merely a pathological condition) to speak of growth as a transformation from necrophilia to biophilia? In other words, is this pathological condition present from the beginning as something to be overcome or transcended through the development of a biophilic orientation? In answering this question it is important to remember that necrophilia is closely related, in Fromm's view, to the other symptoms of regression - narcissism and incestuous fixation. Each contributes to the growth of the other two. Thus it may be surmised that if the narcissism and mother - fixation which characterize infancy and early childhood are not transcended through relatedness and independence, then a necrophilic orientation to life can be expected.

Thus while the symptoms of progression are primary tendencies in the sense that they represent the true goals of normal growth, nevertheless, if one were to view growth in a chronological way, the symptoms of regression appear as primary in the sense that they are the strongest early influence and must be transcended if one is to grow towards life, relatedness and freedom. This becomes possible, in Fromm's view, when environmental conditions are favourable to such growth. Indeed, for Fromm, growth is essentially a proccss of transcendence: the evolution of the human race represents a transcending of the passive creaturely condition, and of the human state of harmony with nature; and the development of the individual human being represents a transcending of the tendency to return or regress to that original state.

I want to suggest, therefore, that , in the context of Fromm's theory of personality, human growth involves a transformation from one type of motivation (necrophilous, narcissistic, incestuous) to a radically different kind of motivation (biophilous, relational, independent). Moreover, it is an authentic transformation since there is a radical discontinuity between necrophilia and biophilia, between narcissism and relatedness, between incestuous fixation and independence. If the symptoms of regression are characteristic of infancy and childhood then the achieving of the true goals of human growth demands the transcending of these orientations, not the development or perfection of them. The seeds of life cannot be found in death, nor the potential for growth in decay.

(iii) *Gordon Allport: From Opportunistic to Propriate Striving:*

As we have seen in the discussion of Adler and Fromm, psychological theories of personality deal primarily with the question of motivation. They ask the question· What arc the dynamics of human behaviour'? What is the basic motivational force behind human conduct? In this respect, Gordon Allport (1897 - 1967) represents a departure from those theories which he found, at the beginning of his career, to dominate psychological thought and practice. These latter might be broadly characterized as "psychoanalytic" and "stimulus - response" theories. In Allport's view, modern dynamic psychology had developed two characteristics which limited the comprehensiveness of its motivational theory. The first of these is the emphasis on the unconscious sources of much of a person's motivations at the expense of conscious values and intentions. Allport sees the beginning of this trend toward "irrationalism" in motivational theory in Schopenhauer's doctrine of the primacy of the blind will and continued in Darwin's theory of the primordial struggle for survival, McDougall's emphasis on instincts and Freud's concept of the "libido."[36] While acknowledging the value of Freud's discovery that much of real motivation is hidden from the light of consciousness, Allport insisted on the role of conscious values and intentions in directing human behaviour. As with those whom we might identify with the tradition of "ego psychology," Allport sought to locate more of the dynamic motivation of personality in the conscious ego rather than the unconscious id. In doing so, he tried to correct what he believed to be Freud's overemphasis on unconscious motivation and the incompleteness of his psychology of the ego. He points out that Freud was a specialist in those motives which "cannot be taken at their face value," that is, in the motivational power of the id. The conscious, accessible region of personality, however, "he regarded as devoid of dynamic power."[37]

Allport also found the dominant psychological theories to be characterized by a belief in what he would later call the "functional continuity" of motives which claims that adult motivation is merely a more sophisticated, socially acceptable version of infantile motivation. This type of "geneticism" assigns a crucial role to innate instincts or early childhood experiences in determining adult behaviour. The behaviouristic, stimulus - response type of theory tends to reduce behaviour to a set of learned responses to external stimuli. Such theories join forces with the Freudian tendency to downgrade the role of consciously motivated and self - propelled behaviour in the adult. In Allport's view, stimulus - response theories, instinct psychologies and psychoanalysis all agree in viewing adult motivations as "conditioned, reinforced, sublimated, or otherwise elaborated editions of instincts or drives, or of an id whose structure, Freud said, 'never changes'."[38] Allport locates the psychoanalytic and behaviouristic views of the human mind within the "Lockean" tradition. Locke saw the mind as a passive receptor of sense impressions, a *tabula rasa.* Moreover, the earlier and simpler these impressions were, the more fundamental and decisive they were in the development of personality. Allport's view is seen to be in the tradition of Leibnitz who saw the intellect as something active, creative, and self - propelled which manipulates sensory data according to its own nature and purposes. The person thus becomes the source of acts, not just their locus.[39]

In this tradition, Allport's theory emphasizes the "ego structure" of personality as opposed to the various forms of instinct psychology, orthodox Freudianism and stimulus - response theories. All of the latter have a basic similarity of approach to the question of motivation, an emphasis on what is innate or learned at an early age. Such theories insist that what motivates the adult is merely a modified, sublimated or refined version of some primary instinct or infantile wish or response. In Freud's view, for example, the religious adult was satisfying an infantile need for a loving, protecting father through his or her religious belief or worship. This view of human motivation insists, as we have seen, on a "functional continuity" between infantile and adult behaviour. Allport's critique of such theories makes three points: First, they do not do justice to what Allport calls "the diversity, uniqueness, and contemporaneity of most adult motivation"[40] which reflects more than sex, aggression and infantile wishes. Secondly, the uniqueness of the person is undermined when motivation is reduced to certain basic instincts which are common to all. Besides the instincts which ensure survival, the individual has "potentialities for adulthood" by which personality becomes a unique structure with a unique style of life.[41] Thirdly, those theories which see all behaviour as having the objective of satisfying a need or reducing tension do not take into consideration the "becoming" aspect of personality growth.

Allport sees the individual as someone who is always in the process of becoming. The goal of growth is not merely to find new ways of reducing tension and thus endlessly reproducing the instinctual cycle of need - effort - satisfaction - need; it is to grow towards the realization of one's capacities, to become what one potentially is. The goal of human growth is self - actualization rather than homeostasis. Such a goal requires what Allport calls "propriate striving" towards a unique style of life. Allport sees this kind of activity whose goal is self - perfection rather than the satisfaction of a primary instinct as characteristic of adult behaviour.

> At low levels of behaviour the familiar formula of drives and their conditioning appears to suffice. But as soon as the personality enters the stage of ego - extension, and develops a self - image with visions of self - perfection, we are, I think, forced to postulate motives of a different order, motives that reflect propriate striving.[42]

Propriate striving is the opposite of instinctually driven behaviour since it maintains tension when necessary rather than reducing it. For this reason, Allport states, the unity or integration it confers on personality "is never the unity of fulfillment, of repose, or of reduced tension."[43] We are speaking, therefore, of a kind of behaviour which is to some degree independent of instincts and infantile needs, because the goal of propriate striving goes beyond the reduction of tension which the instincts seek. Allport suggests that a person is mature to the extent that his motives are thus independent of instinctual drives and infantile needs. The mature individual acts according to motives which are "functionally autonomous."

Functional autonomy means that a particular activity or form of behaviour may become an end in itself in spite of the fact that it was originally engaged in for some further reason. Thus a young man might enter the same profession as his father largely motivated by an infantile identification with the father. What Allport insists upon is that it is entirely possible (and indeed actually happens in most cases) that the young man will develop an interest in his profession for its own sake and for reasons that have nothing to do with any need to identify or compete with his father. His activity in this sphere is no longer dependent on unconscious motivation; he has simply outgrown that type of motivation. There is certainly an historical continuity in his motivation; it evolved from an original need to identify with his father. But Allport insists: "Historical continuity does not mean functional continuity."[44] In other words, the young man's present behaviour does not secure the same purpose or function as his earlier behaviour. In the same way the religion of one who originally acted out of the infantile need for a loving protecting father can become an end in itself, unrelated to such an infantile need. In Allport's view: "Just as we learn new skills, so also we learn new motives."[45]

Allport explains the principle of functional autonomy in this way:

> Just as a child gradually repudiates his dependence on his parents, develops a will of his own, becomes self - acting and self - determining, and outlives his parents, so it is with motives. Each motive has a definite point of origin which may lie in the hypothetical instincts or, more likely, in the organic tension.... Theoretically all adult purposes can be traced back to these seed - forms in infancy. But as the individual matures the bond is broken. The tie is historical, not functional.... The life of a tree is continuous with that of its seed, but the seed no longer sustains and nourishes the full grown tree. Earlier purposes lead into later purposes, but are abandoned in their favour.[46]

It is obvious that the principle of functional autonomy allows for greater emphasis on conscious motivation as opposed to unconscious motives. In Allport's view, much more importance must be given to the conscious intentions, purposes and goals which are contemporary than to the unconscious influence of the past history of the individual. The normal person's behaviour is not just a reaction to the past; it is the result of his intentions and plans for the future determined by his present ego - structure. Allport wants to de - emphasize the "reactive" view of human motivation. We have energies to use, he maintains, "that reach way beyond the need to react."[47]

The achieving of functional autonomy or "propriate striving" represents one aspect of what Allport calls the "proprium," a word which designates the sum total of propriate functions or systems of personality. The concept of the proprium appears in Allport's theory as something of a compromise solution to the question of whether psychology should resort to a concept of the "self" or "soul" to explain the growth, integration and organisation of personality. Is there, at the core of personality, some "mysterious central agency" which directs the growth and integration of personality? Allport points out that modern psychology, since the time of Wundt, has tended to reject such a postulate and to see the individual personality in terms of a stream of experiences and adjustments. The person was identified with his psychological functions rather than a self which was the transcendent subject of those functions. Wundt and his followers believed that the concept of a substantive self or soul was a philosophical or theological postulate which was inaccessible to psychological investigation and, therefore, had no place in an empirically oriented psychology.

Allport attributes the resurgence of the concept of the self in psychology in part to Freud's discussion of the ego. For Freud, the ego was a rational executor of personality, but its role was a passive and restrictive one, reconciling the instinctual demands of the id with the demands of the conscience and the external world. Later theorists, including Allport, saw personality as less instinctively driven and therefore were able to assign a more active and creative role to the ego. This "emancipated" ego became the self. But the problem was to arrive at an understanding of the self which was accessible to psychological analysis rather than a self which is a postulate beyond empirical investigation and which directs personality growth in some mysterious and autonomous way. Allport believed that to revert to such a concept of the self would be, for psychology at least, to retard scientific progress. What he found "unnecessary and inadmissible" was a concept of a self which directs personality growth "in a trans - psychological manner, inaccessible to psychological analysis."[48]

This raises the question of what kind of psychological evidence might support the concept of the self. Allport believed that the beginning of an answer was to be found in what Adler had called the individual's "life style." The self that psychology can deal with is that self which is revealed in a person's unique style of life. For Adler this unique life style was revealed in a person's response to the social challenges of life and the unique way in which each individual strove for the goal of superiority. For Allport, the unique life style is revealed in that kind of activity which can be called "propriate striving" or "oriented becoming." Propriate striving has to do with those things which are matters of importance to an individual, which are vital and central to his or her growth and functioning as a person. These are to be distinguished from those things which are merely matters of fact, mere circumstances which do not touch the core of personality, such as the use of one's native tongue or the innumerable habits which one falls into in the routine of life. It is my propriate activity - my fondest hopes, deepest interests, most cherished relationships and long - range goals - which belong to my unique style of life. It is to the sum total of these central or propriate modes of becoming that Allport applies the term "proprium."

The concept of the proprium conveys a new understanding of the self, one deduced from the observation of a person's "propriate striving" rather than a philosophical postulate to explain what otherwise cannot be explained. Propriate striving reveals the uniqueness of the personality for the propriate functions are aspects of personality which are uniquely one's own. Any account of personality must include hereditary and environmental factors such as conditioned reflexes, habits, skills, language, culture, etc., which each one has in common with others. These elements become "second nature" to the individual; they seldom seem central and important to him. But the uniqueness of the individual person can only be accounted for in terms of what is central and important, what is propriate. This includes "all the regions of our life that we regard as peculiarly ours" and "all aspects of personality that make for inward unity."[49]

If the self is identified with one's propriate striving, then we are speaking of a self which accounts for the growth, maturity and unification of personality, for it is precisely one's conscious plans, intentions and long range goals which give purpose, meaning and direction to life and, therefore, unity to personality. Integrity is achieved when one's strivings and adjustments are given unity and direction by a central mode of adjustment or becoming, that is, by a set of conscious plans and intentions at the centre of personality. Allport sees the presence of such "propriate" long range goals as the mark of maturity and mental health. Motivation, on the other hand, whose aim is the mere reduction of tension through opportunistic satisfaction of instinctual drives results in that fragmented type of personality associated with mental illness. Allport maintains that "the possession of long - range goals, regarded as central to one's existence, distinguishes the human being from the animal, the adult from the child and, in many cases, the healthy personality from the sick."[50]

Allport sees the growth of personality, therefore, as the growth of the proprium, that is, the gradual development of all those ego functions which represent the various aspects of the proprium.[51] These include such things as bodily sense, self - identity, ego - enhancement (the self - affirming, self - preservative aspect of the ego), ego - extension (identification of the ego with loved objects), the "rational agent" (the problem solving aspect of the ego which adjusts to external reality), and self - image. The acquisition of these ego - functions represents the foundation upon which one builds the capacity for that striving or activity which can be called "propriate" or uniquely one's own; activity which is an expression of conscious plans, objectives and values, and, therefore, of one's unique life - style. As such, it is produced by motives which are functionally autonomous, independent of instinctual drive and infantile wishes.

Allport finds a specific example of the functional autonomy of propriate activity in the growth of conscience. Freud believed conscience (the superego) to be the internalized voice of authority which one obeyed out of fear of punishment, whether the punishment came from the authority figure or the superego. For Allport, such a conscience would be an example of "opportunistic becoming," a question of surface conformity which does not touch the core of the personality. Propriate striving or "oriented becoming" on the other hand, involves the conscious pursuit of goals which are seen as meaningful and valuable for their own sake and vital to one's existence. Thus, in the realm of conscience, the mature adult does not merely adjust his behaviour in an opportunistic way to an interiorized voice of authority (as a child does); he consciously pursues goals which are consistent with his values, his self - image and his ego - ideal. Allport points to the fact that, as young adults, we often discard the codes of conduct imposed by parents or culture in favour of a private code of virtue. He interprets this development as a shift from ad hoc habits of obedience to the proprium or "from opportunistic becoming to oriented becoming."[52] This shift involves three important changes.[53] First, the external sanctions give way to internal; the commands and prohibitions of authority - figures are internalized. Secondly, "must" give way to "ought;" the pursuit of values replaces obedience to commands. Thirdly, specific habits of obedience give way to generic self - guidance; conduct is directed not by specific rules but by a broad scheme of values.

This description of the growth of conscience illustrates what is basic to Allport's theory of human growth: the fact that growth and maturity involve a transformation.   Indeed, Allport's theory of personality offers the most explicit description of human growth as a transformation of motives. The transformation from unconscious to conscious motivation means that the mature personality is no longer driven by primitive instincts and infantile needs; he is rather pulled by conscious plans, intentions and ideals.   And it is precisely one's motives which undergo this transformation; for the same activity, originally pursued out of unconscious, infantile motives, may, at the level of mature propriate striving, be pursued no longer for the satisfaction of primitive instinct or infantile need, but for its own sake, as a goal consistent with one's consciously held values.   This is consistent with what we have said about the experience of faith, the essence of which is a transformation of motives. The faith experience is not necessarily a "moral" conversion; the believer may pursue the same ethical ideal as before but from motives which are transformed and self - transcending.

In both human and religious maturity, therefore, motivation has become functionally autonomous, liberated from its unconscious and/or infantile origins. In the context of Allport's theory, the self - transcending quality of maturity consists in the fact that the mature adult is no longer the passive victim of unconscious drives and infantile needs but the creator of a unique style of life through the free and conscious pursuit of values and objectives. Allport is also explicit in describing this transformation in terms of radical discontinuity. Adult behaviour may be historically continuous with infantile behaviour (have its origins in infantile needs and desires) but it is not functionally continuous. It no longer serves the same function of satisfying those needs and drives; it has become functionally autonomous.   Between the motivation of infants or immature behaviour and the motivation of mature adult behaviour there exists that radical discontinuity which is essential to the idea of transformation.

(iv) *Viktor Frankl: From Self - Actualization to Self - Transcendence:*

Viktor Frankl (1906 -) has frequently referred to himself as representing the "Third Viennese School of Psychotherapy." In this way he distinguishes his own psychotherapeutic technique of "logotherapy" and the theory of personality on which it is based from those of Freud and Adler. In Frankl's theory the basic motivating force or tendency of the unconscious is seen as neither the Freudian "will to pleasure" nor the Alderian "will to power" but as the "will to meaning." By this phrase he identified the most basic tendency of the unconscious - the deepest source of human motivation - as the need to find meaning in one's human existence. By implication, the phrase also identifies the most basic kind of anxiety which besets human existence: not the neurotic anxiety which Freud encountered in his patients but the "existential" anxiety, that is, the anxiety which is inherent in human existence itself. Frankl's patients were not suffering from neurotic repression but from a sense of meaninglessness in their lives.

Frankl's hypothesis is that this type of neurosis - "noogenic neurosis" - demands a different kind of treatment the object of which is not to release the energy of inhibiting or repressing forces, and therefore to reduce tension, but to help the patient discover the meaning of his unique human existence. But the pursuit of meaning often involves not the reduction but the maintaining of tension for, in Frankl's view, tension is an integral part of a life that is fully human. The objective we pursue is not to achieve a tensionless state but to fulfil the meaning of our lives in spite of tension. What each person needs, Frankl states, is "not the discharge of tension at any cost, but the call of a particular and potential meaning waiting to be fulfilled by him."[54] It is this sense of meaning and purpose in life which makes tension, and indeed, every other type of suffering bearable. Frankl quotes the works of Nietzsche on this point: "He who has a WHY to live for can bear with almost any HOW."[55] To speak of the human person in this way - as motivated by the absence of meaning - reveals an existentialist understanding of human existence at the heart of Frankl's psychotherapeutic system. His discussion of the principles of logotherapy reveals at least three themes which inform existentialist thought in general.

The first of these is the priority of existence over essence. Existentialist thinking finds the value of the person not in his conformity to some abstract definition of human nature but in his unique, concrete existence. Abstract definitions abstract from a person's particularity and, therefore, from his uniqueness. But the value and dignity of the individual is to be found precisely in this uniqueness. Each individual person is in a constant state of becoming and determines what he or she is to become through personal choices and commitments; it is not predetermined by an abstract system or definition. Frankl insists on this unique value of the individual.

This uniqueness and singleness which distinguishes each individual and gives meaning to his existence has a bearing on creative work as much as it does on human love. When the impossibility of replacing a person is realized, it allows the responsibility which man has for his existence and its continuance to appear in all its magnitude.[56]

It is the assuming of this responsibility for existence through existential decisions and commitments which constitutes the meaning of self - determination. "A human being," Frankl argues, "is not one thing among others; things determine each other, but man is ultimately self - determining."[57]

The second existentialist theme in Frankl's work is the emphasis on freedom. To say that one becomes what he decides to become presupposes the ability to choose freely. This reflects the existentialist theme of the awareness of oneself as a free being in the world. This freedom is not something that can be philosophically demonstrated; it is a matter of immediate awareness. It is balanced, however, by an equally immediate awareness of the limitations of human existence even, and especially, of death. But even in the face of life's limitations one is still free in regard to that attitude one adopts to those circumstances and conditions which restrict freedom. Frankl would refer to this kind of freedom as a way of actualizing "attitudinal values." Human freedom, he asserts, is restricted: "It is not freedom from conditions, but freedom to take a stand toward the conditions."[58] This means that one is never relieved of the responsibility which accompanies freedom, for even in the most restricted circumstances one is responsible for the attitude one adopts. Our freedom is to be used to make responsible decisions. Each person, Frankl states, "is questioned by life; and he can only answer to life by answering for his own life; to life he can only respond by being responsible. Thus logotherapy sees in responsibleness the very essence of human existence."[59]

Finally, Frankl's thought reflects the existentialist emphasis on subjectivity. We have already noted Kierkegaard's insistence that truth must be subjectively as well as objectively true. Truth must be such and stated in such a way that the individual reacts with concern and decision rather than objective detachment. Thus, for Kierkegaard, the question "What is Christianity?" was less important than the question "How does one become a Christian?". In the same vein, Frankl insists that the will to meaning is not satisfied by abstract ideas about the meaning of life in general; what is needed is the discovery of the meaning of one's unique individual existence. The tasks that life assigns us and, therefore, the meaning of life, he says,

> ...differ from man to man and from moment to moment. Thus it is impossible to define the meaning of life in a general way. Questions about the meaning of life can never be answered by sweeping statements. "Life" does not mean something vague, but something very real and concrete, just as life's tasks are also very real and concrete.[60]

Logotherapy aims at the discovery of the concrete meaning of a person's existence. In doing so, Frankl states, it "dares to enter the spiritual dimension of human existence." It deals with spiritual issues, namely, "man's aspirations for a meaningful existence, as well as the frustration of this aspiration."[61]

This mention of spiritual issues reminds us that, for Frankl, human personality is a three - dimensional reality: the physical, the psychological and the spiritual. The physical dimension refers to the operation of the nervous system and glands; the psychological to the instincts and drives; and the spiritual to the striving for meaningful existence. Freud had attributed conscious "spiritual" activity, whether religious, cultural or artistic, to the sublimation of the sexual instinct or the projection of infantile fears and desires. What was consciously spiritual was explained as originating in the unconscious psychological dimension, thus denying the reality of any distinct spiritual dimension of personality. Frankl rejects Freud's explanation of spiritual activity as originating in the instinctual unconscious. In its place he proposes the theory of another and more fundamental source of motivation which he calls the "spiritual unconscious." The spiritual unconscious operates according to the "will to meaning" which Frankl sees as the most fundamental tendency of the unconscious. It is this unconscious tendency which accounts for all human attempts to discover meaning and direction in life. Frankl calls it "the supporting ground of all conscious spirituality."[62]

Frankl refuses to identify the human person with the sum total of his or her biological and instinctual drives. He joins those critics of Freudian psychoanalysis who point out its failure to account for the richness and uniqueness of human personality by explaining it in terms of a set of primitive instincts. In Frankl's view, this failure is the result of ignoring the spiritual dimension of personality; of disregarding the "will to meaning" as the basic motivating tendency of the unconscious, a tendency which is more fundamental to human development than the tendency to gratify instinctual impulses. According to this view, the person who endures the tension of unsatisfied instinctual drives for the sake of a more meaningful existence is acting according to his true nature. Thus the "instinctual renunciation" of which Freud spoke is not merely the result of the repressive force of the superego or of society, but is endured because the will to meaning is more fundamental to human personality than instinctual drives. The search for meaning is a primary motivating force, not a sublimation or "secondary rationalization" of instinctual drives. Frankl writes:

> There are some authors who contend that meanings and values are "nothing but defense mechanisms, reaction formations and sublimations." But as for myself, I would not be willing to live merely for the sake of my "defense mechanisms," nor would I be willing to die merely for the sake of my "reaction formations." Man, however, is able to live and even die for the sake of his ideals and values.[63]

The search for meaning, being the more fundamental need, may demand renunciation on the instinctual level and therefore create inner tension. This tension is however, in Frankl's view, "an indispensable prerequisite of mental health."[64]

Like the instinctual unconscious, the spiritual unconscious is a theoretical construct which is intended to explain observable behaviour and is observed, not directly, but only in human behaviour. What reveals this spiritual dimension of the unconscious is the freedom and responsibility evident in human behaviour. By using both of these words, Frankl makes it clear that human spirituality (the will to meaning) is revealed not only in our freedom of choice but also in the responsibility which freedom implies. Human freedom is limited or conditioned not only by physical, hereditary and environmental factors, but also by the awareness of responsibility. Freedom implies a human mode of existence; responsibility implies self - transcendence. It is the objective of logotherapy to lead the individual to an awareness of responsibility and thereby to self - transcendence.

The concept of self - transcendence is the key to understanding Frankl's view of human existence, human motivation and the transformation of motives implied in human growth. The realization of the will to meaning and hence the achieving of authentic human existence takes place to the extent that one transcends himself by responding to an objective world of meaning and value. For Frankl, meaning and value are not expressions of one's own self (as with some existential thinkers); they are discovered as objective realities which confront and challenge us.

> We have to beware of the tendency to deal with values in terms if the mere self - expression of man himself. For *Logos* or meaning is not only an emergence from existence itself but rather something confronting existence. If the meaning that is waiting to be fulfilled by man were nothing "but a mere expression of the self" or no more than a projection of his wishful thinking, it would immediately lose its demanding and challenging character; it could no longer call man forth or summon him.... I think that the meaning of our existence is not invented by ourselves, but rather detected.[65]

Values have an "intentional referent." We do not create values within ourselves and then live accordingly; we actualize values by the response we make to the tasks and challenges with which life confronts us.

In terms of motivation, this means that one is not driven from within either by his instinctual drives nor by the values one creates for himself. Self - transcendence is achieved by responding to meanings to be fulfilled and values to be actualized in the objective world of reality outside of the self. Frankl applies this idea to the realm of morality. One does not behave morally, he maintains, in order to satisfy a moral drive but for the self - transcending motive of commitment to a cause or to another person or to God. This is the difference between a saint and a perfectionist.[66] Self - actualization is indeed the goal of personality growth but when it becomes a consciously sought goal it is self - defeating. Self - actualization, Frankl insists, can only be achieved as a side effect of self - transcendence. In the words of the New Testament one can only "find himself" by "losing himself" through response and commitment to something outside of himself.

> Self-actualization is not man's ultimate destination. It is not even his primary intention. Self-actualization, if made an end in itself, contradicts the self-transcendent quality of human existence. Like happiness, self-actualization is an effect, the effect of meaning fulfillment. Only to the extent to which man fulfills a meaning out there in the world, does he fulfill himself. If he sets out to actualize himself rather than fulfill a meaning, self-actualization immediately loses its justification... In my view, excessive concern with self-actualization may be traced to a frustration of the will to meaning.

As the boomerang comes back to the hunter who has thrown it only
if it has missed its target, man, too, returns to himself and is intent
upon self-actualization only if he has missed his mission.[67]

To speak of self - transcendence in this way is to remind ourselves
that human maturity involves a kind of "self - forgetfulness" and that
those things which the self most craves - love, happiness, peace of
mind - cannot be directly sought or manufactured. If we experience
them, we do so only as the side - effect or by - product of a self -
transcending commitment to something beyond the self.

Frankl speaks of two modes of self - transcendence. First one may
transcend himself "in height" by actualizing or fulfilling values. In
this context he speaks of three types of values. These are: creative
values realized through artistic creation or by fulfilling a task for
which one feels responsible; experiential values which arise from
emotional experiences such as the appreciation of beauty in art or
nature or the love of another person; attitudinal values which arise
from the attitude one adopts towards those limitations or conditions in
life which limit freedom and which one cannot avoid such as
suffering. This last bastion of freedom, the freedom to assume an
attitude towards one's suffering, prevents these sufferings from
completely tyrannizing life. Frankl summarizes the three types of
values when he states that the meaning of life can be discovered in
three different ways: by doing a deed; by experiencing a value; and by
suffering.[68] Freud, when asked what a mature person should be able to
do, is reported to have answered that a mature person should be able to
"work and love." If the same question were put to Frankl, a third
quality would be added: a mature person should be able "to work, to
love and to suffer."

The second mode of self - transcendence is transcendence "in
breadth." One transcends himself by relating to a community in
which his individuality finds its true meaning. The unique value of
individual existence, which is a theme central to existentialist thought,
is, in Frankl's view, always related to community. Each individual has
a unique value because of the unique role he has to play and the
unique contribution he has to make to a community; and in fulfilling
that role he transcends himself. "In being directed toward
community," Frankl states, "the meaning of the individual transcends
itself."[69] A reciprocal relationship exists then between the individual
and the community. The community is dependent on the unique value

and contribution of the individual; and the individual finds his true value by transcending himself in community.

In speaking in this way of responsibility and self - transcendence logotherapy, as a theory of motivation, proposes a third alternative to Freud's psychoanalytic view and the more humanistic theory of Allport. The psychoanalytic image of the person driven by instinctual necessity suggests the word "must." Allport's stress on the human capacity for self - actualization through conscious goals and objectives suggests the word "can." Frankl wants an understanding of human existence, and therefore of human motivation, which goes beyond the "I must" of psychoanalysis and the "I can" of humanistic psychology and speaks of the "I ought" type of motivation of one who sees himself as responsible for the actualization of those objective values and meanings which challenge him from without. He wants to interpret human existence in terms of our responsibility to something beyond the self. In this way the subjective side of human existence - being - is complemented by what Frankl considers its objective counterpoint - meaning. One may complement being with meaning by interpreting being (the "I am" phenomenon) in terms of necessity ("I must") or possibility ("I can"). But, in Frankl's view, the full dimensionality of being is missed unless we also interpret being in terms of responsibility, that is, interpret the "I am" phenomenon in terms of "I ought."[70]

To interpret being in this way requires a recognition of the spiritual dimension of personality (the will to meaning). Frankl's insistence on a psychology which goes beyond instinctual necessity and self - actualization reveals perhaps his view of human growth and of the transformation that takes place in human development. For these three types of psychology reveal what might be referred to, in the context of Frankl's theory, as three levels of maturity: to be driven by instinctual necessity; to strive for self - actualization; and to respond to an objective world of meaning and value. The attaining of this third level of maturity, the discovery of and response to the meaning of one's existence, involves a transformation of motives. Growth is a progressive experiencing of all three types of motivation: the "I must" of instinctual demands; the "I can" of self - actualization; and finally the "I ought" of the search for meaning. These three types of motivation are clearly analogous to the three stages of faith development we have discussed in chapters one and two.

This transformation of motives moreover implies self - transcendence for one who is motivated by the will to meaning responds freely to something or someone outside of himself such as meaning, value and community; he is not driven by internal necessity. And self - transcendence in turn implies discontinuity. All human attempts to satisfy instinctual demands or achieve self - actualization do not lead naturally or automatically to the kind of self - transcending motivation implied in the will to meaning. Rather, self - transcendence becomes possible only when attempts at self - actualization in some real sense "break down." One does not transcend the self by trying to actualize the self; one transcends oneself by abandoning the self - conscious pursuit of self - actualization and committing oneself to a value, meaning or person outside of the self. In this way a person finds the actualization of his potentialities which he had previously looked for in himself. In "losing himself" he "finds himself."

Let us try to briefly summarize each of our four theorists' description of human transformation:

Adler: Human growth is a movement from motives of self - enhancement to motives of social interest. It involves transcending a self - protective interpretation of life which is private and "useless" and moving towards a striving for superiority or perfection which is directed towards the socially useful side of life.

Fromm: Growth towards maturity is a transformation from the love of death to the love of life, from narcissism to relatedness, and from incestuous ties to independence. Transcendence involves overcoming the desire for the warmth, comfort and security which accompany the state of dependence and accepting independence and autonomy. Transcendence means transcending the pre - human "primary ties" to nature and developing a human type of relatedness through reason and love.

Allport: Human transformation is a transformation from unconscious, infantile motivations to functionally autonomous motivation. There may be an historical continuity but not a functional continuity between the motivation of the child and of the adult. Transcendence, therefore, has to do with breaking out of the cycle or prison of unconsciously, instinctively motivated behaviour. To be a mature adult is to be motivated by conscious values, ideals and long - range goals.

Frankl: Human growth is a transformation from self - actualizing motivation ("I can") to self - transcending motivation ("I ought"). Transcendence means to respond not to one's own needs (even the need for self - actualization) but to something outside of the self, to the meanings and values to be fulfilled in the external world. It is to transcend the striving for self - actualization.

Each of our four theorists, in one way or another, makes this fundamental statement about human growth: human transformation is fundamentally a transformation of motives. Social interest replaces self - enhancement (Adler); the progressive orientations replace the regressive (Fromm); functionally autonomous motives replace functionally continuous motives (Allport); self - transcending motivation replaces self - actualizing motivation (Frankl). In each of these polarities it is obvious that the final stage is not the normal, predictable outgrowth of the preliminary state. There is a radical discontinuity between the two types of motivation; a genuine transformation has taken place. This implies that human growth is an experience of transcendence. In this regard, we can observe in the four theories reviewed a progressively greater emphasis on the self - transcending quality of human growth. Adler and Fromm consider the human person to be less instinctually determined and more socially oriented and assign a more independent creative role to the ego. For Adler this creative self manifests itself in an individual's life - style. But Adler's life - style is still, to a great extent, unconsciously motivated and a reaction against feelings of inferiority. Nevertheless it accounts for a person's uniqueness and Allport, using the uniqueness of the personality as a starting point, developed a theory in which uniqueness is explained in terms of "propriate striving." This term implies that one is able to achieve self - actualization through conscious plans, intentions and goals. In this case it is the closed circle of unconscious and instinctual determination which is transcended. It remained for Frankl, however, to explicitly advance the concept of self - transcendence, that is, to point out that human completeness demands that even Allport's autonomous self must be transcended; that self - actualization takes place only as the by - product of one's self - transcending efforts to respond to meaning and value through commitment to something or someone beyond the self.

What we have said thus far suggests that the theological descriptions of faith and the psychological descriptions of human growth describe the same kind of human experience: a self - transcending transformation of motives. If this be the case, then it should be possible to describe the faith experience and the life of faith in the context of and using the terminology of each of our four psychological theories. This will be the task of our final section.

2.   FAITH EXISTENCE AS TRANSFORMATION

We have seen that the element of self - transcendence which theology ascribes to faith existence implies a transformation of motives; a transformation from self - justifying to self - transcending motives.   Authentic faith existence, therefore, seems to involve the same kind of self - transcending transformation of motives which psychology associates with mature human existence.   It should be possible, therefore, to describe the self - transcending, transforming quality of the faith experience in terms of each of the four psychological theories discussed.   In doing so we are concerned only with pointing out the common elements in both the psychological understanding of human growth and the theological understanding of the Christian faith experience.   The validity of our proposal that the same self - transcending, transforming dynamic is at work in both experiences is obviously contingent upon the validity of these psychological and theological sources which we have used as the basis for comparison.   A critical evaluation of the psychological or theological positions discussed is obviously beyond the scope of this work.   We have merely taken each psychologist or theologian as representing a widely accepted way of describing the dynamics of human growth or of faith.   As such, they have something to contribute to the dialogue between psychology and theology and deserve a hearing.   With this limitation in mind, it seems legitimate to describe the Christian faith experience in terms of the goals of human growth according to the four personality theories we have reviewed.

(i) *Faith and Social Interest.*

"He who loses his life will find it" (Matthew, X: 39).   These words of Christ express the paradoxical Christian view that the fullness of life is achieved not merely through self - awareness and self - actualization but through self - transcendence.   The perfection of human life is achieved not by self - consciously pursuing it but by transcending that very pursuit through commitment to a cause or a person, to something beyond the self and its perfection or fulfillment. By "losing" himself in such a commitment he "finds" himself.   As we have seen, the believer finds the justification or authentication of his life precisely by transcending in faith the self - conscious attempt to achieve it through his moral and ethical striving.   Adler, like Frankl, offers a secular version of this Christian paradox.   Self - actualization in the sense of perfection or superiority is certainly seen as the goal of human becoming; but this goal is only achieved through "social interest," only through commitment to a socially useful goal which transcends the narrow striving   for self - perfection.   Self - actualization comes about only if the individual's striving for perfection or superiority includes social interest; only if it leads one to one's fellow human beings.

For the mature person life means, in Adler's words, "to contribute to the whole." A genius is therefore defined as one who is "supremely useful" to humanity.[71] In Adler's view, one whose life is characterized by social interest achieves a certain immortality in the sense that one's life is thereby given a lasting value. One's life has meaning not just for oneself but also for one's fellow human beings both for contemporaries and posterity. Egocentric self - enhancement, on the other hand, robs life of this lasting value. Life has a meaning only for the individual. This corresponds to the Christian belief that to love one's neighbour (social interest) leads to eternal life while to turn in upon yourself in an egocentric way (to give a "private" meaning to life) leads to eternal death. In St. Paul's description (Romans, XII) the Christian life is clearly one of social interest.   The task of each Christian is to use his unique gifts to contribute to that community of believers of which he is a member and thereby build up the "body of Christ." The purpose of the faith experience is precisely to lift the believer out of the self - preoccupation of the moralistic pursuit of perfection (through the experience of grace) and thereby liberate him for such socially meaningful commitment. The social interest of the Christian is based on the conviction that he and his fellow Christians "in union with Christ, form one body, and as parts of it. ...belong to each other" (Romans, X: 5).

If this is the vocation of the Christian believer, it is in this context that he will finally be judged. In the words of Jesus (Matthew XXV) those who will "enter into life" are those who practice what Christians refer to as the "works of mercy", feeding the hungry, clothing the naked, caring for the sick, etc. In Adlerian terms, eternal life is for those who have become "perfect" through social interest. On the other hand, those who are condemned or excluded from eternal life are those who have given a private meaning to life, who have neglected the needs of their neighbours, which in the context of the Church as the "body of Christ," are the needs of Christ. They are condemned on the Adlerian grounds of "uselessness;" they have no part in the eternal kingdom since they contributed nothing to it.

Then he will say to those on his left hand, "Depart from me you
cursed, into the eternal fire prepared for the devil and his angels; for
I was hungry and you gave me no food, I was thirsty and you gave
me no drink, I was a stranger and you did not welcome me, naked
and you did not cloth me, sick and in prison and you did not visit
me." ...and they will go away to eternal punishment, but the
righteous into eternal life. (Matthew, XXV: 41 - 43, 46).

This passage bears a striking resemblance to a passage in Adler's
What Life Should Mean to You in which he describes the harsh
judgement which life itself will inflict on those who give a private
meaning to life, a judgement similar to that of Jesus on the self -
centred.   After describing the heritage left by those who have
contributed to human welfare in philosophy, science, art, etc., and
thereby pointing out the lasting value of such lives, he then speaks of
those who have lived only for their personal advantage and of the
judgement which life itself pronounces on them.

These results have been left by men who contributed to human
welfare. What has happened to those who never cooperated, who
gave life a different meaning, who asked only, "what can I get out of
life?" They have left no trace behind them. Not only are they dead;
their whole lives were futile. It is as if our earth itself had spoken to
them and said, "We don't need you. You are not fitted for life.
There is no future for your aims and strivings, for the values you
have held dear, for your minds and souls. Be off with you! You are
not wanted. Die and disappear!" The last judgement for people
who give any other meaning to life than cooperation is always, "You
are useless. Nobody wants you. Go!"[72]

The self - transcending quality of faith which makes possible a
genuine and spontaneous love of one's neighbour (a love liberated
from egoistic, self - justifying motives) and which leads to "eternal
life" as opposed to the egoistic love of oneself which leads to eternal
death, finds a parallel in the Adlerian concept of the self -
transcending quality of social interest which gives a lasting value to
life as opposed to the egoistic tendency to give a private meaning to
life which renders life "useless."

For Adler, the striving for superiority or perfection which
characterizes all human life styles may be expressed in an egoistic way
(self - enhancement) or in a self - transcending way (social interest). In
the same way the striving for a self - justifying life which characterizes
all religious life - styles may be expressed in an egocentric way

(through the moralistic attempt to earn justification) or a self - transcending way (faith). Adlerian theory considers such striving for superiority to be, in the final analysis, an unconscious attempt to compensate for the feelings of inferiority inherent in human existence. To overcome such feelings, each individual creates a "fictional goal" of superiority which represents the ultimate compensation for feelings of inferiority. Adler refers to the creation of this fictional goal as the individual's way of "anticipating his redemption." Feelings of inferiority, therefore are not necessarily negative hindrances to human growth. Except when they are abnormally exaggerated they represent a positive starting point for growth towards maturity. The New Testament makes a similar claim; one can enter the kingdom of heaven only through a conversion or a change of heart. This conversion involves an admission of one's guilt, of one's "inferiority," the admission that one is a sinner. This awareness of sin is, as we have seen, the result of the anxiety - producing self - knowledge which is occasioned by one's vain attempts at self - justification and is therefore a necessary preliminary to faith. Thus if Individual Psychology sees the feelings of inferiority as the starting point of human development, Christianity sees a similar phenomenon as the starting point of "life" in the biblical sense.

The Christian experience of awareness of sin and repentance differs, however, from the Adlerian view of human existence in two ways: First, it is not just a question of feelings of inferiority, but a conscious admission of inferiority, of insufficiency, of one's need for redemption. It is what the New Testament calls "poverty of spirit." Secondly, to the believer, faith is not just the creation of a compensating fictional goal; it is an act of trust in an objective event of redemption. It is interesting to note, moreover, that in Adlerian theory the young child sets his goal of superiority unconsciously and thereby establishes a fixed law of growth for the rest of his life; the "life - style" is established. The adult does not have the same creative power over life. "I am convinced" Adler writes "of the free creative power of the individual in his earliest childhood and of his restricted power in later life, once the child has given himself a fixed law of movement for his life."[73] This position perhaps sheds light on the experiential meaning of faith as being "born again" (John, II: 5) and as "becoming a child" again (Matthew, XVII: 3 - 4). Within the context of Adlerian theory such phrases could perhaps refer to the fact that in the self - transcendence of faith one achieves, even in adulthood, that which Adler sees as possible only in childhood: the ability to create a new goal and life - style; a new "law of movement" which Bultmann would call a new understanding of one's existence.

We have seen that Adlerian theory stresses the social meaning of human existence. For Adler, the meaning one gives to life, the degree of social interest in one's strivings for superiority, is revealed in one's life - style. More specifically, it is revealed in the manner in which one responds to the three basic problem areas of life - the occupational, the social and the sexual. Maturity is measured by the degree of social interest and genuine human cooperation one brings to these areas of life. Maladjustment results from the conflict that arises between the private meaning one gives to life and the social demands of these three areas of life. It is also true that Christianity stresses the social meaning of individual existence. Faith is an experience of self - transcendence and transformation but it transforms the believer - liberates him from self - preoccupation - in order to render him capable of a self - transcending commitment to community.

In the context of Adlerian theory, therefore, membership in the community of believers, the Church, must have psychological as well as theological significance. I believe that the imagery by which the Church understands its own nature and function gives some kind of ultimate social meaning to its members' experience of what Adler calls the three problem areas of human life.

First, the Church understands itself as the visible representation of the Kingdom of God. In our discussion of faith we have already seen something of its necessary connection with love and charity. But hope is also basic to the Christian life because that object of Christian faith, the Christ event, contains promise as well as fulfillment. The Christian therefore awaits (as the creed says) and hopes for the future which is promised in Christ and which represents the ultimate and complete realization of the new being or new creation which is revealed in Christ. This last, final and future thing is what Christians call the "Kingdom of God." It is an ultimate state of peace, love, unity, and brotherhood as well as that ultimate victory over death of which Christ's resurrection is seen as a pledge. In the words of the liturgy for the feast of Christ the King, what the Christian hopes for is "a kingdom of truth and life, a kingdom of holiness and grace, a kingdom of justice, love and peace." And the task of the Church, the community of believers, is to communicate this hope to the world. It does so, I believe, in two ways. First, by its preaching, the burden of which is to constantly remind the world of this ultimate goal of all human evolution and therefore, as the theology of liberation has reminded us, to be critical of all social and political ideologies from this more ultimate perspective, the Church becomes not just a bearer of tradition but a source of unrest and an agent of change in human life.

Secondly, the Church communicates its hope to the world by embodying in its own communal life some partial realization of the life of the kingdom that is to come. Thus in answer to the Pharisees who asked him when the kingdom of God was to come, Christ replies: "The kingdom of God is among you" (Luke XVII: 21). Christ is the "new being" and as such is an embodiment of the kingdom; in the same way, the Church as the visible "sacrament" of Christ through time and space, is to be a visible representation of the kingdom to the extent that it participates in the life of Christ, in the reality of the new being. The Church, existing within the human community, is meant to be an embodiment of that life of "justice, love and peace" which is the ultimate destiny of the whole human community. Its obvious failures in this regard are witness to the partial and fragmentary quality of its manifestation of the new being and to the fact that the realization of the kingdom is a divine rather than a human accomplishment. The individual Christian is nevertheless called to cooperate with God in working to bring about the realization of the kingdom both in his own person and life (personal sanctification) and in his world.

This latter is achieved through the contribution that the believer makes to the life of the human community. In this light, his daily occupation takes on an eternal significance. Work is a means of physical survival and of psychological development of our human potential; from the theological point of view it also represents the individual's contribution to the ultimate perfection of the human community, the kingdom of God. From the perspective of faith, even the most humble work is not without this religious and eternal significance. The same is true of that work whose value to the human community is not immediately evident. Hence the Church, speaking from this point of view, has always insisted on the dignity of work as such and does not share the view that only "meaningful" work is of value. In the same way, it has always attached a social value to the cloistered and the contemplative life which involves apparent withdrawal from active involvement in one's world.

All this seems to be in fundamental agreement with Adler's views on the psychological meaning of work. Occupation, he maintains, is one of the areas of life which represents an opportunity to give a social meaning to life and contribute to the welfare of the human community.

Moreover, in agreement with the religious point of view we have been discussing, he insists that contribution to society does not necessarily mean active participation in society. The artist, the philosopher or the contemplative may appear to withdraw from society but may nevertheless be contributing to the advancement of society and therefore, from the religious point of view, the realization of the kingdom of God. For some, assisting humanity towards a goal of ultimate fulfillment does not necessarily involve concrete participation in the circle of one's own time. Social interest, Adler insists, means more than this.

> It means particularly the interest in, or feeling with, the community *sub specie aeternitatis.* It means the striving for community which must be thought of as everlasting, as we could think of it if mankind had reached the goal of perfection. It is never (only) a present day community or society, a specific political or religious formation. It is rather the goal which is best suited for perfection, a goal which would have to signify the ideal community of all mankind, the ultimate fulfillment of evolution.[74]

Such expressions as "the ideal community of all mankind" and "the ultimate fulfillment of evolution" are secularized expressions of the ideal of the "kingdom of God," with this difference: whereas for Adler they may represent an ultimately unrealizable or "fictional" goal, for the Christian it is an article of faith and the object of hope.

Another image by which the Church expresses its self - understanding is that of the "body of Christ." The analogy is used to represent the relationship of the community of believers to Christ. "Just as each of our bodies," writes St. Paul, "has several parts and each part has a separate function, so all of us, in union with Christ, form one body, and as parts of it we belong to each other" (Romans XII: 4 - 5). Among the implications of this truth for the individual believer are the following: His life is lived "in union with Christ," under the direction of Christ's teaching and the movements of his grace, just as the activity of the body is coordinated by the head; the union of each believer with Christ implies union among the believers who thereby "belong to each other" as all members and organs are parts of one body; each member has a unique function to perform by way of contribution to the overall welfare and "building up" of the body; each individual's unique role in the life of the Church manifests the life giving spirit which informs the body of Christ for the contributions of all members "are the work of one and the same Spirit who distributes different gifts to different people just as he chooses" (I Corinthians XII: 11); the union of all with Christ the head overrides all distinctions of race, nationality and social condition, for "in one Spirit we are all baptized, Jews as well as Greeks, slaves as well as citizens, and one Spirit was given to us all to drink" (I Corinthians XII: 13); and finally, the union of all in Christ creates a special bond of empathy among the members whereby "if one part is hurt, all parts are hurt with it" and "if one part is given special honour, all parts enjoy it" (I Corinthians XII: 26).

It is this conviction that one's life is lived as a member of the body of Christ which motivates the Christian believer to give life what Adler calls a "social meaning" and to live a life of social interest. An individual, Adler maintains, whose striving for superiority is characterized by social interest will give life a social meaning. He will choose a goal which is "on the useful side of life," a goal which is useful to human society, and will think of life in terms of service to the community and social cooperation. For the Christian believer the religious source of this kind of social feeling is the faith which liberates him from self - preoccupation and for commitment and his identity and self - understanding as a member of the body of Christ.

Moreover, the identification of the Church as the body of Christ implies that in one's social relationships one is relating, in some sense, to Christ himself and this, I would suggest, gives an ultimate religious meaning to the believer's interpersonal life; to that dimension of life which Adler refers to as the area of social cooperation. The doctrine of the body of Christ implies that if Christ is to be found in the world it is only in his body, that is, in the human face of one's neighbour. The encounter with Christ then takes place within the context of one's interpersonal life. Thus in the parable of the last judgement (Matthew XXV) Christ counts the work of mercy performed or not performed for others as performed or not performed for himself: "I tell you solemnly, in so far as you did this to one of the least of these brothers of mine, you did it to me. ...In so far as you neglected to do this to one of the least of these, you neglected to do it for me" (Matthew XXV: 40 & 45).

In a reading from the official prayer of the Church and attributed to an anonymous "second century author" we find the following passage:

> You are aware, I am sure, that the living "Church is the body of Christ." The Church which is spiritual, was manifested in the flesh of Christ to show us that if any of us serves her in her fleshly

embodiment, he will receive her in the Holy Spirit. No one, then, who refuses the image will receive the archetypal reality. Therefore she tells us, brothers, to serve her in the flesh so that we may share in the Spirit. But if we deny that the flesh is the Church and the spirit Christ, we will, in rejecting the flesh, reject the Church and have no share in the spirit which is Christ.[75]

This passage should give pause to those who want to restrict the meaning of the Church to the purely spiritual community of faith to the exclusion of its all too human dimension including what is for some the much despised or at least embarrassing "institutional Church." To serve the Christ, the author maintains, is to serve his "fleshly embodiment," the Church. To reject "the flesh" is to reject, and therefore have no part in the spirit of Christ, for the flesh is that human reality in which the spirit of Christ dwells. This concern for the very earthly needs of one's fellow human beings who make up the body of Christ is what Adler calls social interest.

A third image which conveys the Church's self - understanding is that of the "bride of Christ." In the person of Christ, dogmatically defined as both God and man, a "marriage" takes place, the union of the human and the divine. The union of the Son of God with his human nature and, through that human nature, with the members of his body, the Church, is viewed by the Christian tradition as a kind of "marriage" in which the Church is the bride and Christ is the bridegroom. (In Jungian psychology this union or "*Coniunctio*" is symbolic of the wholeness which is the goal of the process of human growth.) In Christian tradition this relationship between Christ and the Church becomes the exemplar or prototype for the relationship of husband and wife. Their love is to emulate the love that exists between Christ and the Church (cf. Ephesians, V - 21ff.). It is for this reason that marriage is regarded as a sacrament. If a sacrament is a visible sign of some invisible spiritual reality, then the union of husband and wife in marriage is a visible, "sacramental" sign of the union of Christ and the Church. In the love of the husband and wife the love of Christ and the Church is meant to become a visible reality. Again, therefore, to the psychological meaning which Adler assigns to love and marriage - as an area of life in which the individual gives expression to social interest and the social meaning he gives to life - there is added a religious and theological meaning: marriage is a sacrament in which the love of Christ and his body, the Church, is made visible. Faith existence, then, and existence within the community of faith has the function of giving, even in Adlerian terms, an ultimate social meaning to the life of the Christian believer in all its social dimensions - the occupational, social and sexual.

(ii) *Faith and Progression:*

In Erich Fromm's description, one of the aims of human transformation is "productiveness." The human condition is seen as inherently dichotomous; a dichotomy based on the fact that the human person is part of nature but, at the same time, transcends nature through the human capacity for self - awareness. With the loss of the primary instinctual ties with nature, it becomes necessary to relate to one's world through the specifically human powers of reason and love. This relatedness, however, must not be achieved at the expense of one's individuality and integrity. "Productive" relatedness is relatedness in which one's individuality and self - determination are preserved and one's human potential is realized. Those forms of relatedness in which one's individuality is sacrificed such as authoritarianism, destructiveness and conformity are considered by Fromm to be "non - productive."

This analysis of the human condition highlights that tension between the need to relate to others and the need to affirm one's individuality which characterizes human existence. It is the same dichotomy which Tillich describes in terms of individuality and participation, self and world, the courage to be at oneself and the courage to be as part, autonomy and heteronomy. While Fromm does not offer Tillich's theological solution to this dichotomy - the courage of confidence which results from faith and which transcends one's self and one's world - he does agree that both of these existential needs are so fundamental that one cannot be preserved at the expense of the other. He would quite agree with Tillich that relatedness (participation) at the expense of individuality alienates the individual from his true self. But he would also agree that self - affirmation at the expense of genuine relatedness serves to accentuate and reinforce that awareness of one's isolation and aloneness which is a necessary part of human self - awareness. It is the overcoming of this aloneness and separation which Fromm sees as essential for the preservation of one's sanity. Thus Fromm's position could be stated in terms of a paradox: individuality can only be realized through relatedness or participation. Such things as individuality, freedom and autonomy can be realized not by trying to cultivate them in isolation from one's fellow human beings but only in genuine (productive) relatedness with them. A similar paradox is evident in the theological description of the faith experience we have examined; true individuality, freedom and "courage to be" are not discovered in the false autonomy and self - affirmation of one's moralistic striving for self - justification but in the self - transcending relatedness with God and others which faith makes possible.

This same paradox is reflected also in the biblical injunction: Whoever would be great among you must be your servant, and whoever would be first among you must be your slave" (Matthew XX: 26 - 27). Surely these words cannot be taken as Jesus' prescription for getting to the top of the organizational ladder. In the context in which they occur, they must be taken as a rebuke of the disciples all too human ambition to be "great" or "first." True greatness, Jesus teaches, does not consist in sitting on a throne in splendid isolation or in experiencing despotic power over others, but rather in being a "servant" and a "slave." Fromm might perhaps reject such language as suggesting a decidedly "non - productive" way of relating to others; but allowing for some biblical hyperbole we might also interpret these words as suggesting the kind of care and concern for others which Fromm associates with productive love. And the greatness to be achieved in this way may be called holiness or fulfillment or happiness or authentic selfhood, the very things we seek in the misguided ambition to be "great" or "first." Greatness in this sense is what Fromm calls "productiveness" and the question about relatedness is whether it is productive or non - productive. When applied to human growth the question becomes: will one's growth be progressive or regressive? Will the individual progress toward greater self - awareness and greater transcendence of the primary ties with nature through the development of reason and love; or will he regress toward the pre - human state of harmony with nature? Will he progress in the direction of biophilia, relatedness and independence ("the syndrome of growth"); or will he regress in the direction of necrophilia, narcissism and incestuous fixation ("the syndrome of decay")?

This is also the yardstick which Fromm applies to religion. "Humanistic" religion is that which has human self - realization and growth in one's specifically human powers of reason and love as its aim and is therefore productive and progressive. "Authoritarian" religion, on the other hand, is based on irrational submissiveness to authority; it thus alienates the individual from himself since he projects all his own productive powers onto God and is therefore non - productive and regressive.[76] For Fromm, the ultimate criterion for evaluating religious faith is not the objective validity of the content of one's faith but the human experience of the believer. It is a question of whether one's faith expresses itself in productive or non - productive living; whether it produces growth or decay; whether it helps the believer to become more fully human or to retreat from his humanity. For humanistic religion virtue is defined as "self - realization, not obedience;" faith is "certainty of conviction" but a certainty based on one's own experience and thought, not on submissiveness to a teaching authority; God is "a symbol of man's own powers which he tries to realize in his life, and is not a symbol of force and domination having power over man."[77]   Thus Fromm is equally critical of what he perceives as the emphasis on human powerlessness in the Lutheran and Calvinist traditions and of the emphasis on an infallible teaching authority in the Catholic tradition.   These are viewed as a craving for certainty at the expense of independence and personal responsibility for one's life.

Such a view of religion has implications, both negative and positive, for the kind of dialogue we have been trying to construct between psychology and religion.   In the first place, the application of such an exclusively psychological criterion carries with it the danger of reductionism, a hazard which Fromm does not succeed in avoiding. In his book, *Psychoanalysis and Religion*, he proposes that psychoanalysis and religion should have the same concern - human self - actualization and the realization of human values.   On reading this, the mature religious person may feel that his religion is being put into a psychological straight - jacket; that it is not being allowed to be itself or speak for itself but is being told what it must be.   To the mature believer, striving to serve God and others in a self - transcending way, it may come as a surprise to learn that he should rather be occupied with the more ego - centred pursuit of self - realization.   One is tempted to suspect that, confronted by the believer's claim that in his religious submission and obedience he has discovered his greatest freedom and fulfillment, Fromm would react with bemused incomprehension.   One might further speculate that this is so because Fromm's humanistic thought gives scant attention to the paradoxical nature of religious faith or even human existence.   It should be pointed out further that, in applying a psychological criterion, Fromm fails to differentiate between religion and religious experience.   Religious experience may be judged to be either humanistic or authoritarian since the believer may assimilate his religious tradition in a way that is psychologically healthy or unhealthy.   But for precisely the same reason it is difficult to apply the same criterion to a religious tradition as such.

From another point of view, however, Fromm's view of religion has a valuable contribution to make to the dialogue between psychology and theology. His emphasis on the experience of the believer as distinct from the content of his faith reminds us that in any such dialogue the question under discussion is not whether the objects of faith (God and revelation) have an objective validity or reality but whether the faith response of the believer is psychologically productive in terms of his human growth and existence. It is clear, however, that the transcendent content of theological discourse must be abstracted from and not merely ignored as irrelevant since, for any true dialogue to occur, theology must be heard from, and theology cannot speak of human experience without reference to God and revelation. It is to the kind of human experience implied in such theological discourse (as, for instance, the theological descriptions of faith we have reviewed) that criteria such as "humanistic" and "authoritarian" can be applied. Thus to Fromm's contention that the concept of God is a conceptualization or symbol of a human experience or value and that it is this experience which is important rather than the concept itself, we must hasten to add this qualification: that the concept of God is not unimportant in any absolute sense but only in the context of the dialogue between psychology and theology since it lies beyond the area of human experience which psychology and theology have in common.

Fromm points out that the concept of God, along with the concepts such as love, loyalty, faith, etc., permit us to communicate our human experience but only if those concepts faithfully express the experience to which they refer. But what is the human experience to which the concept of God refers? Fromm believes that the concept expresses the highest human value, an experience of the fullness of growth and productiveness which he designates as the "X" experience. This is essentially a humanistic experience or value which may or may not be associated with a concept of God as its symbol. In his book *You Shall be Gods* Fromm lists some of the main features of this experience.[78] Among these he includes the experience of a "letting go of one's 'ego,' one's greed and, with it, of one's fears."[79] This refers to the willingness to forego the desire to maintain one's isolated ego as a separate entity for the sake of openness and relatedness to others. A further aspect of the "X" experience is what Fromm calls "transcending the ego, leaving the prison of one's selfishness and separateness."[80] In other words, the transcending of the ego involves the overcoming of narcissism, of incestuous fixation and destructiveness, of all those "necrophilous tendencies" by which the ego protects itself.

The "X" experience then is one of self - transcendence. We have seen that faith, as a human experience, involves the same kind of self - transcendence. For the believer this experience of self - transcendence takes place as a result of his faith relationship with his God. For Fromm such reference to God is merely one way of conceptualizing or interpreting a humanistic experience which may be described in theistic or non - theistic terms. It is the experience which is important. "The experience is essentially the same whether it refers to God or not."[81] This is the premise of any dialogue between psychology and theology: that the same kind of experience may be conceptualized or interpreted in non - theistic (psychological) of theistic (theological) terms. The point of the dialogue is to discover the common experiential substratum of psychological and theological discourse.

The very term "X" experience suggests an experience whose meaning cannot be exhausted by one type of formulation or interpretation. In the language of theology what is transcended in the self - transcendence of the faith experience is the ego - centred striving for self - justification. Through this transformation the believer moves beyond the kind of ego - striving and self - preoccupation of one who, living "under the law," tries to earn his justification through moral and religious observance. Experientially this is what Fromm calls a "letting go of one's ego."

In the context of the meaning of faith one would say that the transformation from self - justifying to self - transcending motives, which takes place on the psychological level, is the result of the believer's discovery of the grace or unconditional acceptance of God which takes place on the theological level of faith. For the believer, therefore, this transformation involves that transcending of the ego which Fromm sees as an integral aspect of the "X" experience. The theological interpretation would maintain that this experience results from the believer's discovery of the God of unconditional acceptance or grace. This involves a transcending or going beyond or relativizing of the God of unconditional demand or law. This latter God could be described in psychological terms as the projection of one's superego or, more specifically in Frommian terms, as the "authoritarian" God. On the experiential, psychological level, the result is that a transformation from egoistic, self - justifying motives to outer - directed, self - forgetful and self - transcending motives becomes possible for the believer who is no longer burdened with the task of self - justification.

In this case therefore we may suggest that the theological description of faith does not contradict but complements Fromm's psychological description of the "X" experience. It can be further suggested that, in the context of Fromm's understanding of human growth, the faith experience involves transformation from decay to growth, from non - productiveness to productiveness. More specifically, it is a transformation:

1) *From necrophilia to biophilia.* The transformation of faith may be described as a transformation from a legalistic to a personal relationship with God. The person who lives at that level of existence which is the preamble to faith and which we have described as ethical existence (Kierkegaard), or "religion" (Barth), tends to relate to God in a legalistic way. This is the person who lives "under the law" and for whom the law becomes that self - imposed burden by which he hopes to justify himself before his God. This kind of religious orientation tends to become ever more legalistic since the attempt at self - justification is motivated by the need for security and certainty about God's acceptance and obedience to concrete laws and observances is seen as giving greater certainty than obedience to more generalized moral directives which leave more decision - making to the individual; such concrete rules, therefore, tend to multiply. Legalism is what Fromm would call a "necrophilous" orientation precisely because of this striving for moral and religious certainty. It codifies the relationship with God and others and thereby turns it into something predictable and mechanical; something static rather than dynamic.

The legalist relates to a set of abstract rules and principles rather than to a living person. He does so because it seems to give him greater security, and more reassurance of being in the right and, therefore, justified. At the same time, it turns him in upon himself - perpetually concerned about his moral status - and such preoccupation is the antithesis of true morality. It is what Marc Oraison has called a "neurotic defense against life"[82] because it protects the individual from the risks of real human encounter. Legalism does to the religious life what, according to Fromm, necrophilia does to life in general; it turns life into death by trying to make it certain, predictable and mechanical, in order to avoid the risk and uncertainty which are necessary components of life.

To have faith, on the other hand, means to accept the risk and uncertainty of a personal relationship. The faith relationship is, like any other personal relationship, organic rather than mechanical; it is not the mechanical repetition of unchanging duties and obligations but a relationship which is "open - ended," subject to growth and development. In a personal relationship one's obligation is not to a set of abstract rules but to the needs of a living person. One's response to the other, therefore, must take account of changing needs and circumstances as well as the growth and development of the other. This implies uncertainty rather than security, openness to the new rather than clinging to the old. Fromm maintains that to be an adult means to trade the security and dependence of childhood for the insecurity and independence of maturity. In the same way religious maturity or faith involves the trading of the certainty and security of legalism for the risk and insecurity of faith. In both cases there is an acceptance of life as organic , uncertain, unpredictable and uncontrollable, as risk and adventure, which fulfills the meaning of biophilia.

2) *From Narcissism to Relatedness.* Faith involves the transcending of that preoccupation with self and with one's moral perfection and personal salvation which in turn makes possible an authentic kind of relatedness with others. The person of faith, liberated from the necessity of self - justification is free to love others for their own sake, not in order to prove anything about himself or win the acceptance of God (since that acceptance is already freely given). Thus liberated from the danger of using others for his own moral and spiritual advancement, he is able to relate to others with that genuine care, responsibility, respect and knowledge which Fromm considers essential to productive relatedness.

Faith, therefore is a self - transcending experience which makes possible an altruistic kind of relatedness to others. But is such human relatedness an essential ingredient to the life of faith? Over and above the Christian moral imperative to love one's neighbour there appears to be at least two themes within Christian thought which support a positive answer to this question. The first is the trend in contemporary theology to speak of God less as a supreme being transcending and separate from human existence and more in terms of his immanence within human existence. We have already alluded to Tillich's understanding of God as the ground or depth dimension of being and to Gregory Baum's notion of the "insider God," the mystery present at the heart of human existence. Concepts such as these suggest that God is to be discovered not by looking beyond human existence but at the heart or depth of human existence and of our human relationships. A second theme is the imagery of the church as the "body of Christ" which we have referred to in discussing the theological significance of

Adlerian theory. In the Christian understanding, faith, as a personal relationship is a response to the human person of Christ in whom God is revealed. But the concept of the body of Christ implies that Christ's mode of existence in time is in his body, the church. Therefore faith means to respond to the person of Christ as he exists in his body, in the members of his church. As has already been suggested, one's encounter with and response to Christ is made within the context of one's interpersonal life within the community of believers. Thus that by which, in Fromm's view, we grow humanly - productive relatedness - becomes the means of expressing faith.

3) *From Incestuous Fixation to Independence.* The faith relationship, rightly understood, is not one of dependence and false security but the result of a personal commitment freely made by the believer. Human growth is seen by Fromm as a transition from the security and protection of dependence to the insecurity and uncertainty of independence. In the same way, the dynamics of faith describe a movement from the moral and religious security of legalism and moralism to the moral and religious insecurity of the faith relationship. In faith existence dependence on law and external authority is replaced by personal responsibility and commitment to the demands of a personal relationship with God. As we have seen, that personal relationship at times may well involve what Kierkegaard called the "paradoxical suspension" of those universal ethical norms which are the source of certainty and security for the legalist. In authentic faith the believer does not experience ego - protecting certainty but rather ego - transcending confidence. And, as for Fromm, one can experience true individuality and autonomy only in assuming the care and responsibility of productive relatedness, in the same way, the believer experiences true confidence and freedom by exposing himself to the risk, uncertainty and adventure of the personal relationship of faith.

In addressing the question whether the faith relationship involves dependence and false security or liberation from incestuous ties, it is instructive to consider some of the biblical language in which that relationship is described. Christ's reference to his disciples as "friends" not servants implies not dependence but individual independence and mutual interdependence. Paul's description of the Church as the "bride" of Christ suggests a relationship in which each partner is incomplete but not dependent. And the reference to the Christian believer as a "child" of God suggests what Fromm would call "rootedness" as well as protection and security; but it also suggests a person in the process of growth toward adulthood and independence. In this process of growth, Jesus affirms (Matthew VII: 9 - 11) that we should expect God to display the qualities of a good human father. Surely this includes the wisdom to allow one's children to grow towards maturity and autonomy. Jesus further cautions that the process of becoming a disciple involves "hating" one's parents and family (Luke XIV: 26). This text has been interpreted metaphorically as referring, in an exaggerated way, to the need to put the love of God ahead of all human attachments. Kierkegaard has interpreted it literally as referring to the absolute obedience of faith; that one should, on the grounds of such obedience, be prepared to do even something as ethically repulsive as hating one's parents, just as Abraham was prepared to offer his son as a human sacrifice.[83] But could we not also interpret these words developmentally? Allowing, again, for the biblical hyperbole, we might have here a reference to the fact that discipleship requires human maturity, the acquisition of which requires a "hating" of one's parents by way of adolescent rebellion.

Adolescent rebellion is a way of establishing one's identity, individuality and autonomy; but as long as it is expressed in ways which may be temporarily painful but not ultimately destructive, it can create the possibility of a new relationship with one's parents based on mutual respect and a more realistic view of the parental figures than the idol worship of the young child. To discover this new relationship with his parents the adolescent must first become "independent" of them. In the same way religious maturity or faith involves the outgrowing of the dependence and security of legalistic religion in favour of the freedom and responsibility of the personal relationship of faith. In Frommian terms it is the faith relationship and the confidence it inspires which provides the believer with that "rootedness" which overcomes the anxiety of independence. In discussing the Old Testament concept of God, Fromm speaks of the acknowledgement of God as the negation of idols and obedience to God as liberation from idols. An idol here refers to any person or institution onto which one projects his humanly productive powers thus blocking the development of those powers within himself. If human maturity demands the rejection ("hating"?) of one's parents as idols in this sense, religious maturity also demands the rejection of God as an idol.

(iii) *Faith and Propriate Striving*

We have summarized Allport's view of human becoming as a transformation from opportunistic to propriate striving; from unconscious to conscious motivation; from reactive to proactive behaviour; from functional continuity to functional autonomy. The transition from infantile to adult motivation is a transition from being driven by unconscious forces or infantile needs to the pursuit of conscious goals and self perfection. This latter is what Allport calls propriate striving; the striving for what is genuinely one's own and what is seen as a value in itself and not as a means of satisfying unconscious and/or infantile needs. In this respect, the essence of human transformation in Allport's psychological view corresponds with the theological view which describes the faith experience as essentially a transformation of motives, from self - justifying to self - transcending motives. In this view, authentic human becoming is also seen as being, like faith, an experience of liberating self - transcendence, since it involves the transcending of that passive condition in which the individual is the victim of unconscious or infantile drives in order to become the active creator of a unique style of life. Moreover, just as there is a radical discontinuity between infantile and adult motivation, between functionally continuous and functionally autonomous motivation, so also is there a radical discontinuity between the self - justifying motivation of religious moralism and legalism and the self - transcending motivation of faith. One whose behaviour is motivated by the narcissistic need for self - justification or the infantile need for approval or the unconscious need to expiate guilt is trapped at an immature level of growth, whether the acceptance, approval or forgiveness one seeks is human or divine.

If, as Allport maintains, the behaviour of the mature adult is characterized by motivation which is functionally autonomous - liberated from unconscious and/or infantile drives - then this must also be characteristic of mature religious behaviour. Allport uses the term "religious sentiment" to describe the motivation and the organisation of the religious life. Motivation refers to the emotional, affective wellspring of the religious sentiment (what Allport calls the "go" of mental life); organisation refers to the cognitive force which patterns the life of the individual in accordance with his motives. The word "sentiment" includes both the emotional and cognitive aspects of the religious life.[84]

But what is the source of the religious sentiment? Where does this particular kind of orientation of one's life begin? Looking at this question from the psychologist's point of view, Allport suggests a number of possibilities. He resists the temptation to explain religion by reference to one specific mental mechanism. It is too one - sided, he believes, to dismiss religion as the sublimination of an aim - inhibited sex impulse or as the superego's projection of the image of one's own father. For Allport, the religious sentiment finds its origin not in any one specific mechanism of the psyche but in a complex of needs experienced by the individual in the process of growth.[85] These are: (1) Organic desire, that is, fear of the perils of life and the desire for love and companionship. (2) The temperamental needs of each individual which influences his unique mode of emotional response and, therefore, his unique way of expressing the religious sentiment. (3) Psychogenic desires such as the quest for the spiritual values of truth, goodness and beauty. Religion is seen in part as an attempt to preserve such values. In Allport's view, the most universal spiritual value is the sense of individuality and uniqueness the supreme expression of which the religious person finds in the concept of a personal God. (4) The pursuit of meaning, of a frame of orientation (to use Fromm's term) which will offer an explanation of the world and of human existence, unrest and unfulfilled needs is perceived by many as the purpose of religion.   (5) The need to conform to the culture in which one lives may be experienced as the need to conform to the dominant religious forms, dogmas and rituals of that culture.

The above represents some of the human needs to which religion answers. The question is: Do these needs constitute the only rationale for religion? Is religion "nothing but" a way of fulfilling needs? Allport would answer that, in the mature adult, the religious sentiment, like any other form of motivation, tends to become functionally autonomous; it becomes a value to be pursued for its own sake regardless of its origin as an answer to human or even selfish or neurotic needs. The mature religious sentiment is "derivative yet dynamic;" though it may have originated as an answer to personal needs (derivative) it now supplies its own driving power (dynamic). It is now independent of its origins; it does not serve the same function as it originally did. A religious sentiment originally motivated by the need to satisfy some human need can become an end in itself and supply its own driving power.   Allport maintains that "the most important of all distinctions between the immature and the mature religious sentiment lies in this basic difference in their dynamic character.[86]

In the Christian context, the functional autonomy of the religious sentiment simply means that the believer is approaching the ideal of loving and serving God "for His own sake" and not as a dispenser of rewards or as a source of comfort and security. Religion becomes what

Adrian Van Kaam would call the "central mode of existence" in one's personality.[87] Faith becomes such when the faith relationship gives meaning and direction to all other areas of life or modes of existence and is not the slave of any other pursuit. Security, meaning and value become by - products or side - effects of the religious sentiment, not its goals. The mature religious sentiment does not follow; it leads and transforms.

> A religious sentiment which has thus become largely independent of its origins, "functionally autonomous," cannot be regarded as a servant of other desires, even though its initial function may have been of this order. It behaves no longer like an iron filing, twisting to follow the magnet of self - centred motives; it behaves rather as a master motive, a magnet in its own right by which other cravings are bidden to order their course....
> The power of religion to transform lives ...is a consequence of the functional autonomy that marks the mature religious sentiment.[88]

We have already noted that Allport finds a specific example of this dynamic in the growth experience from surface obedience to the interiorized voice of authority to the conscious pursuit of goals consistent with one's values (from "must" to "ought"). This is but one dimension of that general transformation of motives (including one's religious motivation) which characterizes authentic human growth from "opportunistic" striving or becoming to "propriate striving."

The question which arises at this point is: Can the faith experience of the Christian believer be described in terms of such a transformation and functional autonomy of motives? However one might answer this question on the basis of empirical evidence, the New Testament makes it clear that the life to which the believer is called involves a kind of transformation of personality, a repentance, conversion or change of heart. John the Baptist preaches a message of repentance in preparation for the kingdom of God (Matthew III: 2; Mark I: 1 - 4). Jesus speaks of this conversion in terms of becoming a child again (Matthew XVIII: 3); one must, in some way, become a different or new person. For St. Paul, conversion means to participate in the death and resurrection of Christ and to be transformed in this way (Romans VI: 2 - 4). It also means to pass from a life according to the "flesh" to a life according to the "spirit" (Romans VII: 5; VIII: 3); from the human condition of one who, relying in his own resources, is unable to avoid the egoism of sin to the life of one who is capable of love and commitment through the gift of God's spirit. Conversion is a "new creation" (II Cor. V: 17); it is the destruction of "the old man" and the creation of "the new man" (Col. III: 9 - 10).

This experience of conversion and faith is seen as resulting in a transformation of personality. In the new testament this transformation is described in a series of antitheses which highlight the radical discontinuity between the previous state and the new one: darkness and light, death and life, flesh and spirit, the old man and the new man, Adam and Christ. It would seem legitimate to conclude from this kind of language that the transformation which takes place in the faith experience touches the very core of human personality and therefore includes the transformation of motives of which Allport speaks in his treatment of functional autonomy. Allport himself alludes to the transformation of attitudes which accompanies religious conversion in which "the majority of the previous habits and attitudes may have to be radically altered" and as a result "the 'new' personality seems utterly different from the old."[89]

It is my contention that the theological participants in our dialogue, in describing the faith experience as a liberation from the frustration , anxiety and guilt of religious and moral striving for self - justification, have spelled out the specific nature of the human transformation achieved in that experience. Moreover, the fact that this liberation is attributed to the grace of God by which God's acceptance can be seen as a gift and not as something to be earned points to the possibility of a new kind of religious motivation, a self - transcending motivation which is free of self - concern and self - preoccupation to the extent that it is informed by that same faith. It seems logical to infer from this that the faith experience is for the believer a transformation which involves the achieving of "functional autonomy" since his religious motivation is liberated from the need to earn something for himself or fulfill some human need.

In both human and religious growth, therefore, it is precisely the transformation of *motives* which constitutes maturity. The Christian experience of conversion is not simply that of moral conversion, the abandoning of a sinful life; the call to repentance and faith is addressed even (and specifically) to those already striving to live a morally good life. It is precisely to the person striving to justify himself before God through such moral observance that the call to faith is addressed. In the light of faith such moral effort is perceived as an egocentric attempt to do the impossible, to command God's love and acceptance through one's human efforts and reliance on one's human resources; it is "living after the flesh." For such a person faith makes possible a love and service which is rendered from a purified, spontaneous, self - transcending motive. To the person justified by grace and faith the goal he seeks in his moral striving, the object of his commitment, is God and others; it is not an infantile goal (comfort, security) nor a neurotic one (expiation of guilt feelings)   nor a narcissistic one (self - justification). Faith reveals to the believer that acceptance, forgiveness and justification are gifts from God, not prizes to be earned. The religious sentiment is therefore freed to concern itself with God directly; it does not have to serve the purpose of achieving these other goals. It is "functionally autonomous." Faith liberates the believer to follow the injunction of Christ: "Set your hearts on (God's) kingdom first, and all these other things will be given to you as well." (Matthew VI: 33)

The theological meaning of the Christian faith - experience is that the believer is justified by his faith in God's acceptance of him which is revealed in Christ, and which renders all human attempts at self - justification pointless.   And this is precisely why the   religious sentiment (faith) of the mature Christian is functionally autonomous, because all the self - seeking motives in which it might originate - security, self - justification, self - gratification - have become, in the view of faith, pointless. Psychologically, it means that the believer is liberated from the need to prove himself worthy or deserving of that love and acceptance through his moral and religious efforts. This revelation from without is intended to free him from any inner compulsions to act out of self - preserving of self - justifying motives. Religious motivation has become functionally autonomous, concerned with God and others and not with the satisfaction of one's own needs. The relationship with God has become a value in itself, not a means to gratify some human need; for the most fundamental human need (love and acceptance) has been fulfilled. And it is because this deepest human yearning has been satisfied that the believer is warned that religion must not be put at the service of egoistic or narcissistic human needs. One must not seek to earn or achieve what has already been given freely. Accordingly, Jesus demands of the believer a "purity of heart" (singleness of intention) by which he seeks God alone and the good of his neighbour in his good works and not the gratification of an infantile need for the approval of others, for the "Father who sees in secret" will reward him. (Matthew VI: 18)

In this same passage (the sermon on the mount) Jesus says to his disciples: "For I tell you, if your virtue goes no deeper than that of the Scribes and Pharisees, you will never get into the kingdom of heaven"

(Matthew V: 20). In a sermon by Pope Leo the Great we read the following commentary on these words:

> The uprightness of the Christian comes to exceed that of the Scribes and Pharisees, not by doing away with the law but by going beyond a carnal understanding of the law. Thus the Lord, in telling his disciples how to fast, says: "when you fast do not imitate the hypocrites and be sad. They distort their faces so that men will see they are fasting. I tell you, they already have their reward." What reward? Praise from men! Desiring this, they don the appearance of uprightness; with no concern for their inner state of mind, they cherish an unfounded reputation.[90]

Here we have a description of religious motivation which is "functionally continuous" with the infantile need for the acceptance and approval of others. It also describes a religious orientation which Allport would describe as "extrinsic," that is, one whose goal and purpose is something beyond, foreign to, or extrinsic, to religion itself. Pope Leo refers to it as a "carnal understanding" of the law, the keeping of the law for the sake of earning a reward. The Christian's virtue is supposed to go deeper than this "not by doing away with the law" but by observing it from a different motive. The Christian is to fast just as "the hypocrites" do but not for the sake of the human reward it might bring.

> If a man loves God, it is enough for him to please his Beloved; he expects no greater reward than the joy of loving. For love is from God who is Love. The devout and pure soul yearns to be filled with that love and to delight in it alone. "Where your treasure is, there your heart is too."[91]

The type of religious motivation described here is "functionally autonomous," liberated from the infantile need for approval or ego - centred desire for reward. And what makes this kind of self - transcending motivation possible is the faith which acknowledges that "the Creator effected the reparation and sanctification of believers through forgiveness of sins, so that the threat of stern revenge and torment was removed, the guilty were restored to innocence, and virtue succeeded vice."[92]

The Christian experience of transformation through faith as an objective event of redemption is analogous to the common human experience as Allport describes it. He draws the conclusion from modern industrial relations that everyone has an "affiliative need," a need for warm friendly relations with others through love and acceptance. When this need is frustrated a person suffers indignity and humiliation and becomes depressive; love turns into hate. Thus the ability to forget oneself and to enter into loving and cooperative relationships with others depends, to a great extent, on the degree of love and acceptance one receives from others. Acceptance leads to what Allport calls an "inclusionist" attitude and way of life, an openness to others; rejection leads to an "exclusionist" attitude, the exclusion of segments of humanity from one's affiliative tendencies. Prejudice and bigotry are examples of this. Allport concludes that "each person, through circumstances and training, develops an exclusionist, an inclusionist or mixed style of life that guides his own human relations."[93] Applying this principle to our understanding of the Christian faith - experience suggests the following conclusion: As a human experience, grace is essentially an experience of love and acceptance which opens the one who accepts it in faith to an affiliative style of life. And the community of believers, the Church, is intended to be that community in which the love and acceptance (grace) of God which is at the heart of the Christian message is given human expression and therefore to be a model of "inclusionist" community within the human community.

(iv) *Faith and Self - Transcendence.*

If Allport's concept of "functional autonomy" serves as an interpretative tool for understanding the transforming quality of the faith - experience, the personality theory of Viktor Frankl lends itself to a description of the dynamic of self - transcendence which characterizes the faith - experience, since it describes human growth and maturity essentially in terms of self - transcendence. We have described faith as a radical act of trust by which the believer transcends the anxiety and frustration involved in the pursuit of moral self - justification or of self - actualization. In the same way, Frankl maintains that while self - actualization (the realization of one's human potential) is the goal of human growth, nevertheless the conscious pursuit of self - actualization is self - defeating; self - actualization must be a side - effect of self transcendence, that is, of self - commitment to objective values and meanings, to something or someone outside of the self.

Frankl himself applies this principle of self - transcendence to faith when he remarks that the truly religious person - the saint - does not directly seek moral perfection or a "good conscience" as an end in itself; such moral perfection is the result of a self - transcending commitment to God and/or one's fellow human beings. Saints are people who "lose themselves" in the service of God; they are not people who set out to become saints, whose goal is self - perfection. "If that were the case," Frankl argues, "they would have become only perfectionists rather than saints."[94] In claiming that authentic human existence exhibits the same kind of self - transcendence which characterizes the life of the authentically religious person, Frankl posits the existence in the human person of an "unconscious religiousness," that is, "a latent relation to transcendence inherent in man"[95] which we might read as his version of *homo naturaliter religiosus*. By the use of this phrase Frankl wants to assert that life is not self - expression but a meaning to be discovered in the world of objective reality: a God to be served, a person to be loved, a task to be fulfilled, a suffering to be endured, etc. Human existence always has an "intentional referent;" whether that intentional referent is God or not, it is a transcendent reality in the sense that it transcends the self and its actualization. Frankl finds the empirical evidence for this view of human existence in the responsibleness to which conscience leads us; for the transcendent reality which gives meaning to life - whether it be God or not - is that to which we are responsible. Conscience, therefore is not the voice of myself; it mediates the voice of something other than myself. Frankl would describe conscience as the voice of transcendence.[96]

Frankl's principle that human life must transcend itself, that one can actualize the self only by transcending the self, seems to be the most explicit psychological reflection of the biblical paradox that one must "lose himself" in order to "find himself" (Matthew X: 39). It is a paradox which is reflected not only in Frankl's psychological theory but also in his therapeutic technique of "paradoxical intention" which is based on the premise that "fear makes come true that which one is afraid of and that hyper - intention makes impossible what one wishes."[97] Readers of Frankl will recall the case of the concert violinist whose hyper - intention rendered him eventually incapable of performing. Everyday life suggests other examples of human endeavours (athletic, artistic, social, etc.) which are rendered ineffective because the performer "thinks too much" or "tries too hard." We may add that in the life of faith the same paradoxical intention is at work; the believer must abandon his over - driven pursuit of what he wants most, justification, in order to receive it. There is certainly an analogy between Frankl's description of one

seeking self - actualization and psychological health and unable to
achieve it because of his "hyper - intention" and theological
descriptions of one whose pursuit of self - justification (religious self -
actualization) through moral and religious observance not only serves
to intensify and reinforce his sense of unworthiness and lack of self -
sufficiency but also aggravates his moral condition by stimulating him
to greater transgressions.

It is, in Frankl's view, this self - defeating pursuit of self -
actualization - religious or nonreligious, with or without reference to
God - which must be transcended. As a psychologist, Frankl would
agree with Erich Fromm that whether or not this transcendence takes
the form of a commitment to God is psychologically irrelevant; what is
important is the experience of self - transcendence.   From the
psychological point of view our question has to do with the human
experience of faith and, in the present context, that question becomes:
May one describe the human dimension of the faith experience as an
experience of self - transcendence according to Frankl's understanding
of self - transcendence? I want to suggest that an affirmative answer
to this question would be based on a threefold similarity between the
self - transcendence which Frankl describes as necessary to human
growth and the self - transcendence achieved in the faith experience.
Each experience would appear to have the same dimensions (height
and breadth), is based on the same basic view of the human condition
and is arrived at by way of the same kind of dynamic or transformation
of motives. Let us examine these three similarities in more detail.

(1) *The Same Dimensions.* Frankl speaks of transcendence as two
dimensional. One achieves transcendence "in height" by fulfilling
creative, experiential and attitudinal values and transcendence "in
breadth" by relating to and fulfilling a unique role in community.[98]
The same twofold transcendence obtains also in the faith experience
for faith has both a "vertical" and a "horizontal" dimension. Through
faith the believer transcends the self - preoccupation of moralistic and
legalistic religion and enters into a personal relationship with God,
which like all personal relationships is based on faith (trust) rather
than observance of law. In responding to the demands of that personal
relationship the believer achieves a degree of what Frankl calls
transcendence in height by fulfilling the values associated with it.
Again these values are creative, experiential and attitudinal.   The
believer fulfills or actualizes creative values when he sees himself as
having a unique task or vocation to fulfill.   Legalism tends to
depersonalize since everyone is subjected to the same universal moral

code; the believer, on the other hand, sees himself called to a unique set of responsibilities.[99] Ethics speaks of universal moral principles; religion speaks of personal "vocation" or calling. Secondly, the "experiential" value associated with the faith relationship consists in the fact that it is primarily a relationship of love and gratitude rather than law and obedience. If faith were not an experiential value the whole passive, mystical, contemplative dimension of the Christian life would be without meaning. Finally, Faith involves the actualizing of attitudinal values since it demands an attitude of trust and confidence "in spite of." Both God's grace or acceptance and the believer's belief in that acceptance are maintained in spite of what Tillich calls his "unacceptability." This refers to those limitations inherent in human existence of which one becomes painfully aware in the attempt to live a self - justifying life. The attitudinal value of faith consists in the acceptance of these negative elements which remain a part of human existence in spite of one's best efforts to overcome them: egoism, destructiveness, passiveness, lack of moral rectitude and self - sufficiency. To the believer, it is God's acceptance of him "in spite of" these realities which makes the attitudinal value of self - acceptance and self - affirmation "in spite of" possible.

Faith then is an attitude of trust which transcends the existential conflict between awareness of freedom and responsibility and those limitations of freedom which one's moral effort reveals and which the New Testament refers to as bondage or slavery. But faith also has a horizontal dimension by which the believer achieves transcendence "in breadth." We have seen that the purpose of the transforming experience of faith is to liberate the believer from self - preoccupation so that he becomes capable of some degree of altruistic, self - transcending love and service towards others which is free of egoistic motives of self - justification. The personal experience of faith, therefore, prepares the believer for life within a community of faith and love. The ultimate significance of faith has to do with community. In the view of St. Paul, the gift of the Spirit which is associated with faith and makes self - transcendence "in height" possible, also makes transcendence "in breadth" possible since the same spirit which is given to each believer enables him to perform a unique task within the community of believers for the purpose of building up the body of Christ (I Cor. XII).

(2) *The Same Basic View of Human Existence.* Frankl's understanding of human personality revolves, as we have seen, around two points. The first is that the most basic motivating force in human

personality is the "will to meaning," the desire to live a meaningful existence, to discover the "why" of one's personal existence. The second is that the will to meaning reveals a spiritual dimension of human personality in addition to the physical and psychological (instinctive) dimensions. Hence conscious spiritual activity, the search for meaning, is not merely a sublimation of the instinctual unconscious but springs from the "spiritual unconscious," the locus of the will to meaning which is more fundamental to human existence than the instinctual will to pleasure. Self - transcendence takes place when one discovers the meaning of his existence and commits himself to it.

Two aspects of this dynamic of self - transcendence are analogous to the self - transcendence achieved in the faith experience. First, it is not the meaning of life in general that one seeks through the will to meaning but the particular meaning of his own concrete existence. When the unique meaning of one's individual existence is discovered, transcendence of all dehumanizing and depersonalizing forces which tend to destroy individuality becomes possible. A sense of the meaning of one's personal existence mitigates the depersonalizing effects of abstract philosophical systems, mass movements, social pressures and totalitarian or collectivist political systems. In the same way, as we have already noted, faith implies a personal relationship with God in which the emphasis is on the believer's unique task or vocation and unique set of responsibilities. The basing of one's religious life entirely on universal moral or ethical principles fails to do justice to the individual's unique relationship to the absolute and to his need to express his individuality within that relationship. Faith involves the transcending of the depersonalizing effects of this kind of religion. The philosopher asks, "What is the meaning of life?" The theologian asks, "What is the meaning of Christian life?" The believer asks, "What is the meaning of my life?"

Secondly, the search for meaning is a tension - maintaining rather than a tension - reducing dynamic. The will to meaning leads one to endure tension rather than to reduce tension and seek equilibrium or homeostasis through instinctual gratification. According to Frankl, this is so because the will to meaning is more fundamental to human existence than the will to pleasure. In the life of faith the same tension - maintaining dynamic obtains. To use Kierkegaard's terminology, faith becomes possible only when the enjoyment - seeking motivation of the aesthetic life gives way to the more fundamental desire to have a self - justifying, self - authenticating life at the ethical level of existence, and finally, when the tensions of the self - justifying efforts of ethical existence give way to the tensions involved in the risk, adventure and uncertainty of religious existence or faith.

(3) *The Same Transformation of Motives.*

Frankl speaks of three types of motivation represented by the words "must," "can" and "ought."[100] These types of motivation correspond respectively to three basic theories of motivation: the psychoanalytic, the humanistic and the existential. They can also be taken to represent Frankl's view of three levels of maturity: the level of the instinctual drives, the level of the conscious pursuit of self - actualization and the level of self - transcending response to meaning and value.

The same three types of motivation can be recognized in the three stages of faith development we have proposed. The believer sees himself in retrospect as having passed through three levels of existence characterized by the same three types of motivation. The first level refers to that state in which he is enslaved or in bondage to that basic egoistic self - seeking which the New Testament calls "sin." Sin is perceived as dominating human existence. The second level is that of commitment to ethical or moral principles as a means of self - justification. This attempt at self - authentication through reliance on one's own human resources reflects the "I can" type of motivation characteristic of the humanistic pursuit of self - actualization. The third level is the level of faith existence in which the egoism and narcissism of self - justification is transcended. This corresponds to the self - transcending "I ought" type of motivation described in Frankl's existential psychology. This type of motivation seeks to fulfill not an egoistic and self - defeating desire for self - actualization but a value and meaning which challenges from without. The believer, relieved of the human burden of self - justification, is also free to operate on the "I ought" level of motivation by acting out of motives of responsibleness towards the transcendent source of that acceptance or justification which he could not fashion for himself. Frankl's self - transcending person actualizes himself by transcending the desire for self - actualization. The person of faith, in the same way, achieves justification by transcending the desire to justify himself.

I have suggested throughout this work that the dynamics of self - transcendence, which involves a radical transformation of motives, is common to both the experience of authentic human growth and the authentic faith experience of the Christian believer. In order to avoid any kind of reductionism it must be emphasized that the point of comparison is not the reality of human growth and the reality of faith in themselves, but rather the manner in which these two realities are experienced. The four psychological descriptions of the Christian faith experience given in this last section are not to be taken as descriptions of faith itself (which would be a theological enterprise), but as psychological reflections on the manner in which faith is experienced, that is, of the human transformation effected by faith. Thus to speak of faith as "social interest" or "progression" or "propriate striving" or "self - transcendence" is not to exhaust the meaning of faith within psychological categories but rather to find various ways of describing the human experience of the believer which results from his act of faith.

If one were to reduce the argumentation of the preceding pages to the formula of the classic three - term syllogism, the common or middle term would be self - transcendence or transformation. Thus the argument would run: Human growth may be described in terms of self - transcendence. The faith experience may also be described in terms of self - transcendence. Therefore the faith experience may be described in terms of human growth. The psychological descriptions of the faith experience we have proposed in this final section become possible only in the light of the findings of the previous sections. These findings might be summarized thus: In those disciplines which articulate and conceptualize the dynamics of human growth and of faith (psychology and theology) there has been a growing emphasis on the dimension of self - transcendence in both experiences. Self - transcendence (and the transformation of motives it implies) becomes, in this case, the common ground of both disciplines and the bridge over which dialogue may take place.

The author feels compelled to beg the indulgence of the reader for whom the central point of our refections - the human experience of transformation and self - transcendence inherent in the experience of faith - may be a matter of deep conviction and everyday experience. It is hoped however that for those for whom the traditional concepts of the Christian tradition, if not God himself, are dead, these reflections might restore some kind of experiential meaning to the much abused, overworked, but finally irreplaceable, concept of faith.

ENDNOTES

1.   *U.S. Catholic and Jubilee*, XXXV:7, July 1970, pp. 6 - 9.
2.   A. Adler, "Zartlicheitsbedurfnis," quoted in H.& R. Ansbacher, *The Individual Psychology of Alfred Adler* (New York: Harper and Row,

1964), p. 42.

3.   A. Adler, "Hermaphroditismus," quoted in H. & R. Ansbacher, *The Individual Psychology of Alfred Adler*. p. 48.

4.   A. Adler, "Progress in Individual Psychology," in *British Journal of Medical Psychology*, vol. 4, 1924, p. 23.

5.   A. Adler, *The Science of Living* (New York: Greenberg, 1929), p. 34.

6.   A. Adler, *What Life Should Mean to You* (New York: Capricorn Books, 1958), p. 51.

7.   *Ibid.*, p. 7.

8.   *Ibid.*, p. 10.

9.   A. Adler, "Individualpsychologie und Wissenschaft," quoted in H. & R. Ansbacher, *The Individual Psychology of Alfred Adler*, pp. 157 - 159.

10.   A. Adler, *What Life Should Mean to You*, p. 37.

11.   *Ibid.*, p. 10.

12.   A. Adler, "Der Nervose Charakter," quoted in H. & R. Ansbacher, *The Individual Psychology of Alfred Adler*, p. 114.

13.   *Ibid.*

14.   A. Adler, *The Science of Living*, p. 104.

15.   A. Adler, "Der Komplexzwang als Teil der Personlichkeit und der Neurose," quoted in H. & R. Ansbacher, *The Individual Psychology of Alfred Adler*, p. 185.

16.   E. Fromm, *The Heart if Man: Its Genius for Good and Evil* (New York: Harper and Row, 1964), p. 117.

17.   E. Fromm, *Man for Himself* (Greenwich, Conn.: Fawcett Publications, 1965), p. 49.

18.   E. Fromm, *The Art of Loving* (New York: Bantam Books, 1963), p. 8.

19.   E. Fromm, *The Sane Society* (Greenwich, Conn.: Fawcett Publications, 19650), p. 36.

20.   E. Fromm, *Escape from Freedom* (New York: Avon Books, 1965), p. 35.

21.   This is the theme of Fromm's book *Escape from Freedom* first published in 1941. In it, he accounts for the appeal of totalitarian systems such as Nazism and Fascism by pointing out that they offered the individual an "escape from freedom," that is, an opportunity to escape from the insecurity of being an individual by finding a sense of belonging and relatedness in abject submission to a strong leader but at the cost of his individuality and integrity.

22.   E. Fromm, *Man for Himself*, p. 109.

23.   E. Fromm, *The Sane Society*, pp. 36 - 37.

24.   *Ibid.*, p. 37.

25.   E. Fromm, *The Art of Loving*, p. 22.

26.   E. Fromm, *Man for Himself*, p. 107.

27.   E. Fromm, *The Art of Loving*, p. 19.

28.   E. Fromm, *Man for Himself*, p. 53.

29.   *Ibid.*, p. 49.

30.   E. Fromm, *The Heart of Man*, chapters 3, 4 and 5.

31.   *Ibid.*, p. 42.

32.   *Ibid.*, p. 47.

33.   *Ibid.*, p. 77.

34.   *Ibid.*, p. 88.

35.   *Ibid.*, p. 98.

36.   G. Allport, *Personality and social Encounter* (Boston: Beacon Press, 1960), pp. 95 - 96.

37.   *Ibid.*, p. 103.

38.   *Ibid.*, p. 96.

39.   G. Allport, *Becoming: Basic Considerations for a Psychology of Personality* (New Haven: Yale University Press, 1955), chapters 1, 2, and 3.

40.   G. Allport, *Pattern and Growth in Personality* (New York: Holt, Reinhart and Winston, 1961), p. 208.

41.   G. Allport, *Becoming*, p. 26.

42.   *Ibid.*, p. 48.

43.   *Ibid.*, p. 67.

44.   G. Allport, *Personality and Social Encounter*, p. 137.

45.   *Ibid.*, p. 149.

46.   G. Allport *Personality: A Psychological Interpretation* (new York: Henry Holt & Co., 1937), p. 194.

47.   G. Allport, *Pattern and Growth in Personality*, p. 251.

48.   G. Allport, *Becoming*, p. 55.

49.   *Ibid.*, p. 40.

50.   *Ibid.*, pp. 50 - 51.

51.   *Ibid.*, pp. 41 - 54.

52.   *Ibid.*, p. 72.

53.   *Ibid.*, p. 73.

54.   V. Frankl *Man's Search for Meaning* (New York: Washington Square Press, 1963), p. 166.

55.   *Ibid.*, p. 121.

56.   *Ibid.*, p. 127.

57.   *Ibid.*, p. 213.

58.   *Ibid.*, p. 205.

59.   *Ibid.*, pp. 172 - 173.

60.   *Ibid.*, pp. 122 - 123.

61.   *Ibid.*, p. 160.

62.   V. Frankl, *Handbuch der Neurosenlehre und Psychotherapie* (Wien: Urban and Schwarzenberg, 1957), p. 974. Quoted in Donald F. Tweedie Jr., *Logotherapy and the Christian Faith* (Grand Rapids: Baker Book House, 1965), pp. 56 - 57.

63. V. Frankl, *Man's Search for Meaning*, pp. 154 - 155.
64. *Ibid.*, p. 164.
65. *Ibid.*, pp. 156 - 157.
66. *Ibid.*, p. 158.
67. V. Frankl, *The Will to Meaning* (New York: New American Library, 1969), p. 38.
68. V. Frankl, *Man's Search for Meaning*, p. 176.
69. V. Frankl, *The Doctor and the Soul* (New York: Bantam Books, 1967), p. 57.
70. V. Frankl, "Logotherapy and the Challenge of Suffering," in *Review of Existential Psychology and Psychiatry*, I:1, 1961, p. 3.
71. A. Adler, *What Life Should Mean to You*, p. 9.
72. *Ibid.*, p. 11.
73. A. Adler *Der Sinn des Lebens* (Vienna, Leipzig: Rolf Posser, 1933). Quoted in H. & R. Ansbacher (editors), *The Individual Psychology of Alfred Adler;* p. 186.
74. A. Adler, "Uber den Ursprung des Strebens nach Uberlegenbeit und des Gemeinschaftgefuhles," quoted in H. & R. Ansbacher, *op. cit.*, p. 142.
75. Matins, Thursday of Week 31, Reading II.
76. Erich Fromm *Psychoanalysis and Religion* (New Haven: Yale University Press, 1950), chapter 3.
77. *Ibid.*, p. 37.
78. E. Fromm *You Shall Be as Gods: A Radical Interpretation of the Old Testament and its Tradition* (New York: Holt, Reinhart and Winston, 1966), pp. 57 - 60.
79. *Ibid.*, p. 59.
80. *Ibid.*, p. 60.
81. *Ibid.*, p.60.
82. M. Oraison *Morality for Our Time.* (Translated by Nels Challe, Garden City, N.Y.: Doubleday & Co., 1969), p. 65.
83. S. Kierkegaard *Fear and Trembling.*, Translated by Walter Lowrie (Princeton, N.J.: Princeton University Press, 1968), pp. 82 - 86.
84. G. Allport *The Individual and His Religion* (New York: MacMillan, 1960), pp. 62 - 65.
85. *Ibid.*, chapter 1.
86. *Ibid.*, pp. 71 - 72.
87. A. Van Kaam *Religion and Personality* (Englewood Cliffs, N.J.: Prentence - Hall, 1964), chapter 1.
88. G. Allport *The Individual and His Religion*, pp. 72 - 73.
89. G. Allport, *Personality : A Psychological Interpretation* (New York: Henry Holt and Co., 1937), p. 211.
90. Pope Leo the Great, *Sermon 92*
91. *Ibid.*
92. *Ibid.*

93.   G. Allport *Personality and Social Encounter*, p. 202.
94.   V. Frankl *Man's Search for Meaning*, p. 158.
95.   V. Frankl *The Unconscious God*. (New York: Simon and Schuster, 1975), p. 61.
96.   *Ibid.*, chapter 5.
97.   V. Frankl *Man's Search for Meaning*, pp. 195 - 196.
98.   V. Frankl *The Doctor and the Soul*.; pp. 55ff.
99.   Frankl himself speaks of the religious person as not only seeing life in terms of a task to be performed but as a task assigned to him by God. Cf. *The Doctor and the Soul*, pp. 46 - 47.
100. V. Frankl "Logotherapy and the Challenge of Suffering", pp. 3 - 7.

SELECTED BIBLIOGRAPHY

Adler, Alfred. *What Life Should Mean to You.* New York: Capricorn Books, 1958.

Allport, Gordon. *Becoming: Basic Considerations for a Phycology of Personality.* New Haven: Yale University Press, 1955.

_____. *The Individual and His Religion.* New York: Macmillan, 1986.

_____. *Pattern and Growth in Personality.* New York: Holt, Reinhart & Winston, 1961.

Althaus, Paul. *The Theology of Martin Luther.* Trans. by Robert C. Schultz. Philadelphia: Fortress Press, 1966.

Ansbacher, Heinz and Rowena (eds.). *The Individual Psychology of Alfred Adler.* New York: Harper & Row, 1964.

Armbruster, Carl, S.J. *The Vision of Paul Tillich.* New York: Sheed & Ward, 1967.

Augustine, St. *Confessions.* Trans. By F.J. Sheed. London: Sheed & Ward, 1948.

Bainton, Roland. *Here I Stand: A Life of Martin Luther.* New York: New American Library, 1950.

Barth, Karl. *Dogmatics in Outline.* New York: Harper and Row, 1959.

_____. *Epistle to the Romans.* Trans. by Edwyn C. Hoskyns. London: Oxford University Press, 1933.

Bultmann, Rudolf. *Jesus Christ and Mythology.* London: S.C.M. Press, 1960.

_____. "The New Testament and Mythology", in *Kerygma and Myth: A Theological Debate*. Trans. by R.H. Fuller and edited by Hans Werner Bartsch. New York: Harper and Row, 1961.

Dillenberger, John, ed. *Martin Luther: Selections from his Writings*. Garden City, N.Y.: Doubleday, 1961.

Dunne, John. *A Search for God in Time and Memory*. London: Macmillan, 1967.

Duska, Ronald and Mariellen Whelan. *Moral Development: A Guide to Piaget and Kohlberg*. New York: Paulist Press, 1975.

Erikson, Erik. *Identity and the Life Cycle*. New York: W.W. Norton and Co., 1980.

_____. *Young Man Luther: A Study in Psychoanalysis and History*. New York: W.W. Norton and Co., 1962.

Evans, Donald. *Struggle and Fulfillment: The Inner Dynamics of Religion and Morality*. New York: Collins, 1979.

Evans, Richard. *Dialogue with Erik Erikson*. New York: W.W. Norton and Co., 1969.

Faber, Heije. *Psychology of Religion*. Philadelphia: Westminster Press, 1975.

Fowler, James. *Stages of Faith: The Psychology of Human Development and the Quest for Meaning*. San Francisco: Harper and Row, 1981.

Frankl, Viktor. *The Doctor and the Soul*. New York: Bantam, 1967.

_____. *Man's Search for Meaning*. New Yrok: Washington Square Press, 1963.

_____. *The Unconscious God*. New York: Simon and Schuster, 1975.

From, Erich. *The Heart of Man: Its Genius for Good and Evil.* New York: Harper and Row, 1964.

_____. *Psychoanalysis and Religion.* New Haven: Yale University Press, 1950.

_____. *You Shall Be As Gods: A Radical Interpretation of the Old Testament and its Tradition.* New York: Holt, Reinhart and Winston, 1966.

Kierkegaard, Soren. *Fear and Trembling.* Trans. by Walter Lowrie. Garden City, N.Y.: Doubleday, 1954.

_____. *Training in Christianity.* Trans. by Walter Lowrie. Princeton: Princeton University Press, 1944.

Kohlberg, Lawrence. *The Philosophy of Moral Development: Moral Stages and the Idea of Justice.* San Francisco: Harper and Row, 1981.

_____. *The Psychology of Moral Development. The Nature and Validity of Moral Stages.* San Francisco: Harper and Row, 1984.

Mackintosh, H.R. *Types of Modern Theology.* London: Fontana, 1964.

Macquarrie, John. "Philosophy and Theology in Bultmann's Thought", in *The Theology of Rudolf Bultmann.* Edited by C.W. Kegley. New York: Harper and Row, 1966.

Meissner, William, S.J. *Life and Faith: Psychological Perspectives on Religious Experience.* Washington: Georgetown University Press, 1987.

O'Connell, R.J. *St. Augustine's Confessions: The Odyssey of a Soul.* Cambridge, Mass.: Harvard University Press, 1969.

Ottley, R.L. *Studies in the Confessions of St. Augustine.* London: Robert Scott, 1919.

Pelikan, Jaroslav. (ed.). *Interpreters of Luther.* Philadelphia: Fortress Press, 1968.

Piaget, Jean. *Six Psychological Studies.* New York: Random House, 1967.

Roberts, David. *Existentialism and Religious Belief.* New York: Oxford University Press, 1959.

Tillich, Paul. *A History of Christian Thought.* Edited by Carl E. Braaten. London: S.C.M. Press, 1968.

_____. *The Courage To Be.* London: Fontana, 1962.

Wilcox, Mary. *Developmental Journey: A Guide to the Development of Logical and Moral Reasoning and Social Perspective.* Nashville: Abingdon, 1979.

INDEX OF NAMES

INDEX OF SUBJECTS